ON A SILVER DESERT

On a Silver Desert

THE LIFE OF

Ernest Haycox

by ERNEST HAYCOX JR.

Foreword by RONALD L. DAVIS

UNIVERSITY OF OKLAHOMA PRESS NORMAN

Library of Congress Cataloging-in-Publication Data

Haycox, Ernest Jr.

On a silver desert: the life of Ernest Haycox / by Ernest Haycox Jr.; foreword by Ronald L. Davis.

p. cm.

Includes bibliographical references and index.

ISBN 978-0-8061-3564-9 (hardcover) ISBN 978-0-8061-9485-1 (paper)

1. Haycox, Ernest, 1899–1950. 2. Authors, American—20th century—Biography.
3. Western stories—History and criticism. 4. West (U.S.)—In literature. I. Title.

PS3515.A9327Z68 2003
813'.53—dc21
[B]

2003042650

The paper in this book meets the guidelines for permanence and durability of the Committee on Production Guidelines for Book Longevity of the Council on Library Resources, Inc. ∞

To Marylou

CONTENTS

ILLUSTRATIONS

Illustrations are all courtesy the Haycox Family Collection.

FOREWORD

WESTERN ADVENTURE WRITER ERNEST HAYCOX IS PROBABLY BEST remembered for his short story "Stage to Lordsburg," which appeared in *Collier's* magazine in 1937 and two years later became the basis of John Ford's *Stagecoach*, the film that propelled John Wayne to major Hollywood stardom. *Union Pacific*, *Canyon Passage*, and *Abilene Town* are other classic movies drawn from Haycox's fiction, and the writer's popularity was great enough by 1940 that *Collier's* reputedly increased its issue by fifty thousand any time a Haycox story was included in its contents. A commercial writer dependent on a mass market for financial security, Haycox published some three hundred short stories and twenty-four novels during his career, and struggled to produce profitable fiction of artistic worth. No less a stylist than Ernest Hemingway admired Haycox's craftsmanship, which set standards in both pulp and slick magazines during the 1930s and 1940s.

Born in 1899 in Portland, Oregon, Haycox grew up listening to tales of old-timers who had experienced the frontier West a generation before him. By the time he entered the University of Oregon, he knew that he wanted to write adventure fiction and soon began sending out student efforts to all but the most lurid periodicals, receiving sufficient recognition to validate his commitment. Haycox's initial success came with supplying adventure yarns to pulp magazines, which the novice considered a training ground. Yet from the beginning he aspired to art and possibly greatness.

Pulp magazines in the 1920s, most notably *Western Story*, specialized in adventure tales intended for a largely male readership. Editors encouraged writers to comply with established formulas, which resulted in predictable plots, exciting action, and fantastic heroism rendered in a disreputable vernacular style. Although Haycox was forced to conform to standard conventions, his integrity as a writer quickly distinguished his work from the usual pulp hack. Not only did Ernest have a university degree and formal training in writing, he showed a persistent determination to improve his craft and assume a philosophical position in his work. From the outset, Haycox treated the western past with respect. He admired frontier values and, like Owen Wister, thought westerners demonstrated a vibrancy that easterners had lost.

Although Haycox obeyed the mandates of the pulp tradition, he looked for meaning behind surface action. He recognized the challenges that the frontier West offered his characters, the brutality of violent actions, the toll extracted by contests and conquest. The writer's early stories are set in rural Oregon and deal with homesteading and farming. Rather than struggles between heroes and villains, much of Haycox's action is inner conflict. In his early output the writer seems more strongly influenced by American naturalist Jack London and British adventure writer Robert Louis Stevenson than by Owen Wister and the writers of western romances.

During the 1920s Haycox published regularly in *Western Story* and *Short Stories*. Although he continued writing for pulp magazines until 1934, he made an important leap forward in February 1931, when his first story appeared in *Collier's*, one of the major glossy periodicals of the time. While publishing in *Collier's* and later the *Saturday Evening Post* contributed to Haycox's prestige and prosperity, it added to his conflict between financial and artistic objectives. A member of the Republican Party's elite in Oregon, the seasoned writer lived in a grand estate in the hills west of Portland and demanded economic security. An assured income meant adhering to the formulas that had won him fame as a top western writer, yet Haycox became increasingly dissatisfied with repetition. He added variations but feared a loss of marketability should he stray too far from the mold expected by editors of magazines with a mass circulation. Haycox yearned to produce works of lasting value and tortured himself when, for commercial reasons, he turned to writing about cowboys rather than the pioneer experience in Oregon, which remained his major interest.

Despite his aspirations, Haycox was doubtful of inspiration and viewed his literary development as coming more from hard work than from any natural talent. His was a businesslike approach of simply sitting down before his typewriter and forcing himself to create. Gradually his technique improved, and refinement came, he felt, not from intellectual planning but from never being complaisant about the work he was doing. The writer wanted to entertain readers but yearned to bring social and moral concerns into his stories. Haycox frequently wrote about the code of the West, individual duty, and increasingly about free will versus fate. His typical hero is a self-motivated leader, a man of action doing what he has to do with a somewhat melancholy, fatalistic attitude. The writer often laments the frailty of human life when contrasted with the vastness of nature and immeasurable time.

By the time "Stage to Lordsburg" appeared, Ernest Haycox had joined Zane Grey and Frederick Faust, who published under the name Max Brand, as the three most successful and prolific authors of popular western fiction. All three of these writers lived by the market, yet each had a yearning for artistic development. Zane Grey, who hailed from Zanesville, Ohio, traveled extensively throughout the West, wrote romantically about the desert landscape, and remained the most widely read writer of western tales until Louis L'Amour's success after World War II. Frederick Faust, who was born in Seattle but spent his youth on farms in the San Joaquin Valley of California, became a consummate pulp writer, emphasizing action over reflection without adopting the common vocabulary and hackneyed excesses of the dime novelists, who targeted their output at juvenile readers. Ernest Haycox, whose body of work was slimmer than either Grey's or Faust's, preferred more challenging themes than his competitors and heroes who were more psychologically complex.

Haycox started publishing serialized novels in December 1928 with *Free Grass*, a story that originally appeared in installments in *West*, one of the pulp magazines. In *Free Grass*, Haycox has the hero state his credo: "Shoulder to shoulder, fist to fist . . . . Play your own hand, ask no favors, ride straight, shoot fast. Keep all obligations." Doubleday subsequently brought the volume out in hardback, and the book enjoyed popularity in both the United States and England.

By 1936, with *Trouble Shooter*, the novel that director Cecil B. DeMille filmed as *Union Pacific*, Haycox turned seriously to the historical western, putting his love for thorough research to advantageous use. For the first time he based a novel on an actual event, the building of the Union Pacific Railroad, and included historical personages. By that point in Haycox's career, the writer's language had become less clichéd, and he introduced more characters and subplots.

Breaking into the pages of the *Saturday Evening Post*, the most widely read glossy magazine of them all, had been Haycox's goal for two decades, and he was delighted when *Bugles in the Afternoon*, perhaps his best historical novel, appeared in the popular periodical in serialized form in 1943. *Bugles in the Afternoon*, which deals with the Battle of the Little Bighorn, reached an estimated 3.5 million readers through the *Saturday Evening Post* and over time sold almost another 1.3 million copies in book format. Haycox interpreted Custer as a complex man, permanently adolescent, driven by energy and ambition to seek fame in a predatory world.

Although Haycox had become a master at writing commercial fiction, he knew that westerns were considered a second-rate genre and desired to move beyond the magazine audience and devote himself to producing serious novels about the West that would attract non-western readers. Aware of the financial risk involved, Ernest redirected his creative powers during his final years to writing three books with literary merit, none of them serialized. *Long Storm*, which appeared in 1946, is rife with the rhetoric of social Darwinism, a point of view that haunted Haycox, and focuses on the struggle of the weak against the strong. Almost a half-century after Frank Norris and Theodore Dreiser arrived on the literary scene, Haycox fully embraced the naturalism of those earlier American writers, even though their outlook was no longer in vogue.

In *The Earthbreakers* (1952), Haycox returned to frontier Oregon, the subject nearest his heart, and devoted months to researching pioneer records and memoirs. The result is a long, multidimensional novel about a frontier community, a combination of history and imagination, but a story in which women assume a dynamic role.

The Adventurers, like *Earthbreakers* published after Haycox's death, begins in 1865 with a shipwreck off the Oregon coast and again shows the writer's fascination with the Darwinian contest. The novel's characters are governed by animal instincts and survival becomes their principle concern. Unhappy with the book, Haycox set it aside in 1948, as he struggled to find a new style, and the novel did not reach print until 1954.

Throughout his life Haycox agonized over perfecting his craft, vacillating between commercialism and an urge for literary stature. To lead a life of comfort, the writer made compromises yet remained convinced that quality and marketability need not be exclusive. Frustrated, torn between confidence and doubt, Haycox searched for a better means of expression that would capture honestly the pioneer experience without sacrificing a mass readership. Behind the action in his adventure fiction was a philosopher struggling to improve himself as an artisan, a dedicated workman who longed to lift himself into the ranks of literature.

Haycox lived at a time when critics viewed westerns as mere entertainment. John Ford, widely regarded as the greatest of Hollywood's Western directors, won four Academy Awards for feature films and two for documentaries, yet none of his Oscars was for westerns. The literary world until after Haycox's death tended to ignore western writers, even though some were well regarded by such historians as Bernard De Voto and Walter Prescott Webb.

Undoubtedly Ernest Haycox's narratives, like those of Owen Wister, Zane Grey, and Frederick Faust, helped shape the popular conception of the frontier West. Later western writers—Luke Short, Frank Gruber, and D. W. Newton, among others—attested to Haycox's influence, and Haycox led the way for Alan LeMay (*The Searchers*) and Jack Schaefer (*Shane*), who brought unique creativity to the western genre. It was appropriate that for years the Western Writers of America called their annual awards, what is now named the "Spur" awards, the "Erny."

Ernest Haycox Jr. has written an amazingly frank and perceptive biography of his father, presenting the man both as a successful writer and as a private person—parent, husband, responsible community leader. Shortly before his death in 1950, the popular western author, terminally ill with cancer, lamented, "I hope I'm remembered." This biography brings Haycox's life, effort, and accomplishment into focus and adds to the popular storyteller's claim to worth and remembrance.

RONALD L. DAVIS

Dallas, Texas

PREFACE

FIFTY YEARS AGO, SHORTLY AFTER MY FATHER'S DEATH, HIS COLLEGE writing instructor proposed to write a book about his gifted, one-time student. My mother resisted the idea, explaining that any honest account would have required mention of his unpleasant childhood and thus reflected poorly on his parents, both living. In addition, her son was considering a book about his father and, she said, "he should have first crack at it."

Obviously, I'd said something to her along that line, though I don't recall it now. What is clear is that I took inordinate time addressing the project, which didn't get off the ground until I'd retired from a career in corporate journalism. And even then, with abundant time theoretically available, it did not move swiftly.

My first thought was to build a brief narrative around excerpts from his 1947–50 correspondence, which, at one time, appeared to be the only personal record remaining of a life that, while not long, was conspicuously energetic and accomplished. He had cheerfully burned most of his earlier records when he and my mother moved from their impractically large house in Portland's West Hills to more manageable quarters in 1949.

It was only a slice of the man's life but a pretty good one because he had now been, for a decade or more, one of the country's most popular producers of western adventure fiction, particularly well known to the millions of weekly readers of *Collier's* magazine and the *Saturday Evening Post*. By 1947, he had 22 novels and about 250 short stories to his credit and a good handful of motion pictures, notably *Stagecoach* in 1939. He was probably Oregon's best-known private citizen for, beyond the writing, he was a busy public man, a frequent speaker at events large and small, a stalwart Republican spokesman (and, to some minds, gubernatorial prospect), and the head of his college alumni association—a board member, fund-raiser, figurehead, or counselor a dozen times over.

It is true that western fiction was not then, and is not now, widely regarded as a venue of literary merit. Many critics and scholars have said that he was as good a hand at the business as ever came along, and that he did more than any other to give the western theme style and substance—a degree of credibility, an occasionally lustrous passage. But in these years, it wasn't uncommon for some reviewer to observe that, yes, that was a good book but then ask why this fellow didn't apply his considerable talent to better material.

He had asked himself the same question and, for that reason, the late 1940s were for him a time of immense frustration. There were days when the grand scheme of the panoramic novel seemed clear and bright, but also days in which his characters appeared leaden and frivolous to him and the next rung on the literary ladder seemed hopelessly beyond grasp. He wrote two novels in this period that were in his mind failures; the short story output faltered and his income fell by half. He did not live to know how his final effort, *The Earthbreakers*, would be seen, and no one knows how he might be regarded today if there had been time for the half-dozen major works he'd framed in his mind and not just the one.

What appears here is a fuller account than first contemplated, for, after my mother's death in 1993, more of the personal record surfaced. She discarded nothing and he'd not been quite the destroyer that I remembered standing by that bonfire. His speech and research files remained intact and among his unpublished manuscripts were several pieces that were to some degree autobiographical. There was a long soldier's lament from 1917 and a loose-leaf diary in which, when the very occasional mood struck, he would examine his progress and that of his world. And I would find that recipients had preserved some of the correspondence that he had thought not worth saving. From these and some other sources came the longer story.

I have, of course, exercised the normal editorial prerogatives. His letters, scattered throughout this volume but particularly concentrated (covering 1947–50) in the final five chapters, are generally excerpted rather than presented full. Sentences are sometimes condensed and paragraphs have been combined here and there to connect a train of thought more closely. A few spellings have been modernized and a few commas excised. Otherwise, all quotations in this book and all of the passages lifted from his published and unpublished works are unexpurgated and unvarnished originals. From chapter 12 on, I have reduced my role as a narrator and allowed the letters to tell much of the story because they express vividly the concerns of his last years.

The title of this volume was suggested by his 1935 novel, *The Silver Desert*, a contemporary western incorporating Hollywood personalities that foreshadowed by about two years his own lengthy association with the silver screen. He was only a "Hollywood writer" once, for a couple of months, and found the interlude cautionary. Still, a string of motion picture sales in the late 1930s and the 40s contributed greatly to his reputation and bank account. He was one of those artists, he would have admitted, "who disliked everything about Hollywood but the money."

This account describes a deliberative man who knew himself to be a competent professional but did not consider that profession beyond the reach of many others. Writing was mostly a matter of unrelenting, repetitive labor, he said, and when I once insisted that some exceptional manner of talent had to loom large in the equation, and asked him to quantify what part that might be, he responded after a moment's contemplation: "Fifteen percent. No more than that. If that."

He was probably laughing when he said it. He was amused by many things, his own afflictions foremost. Introductions were often awkward, he said, for a good many people were expecting a weather-stained and taciturn westerner or, if not that, a moody and mercurial aesthetic; and what they found, with evident suspicion and disappointment, was a little guy with a bald head and a Roman nose. Hauled before a packed movie house at the world premiere of *Canyon Passage* in Portland in 1946 and expected to say something profound, he settled for small talk. "Well," he said, "this is the first time I have ever gotten into the Broadway Theater for nothing." He overheard a conversation at the Multnomah Athletic

Club that kept him chuckling for hours. The conversation was about him: wasn't it nice, some chap said to a companion, that the club had finally elected "one of them" to its board of trustees. He probably wasn't "one of them" despite appearances; but he wasn't affronted by the suggestion or by many other small matters of conflict or criticism or misunderstanding, of which authors get a full share. Near the end of his life, he regretted the lack of time to do more. That was worth a complaint. But he also knew that he'd done about as much with the time available as a man can. He had played the hand as well as he knew how, and with a good deal of success; and on that frontier which he knew so well and had described so often, that was all you could ask.

This book could not have been written without the assistance of many other individuals or the resources of several institutions. They are gratefully acknowledged at the end of the story.

ERNEST HAYCOX JR.

Mosier, Oregon

ON A SILVER DESERT

—1—

On a Late Frontier

FOR SEVERAL OF HIS YOUNG YEARS, IT WAS THE BOY'S AMBITION to farm in the Barton district, which lies along the Clackamas River about thirty miles east of Portland. This was where his maternal grandfather had established himself and, although the vernal Ernest Haycox could not have known Ernest Burghardt well, he seems to have been that relative the young man most admired and most closely resembled in later life. The two Ernests shared energetic and optimistic dispositions and both were incessant toilers. They were also both of modest height, although otherwise dissimilar, the grandfather being heavyset from the healthy appetite of hard labor while the grandson (addressed by all who knew him as Erny) seldom passed 150 pounds in his maturity. He was a lithe and respectably constructed fellow—just never a very big one.

Ernest Burghardt and his wife, Emelia, and her parents were the first of the forebears to reach Oregon, to which the grandson's name will long be attached. They had stepped ashore at San Francisco in early 1876 after a hard six-month voyage from the East Coast, but were dissatisfied with this first landfall. The lack of cascading streams in the vicinity may have been a factor, for Ernest was by training a miller and falling water was the foundation of such enterprise. Then, too, there was perhaps a feeling that earlier arrivals had skimmed the cream of opportunity here and that the present residents were a sharp, grasping lot, particularly in the presence of those newly landed with evident resources. It was not at all like their previous habitat, which was rural Wisconsin.

In any event, the original idea had been to come to Oregon, which they understood to be much like the upper Midwest, though less severe in climate. They continued on to Portland, where it was raining hard and desperately muddy and the Willamette River, to which the city clung, had overrun its banks. Alternately walking and wading, twenty-six-year-old Ernest and father-in-law Henry Melcher explored thirty miles up the river, passing Oregon City where a great rock ledge interrupted navigation and produced waterpower in abundance.* Ernest bought a homestead a dozen miles east of that community and, having spent his entire $2,000 bankroll, found employment sharpening the stone buhrs of an Oregon City flour mill, walking home on weekends to comfort his isolated wife and the first of their nine children.

When his financial situation improved, Ernest stayed home and cleared land, soon discovering that a single man, however industrious, was no match for two hundred acres of matted brush and old-growth fir. In 1878, he sold a part of the homestead and bought a half interest in a rundown gristmill several miles east on the Clackamas River. He renovated the Eagle Creek mill and, though he soon sold out, continued to run it for wages while farming and stock raising in other locations near the river. One of these was the Palmateer settlement (later christened Garfield), the apex of several land claims of a large French-Canadian family; and it was probably here in 1881 that daughter Bertha Mary, the fourth of Ernest and Emelia's offspring and the future mother of Erny, was born.

In 1887, the Burghardts moved again—for the sixth time, according to the remarkably tolerant Emelia, who was not often consulted on such matters. This time it was to Deep Creek, a few miles west of Eagle Creek and a half-day wagon ride east of Portland. Here, Ernest turned another sagging collection of parts and pieces into a first-rate flour and feed mill that would shortly attract grain-laden farm wagons from a thirty-mile

* Many Oregonians have at least one story associated with the famously damp and dreary winters and early spring in the western portion of the state. Ernest's involved that walk along the river with his father-in-law. The young man observed a woman in high boots in a flooded farmyard, a stick in one hand, a bucket in the other. What could she be doing? "Well, Ernest," Henry Melcher replied, "she is looking for the well."

radius. He added a sawmill to keep himself occupied before the fall harvest, opened a general store, continued his farming and raised hogs, a fine supply of feed for the porkers being provided by his miller's toll. Shortly, he also began accumulating land on flat ground a mile east of the mills, plotting a town there, which he named Barton in honor of a pleasantly remembered Wisconsin community. He built a larger store in Barton and, at the time of his grandson's birth in 1899, he was the community's postmaster as well as its promoter and principal supplier of flour, feed, and general merchandise.

He was about as self-made as they come, albeit touched by fortune occasionally. Born in 1850 in Berlin, Kingdom of Prussia, Ernest had survived passage to the New World in 1856 on a vessel that surrendered about 30 of its 250 passengers to cholera, his father and an older brother among them. There was a near miss during the Civil War when he was enveloped by Confederate cavalry and trampled, forever after carrying the mark of a horse's hoof on his chest. He was officially a drummer for a volunteer company of Wisconsin's Fourteenth Infantry Regiment, but said his principal duty was scavenging—raiding beehives and stealing chickens and piglets and such from farms along the route of march—and trading across lines for coffee and tobacco and sugar when the Fourteenth was closely engaged. It can be assumed that he was shot at occasionally, by farmers or Johnny Rebs or perhaps both.

He was in many respects an ideal colonist, his skills abetted by a restless and self-reliant nature, documented at age eleven when he rebelled against the stern discipline of stepfather Silas Doernbecher and left home. He came to Oregon because his wife's parents offered to pay the way, but sooner or later, driven by unconfined curiosity, he would have gone somewhere. The western frontier was, of course, full of those who were never certain that a present opportunity, however rewarding, was the best obtainable. The paternal grandfather, Thomas Haycox, was like Ernest Burghardt in that respect, but in almost no other. ◆

Grandfather Tom, a painter of wagons and houses and scenic murals on occasion, and a moody socialist, arrived in Oregon in 1890. A Shropshire lad, he was now in his fifties and had been in the United States for about three dozen years. The family settled in Cleveland about 1855 but Tom wasn't with them for long, if at all. Some heard that he was deemed to have disgraced the Haycox name by running away from an apprenticeship in England and stealing aboard the ship that carried his parents to America, and was cast out for this atrocious act. Whatever the circumstances, it seems to have been firm and final parting, for apparently neither mother nor father ever again saw or heard from their fourth son.

Tom did not apply for citizenship and, for this reason, probably avoided military service in the Civil War. In later years, he deflected questions about his status by declaring in various records that he was born in New York state. He did live there for a time, marrying Mary Hill of Utica about 1870, but he also painted wagons in Chicago for Studebaker and may have lived in Kansas for a spell, and was in California by 1877. His third and last child, William James (who would father Erny), was born in Stockton that year and, not long after, twenty-six-year-old Mary Haycox died there. Then or later, her sister Laura, who worked in a textile mill in Utica, came west to help Tom raise his brood, which, in addition to the baby, included son Frank and daughter Lily.

In Stockton, Tom was by turns foreman of a Southern Pacific Railroad paint shop, a painting contractor, and the operator of a home-decorating store. No extended description of him survives, but son Frank remembered a brooding and largely uncommunicative father. Another relative said Tom "was the splitting image of John Bull" and his grandson would put it this way: "He was the toughest Englishman I ever knew."

Tom must have been a burly fellow and, as was said of a couple of his six brothers, probably inclined to use his fists when no better solution offered. That may help explain why he changed jobs frequently. He is next found in Tucson, where he and Laura were married and his grandson was told that Tom had abandoned the painting profession for a time and was a lawman. In the late 1880s the family returned to Utica briefly, where Tom worked for a streetcar company and son WJ joined a street gang, the Twelfth Ward Sluggers. And then it was on to Oregon and the promised purity of communal living in a cooperative society that had been established (or perhaps *was* established with Tom's assistance) in the timbered wilds above the Nehalem River Valley. That place is not much farther west of Portland in a straight line than Deep Creek is east, but it was, and remains, incomparably more difficult to reach. To describe the Nehalem country as remote requires generosity.

Sparked by religious conviction or political views that veered from the mainstream, or by a resentment of oppressive labor conditions or depressed agricultural prices, or by some combination of these and other indignities borne by the common man, Utopian communities thrived in the late nineteenth-century Pacific Northwest. Some had fairly long runs but this one, of which there is almost no record, did not. Tom and his associates evidently built a sawmill and hired a business agent to sell their output; but it was a poor location for that purpose, the local market being small and the distant one hard to reach over wagon tracks that were often impassable in winter. The precise reason for the cooperative's failure, however, may have been social rather than economic. The grandson was told that the community flew apart when its men wisely pronounced that its women should prepare meals in the harmony of a communal kitchen.

Tom was in Portland briefly in 1892–93 with sixteen-year-old WJ. The boy landed his first steady job about this time, as a fireman on a Southern Pacific Railroad switchyard engine, and he stayed on when Tom returned to the Nehalem to homestead for several years. Son Frank had remained there, raising a family and manufacturing shingles, as had daughter Lily for a sadly short time. Lily's story is misty; all that's remembered with certainty is that she and her baby daughter Georgie rejoined the family after her husband, George Latimer, perhaps a logger, was killed in railroad accident. Lily died a short time later. With Georgie in tow, Tom and Laura moved to Portland about 1899 and he was once again a painter of wagons and houses when his grandson was born.

In contrast, the last decade of the nineteenth century was the only extended period of Ernest Burghardt's life during which he did not wander away on some new quest. Deep Creek and a growing family had him fully occupied, indeed overworked during harvest when both farm and gristmill demanded more or less continuous manual effort. The entire family labored and while Bertha and her sisters avoided their father's dusty, sweaty flour factory, there were tasks at hand, all year long—abundant housework and kitchen duty, and a large vegetable garden, and there were chickens and hogs to feed and the store to clerk. As this was a typically self-sufficient farm family, the summers and falls were a steady procession of preserving and pickling and butchering and curing and, of course, the women made most of the family's clothing. They were also handy with the horses and Emma, who was two years older than Bertha, helped brother Charlie break a pair of black bull calves to the yoke. Ernest would return from his Portland deliveries of flour and dressed pork with necessities like sugar and coffee, and boots and lengths of cloth and the occasional sack of hard candy. But most of what this large family consumed, including the dandelion and berry-flavored wines, was homemade.

It was by all accounts a cheerful and supportive household. Rejecting stepfather Doernbecher's stern discipline, Ernest did not punish his offspring for sins as minor as talking back or scattering tools. Son Charlie would recall that for a time Bertha was given some slack in the matter of doing dishes—she did not like to get her hands wet, he said—and that brother Eddy was allowed to sleep late and did so until he tired of limp pancakes and cold coffee. Education suffered, though that was unavoidable. Ernest cut and donated the lumber for the Barton area's first schoolhouse, but it was difficult to attract competent instructors to this near wilderness. Some who came, including one gentleman who dedicated afternoons to independent study while he snoozed behind a log, were hardly more useful than some neighbor's bright teenage daughter. At one point, the Burghardts sent Eddy, the oldest, to stay with Emelia's parents for several months. They lived a bit closer to civilization but, said Charlie, "all Eddy ever learned to do there was chew tobacco."

Bertha fondly recalled her parents and Deep Creek in later years but by sixteen or so was ready to make her own way. Generations of Oregon farm daughters of that age—those not yet married—found their way to Portland, where there was a steady market for domestic help. More likely, though, Bertha migrated to Oregon City, where her family probably had friends. A capable and confident young lady, already schooled in the retail trade, Bertha would have had no difficulty securing employment there.

Meanwhile, after feeding the firebox of a steam locomotive for a time, WJ had gone to work on the river, serving alternately as a deckhand or fireman on various steamboats that operated on the lower Columbia River system. These included the *R. R. Thompson,* the largest sternwheeler on the river, and the swift sidewheeler *T. J. Potter,* which incorporated the gingerbread style and commodious accommodations of an elegant Hudson River packet. Both operated between Portland and Astoria on the coast, the *Potter* accomplishing the roughly hundred-mile, one-way passage, which included intermediate landings for fuel and freight, in nine busy hours. WJ and his mates worked their tails off; three firemen on six-hour shifts fed twenty-seven cords of wood into the firebox on each round trip while the deckhands, six to a shift, loaded the fuel and trucked the cargo on and off and, in addition to their line-handling and navigational duties, assisted passengers with their baggage and kept the *Potter* shining with brushes and brooms.

The *Potter's* transits were often eventful, for there were cardsharps at many of its tables and the occasional drunken logger slumbered in the ladies' saloon. In the late 1890s, some of these daily excursions were additionally spiced by rumors associated with the Spanish-American War (Astoria Bay had been mined, according to one) and tales spun by travelers to and from Klondike gold fields. There were also genuine dramas afloat, typically involving the swift-churning boats of competitive lines seeking right-of-way or obdurate Finnish fisherman along the lower Columbia who were disinclined to yield it.

WJ would recall one occasion when the *Potter* pushed through a cluster of fishing boats near its Astoria terminal, nearly swamping several. "The aroused fishermen . . . appeared in a frenzied and threatening mood," he wrote, "[and] the deck crew assumed strategic positions at the bow, guard rail and amidships to prevent the Finns from boarding the steamer while the passengers crowded forward on the upper deck, watching developments. One Finlander with a rifle in his hands shouted from his boat to the steamer's captain: 'You better build an iron fence around that pilot house before you make another trip down here.'" On an earlier run, he added, a bullet from an unseen rifleman had pierced the house. ◆

At twenty-one in 1898, young WJ Haycox was a slender six-footer with straight and pleasant features and a light step to which, mostly likely, the slight swagger of a prideful riverman had been added. He strummed a guitar with some skill and had a gift for conversation and storytelling, and Bertha surely wasn't the first young lady he charmed with his sociable manner and worldly knowledge. However, although only seventeen, she may have been the first he had known who could give equally good account. She was a gangly girl with large dark eyes—no great beauty but, based on photographic evidence, a suitably striking presence in the high-necked, tight-wasted costumes of fin-de-siècle fashion, with her dark tresses swept up under the wide brim of a commanding headpiece. Her manner was both dramatic and coquettish and, if you believed her, she was sometimes followed by strange men. She and WJ were, at very least, an interesting combination.

They may have met in Oregon City, where WJ landed occasionally while working on the steamer *Elmore*, which was small enough to squeeze through the navigation lock at the falls of the Willamette and trade along the upper river. Perhaps it happened at one of the weekly public dances in the city or when Bertha was a passenger on some weekend excursion or on a commuter run downriver to Portland. All that is certain of the affair, however, is its conclusion. Bertha and WJ were married in Oregon City on December 5, 1898, in the office of the distinguished lawyer and political activist William S. U'Ren. The ceremony was performed by Justice of the Peace Christian Scheubel, U'Ren's law partner and later a legislator of considerable standing in his own right, and witnessed by U'Ren and sister Emma. The couple located in Portland immediately after the wedding; and ten months following, in a house near the Willamette a few blocks south of Portland's center, their son was born. They named him Ernest James, honoring her father and someone on the Haycox side—perhaps both father and grandfather, as James was Tom's middle name too.

Either by edict or common consent, the day of his birth—Sunday, October 1, 1899—was one of national celebration, marking the victorious return to New York City of Admiral George Dewey, the hero of Manila Bay. Flags flew high, there was great naval review in New York harbor, and many Portland merchants marked the event with Dewey Day sales on Saturday. Triumph and conflict dominated that Sunday's papers: in the Philippines, the Spanish-American War had been followed by indigenous resistance to American occupation, in which a recently returned regiment of Oregon volunteers had taken casualties; and in South Africa, where the shooting had started two weeks earlier, British troops were now in some places cut off by columns of fierce and mobile Dutchmen.

That fall Sunday was probably a joyous occasion, the new parents at least momentarily flattered by the appearance of an heir. However, the event was most likely unplanned and unsolicited. They did not obtain a birth certificate for the boy, nor did they observe the custom of that time of providing notice to local newspapers. One can theorize, of course, that the lack of publicity was justified; given WJ's recent problem (he had been arrested shortly after the wedding for stealing a guitar, and jailed for twelve days), perhaps it made no sense to him to advertise his presence. However, the later record is undeniably one of two people for whom parenthood held no great appeal, for they abandoned the boy when they separated a few years later and there were no more children by that marriage or by any of those following. Youthful imperfections are forgivable, of course, and Bertha and WJ were hardly more than adolescents when their son was born. Still, maturity is a process by which, sooner or later, the self-absorbed and fanciful tendencies common to youth are tempered by judgment and responsibility. In many ways, these two never did grow up.

WJ retired from the river after marriage and in 1899 was a fireman in the powerhouse of a Portland streetcar company, and this was the beginning of an odyssey of mostly unsatisfactory positions in unsatisfactory places that would persist until, at about age fifty, he no longer sought employment. Had Erny's father achieved something more than a rural grade school education, he might have had better luck, but this is uncertain. For while he was an affable and presentable man with a quick mind, he was also destructively impatient, noisily opinionated and easily offended, particularly by the manner of his employers. Recurring poverty was the fact of his life, but it never diminished a mood of self-righteous importance that made no other man, the son included, quite his equal.

In womanhood, Bertha was dismissed as flighty and frivolous by some of her sisters and brothers, described by them as given to adventurous stories about her life which they did not entirely believe. Some probably were true, for her second husband, Billy Pond, was a gambler who died in puzzling and perhaps premeditated circumstances. But some certainly were not, for she told them that her third husband was a titled Englishman. This was a remarkable promotion for Joel Cartwright, who was English but had been an ordinary seaman and, during the Spanish-American War, a medical corpsman in the U.S. Army. Maybe he was from a good family but, according to story, he had fled England after killing a man in a fight.

Bertha's facial features were dominated by a powerful nose (which the boy inherited), suggesting to many that she was one of Zion's daughters. She was clever enough to realize that vigorous denial was pointless and perhaps incriminating, but the condition gravely affronted her vanity and caused lifelong aggravation. The imaginary world she sometimes sought was explained to some degree by a real one that, in her mind, had burdened her unfairly. ◆

Had Ernest Burghardt remained on Deep Creek, he and Emelia might have grown old pleasantly enough, surrounded by a spreading family and the material comforts of a good life's work. However, about 1905, he traded the Barton store for a commercial building in Portland and, a year or so later, bargained this structure for a quarter-section of virgin farmland in southern Idaho, on which, he was assured, water could be plentifully supplied. Leaving Emelia at home, he went to Idaho with three of the boys, discovering there a sagebrush desert on which there was no water at all and no prospect of getting any. Ernest gave up on the project after a couple of hopeless years and was ill and financially pressed when he retreated to Deep Creek. The Idaho venture had drained the family's resources and Ernest was not much of a hand at collecting his own receivables, which at the time included notes from a number of land sales. He died a dispirited man in 1912 and most of the family's Deep Creek holdings were attached by a creditor and later disposed of in a sheriff's auction. Emelia remarried, not wishing to burden her offspring. Her new husband's name was Turner but she asked to be remembered as Ernest's wife and, when she died in 1934, she was buried next to him in the pioneer cemetery at Damascus, which is a short distance northwest of Deep Creek.

The city of Barton has not yet materialized. A railroad and trolley line from Portland arrived in 1903 but was later abandoned. It is but a small crossroads community today, with a store and post office and a few other buildings and flat fields running away in every direction. The approximate location of the gristmill, where state highway 224 bridges Deep Creek, is still identified as Burghardts Mill on some maps.*

As for the Haycox elders, Tom and Laura moved from Portland to Seaside on the Oregon coast in 1906. Though near seventy, he continued working and for several years operated a retail paint store where Georgie clerked. He was elected to the Seaside City Council in 1907, serving two years; and grandson Ernest, now being passed around to relatives, attended the fifth grade at Seaside in 1910–11. Tom's artistic hand remained firm for a long time. A generous reporter observed in 1910 that his newly executed mural on the Pythian Hall's drop curtain was a "humdinger . . . he has excelled all former efforts as a scenic artist."

*A far more visible reminder of the old family is associated with Frank Silas Doernbecher, who was Ernest's half brother, born to his mother, Johanna, and stepfather in 1861 (about the time Ernest left home). Frank came west in the 1880s, establishing a furniture manufacturing company in Portland that was one of the country's largest in the early twentieth century. He directed that a quarter of his estate be used for public benefit, and this bequest founded the city's magnificent Doernbecher Children's Hospital.

He and Laura were now spending summers on the homestead and about 1917 they moved back to the Nehalem country for good. Georgie, married in 1913, followed with her husband and the four of them were living there, planting fruit trees and berries, when the old man's heart failed in 1920. He was buried in the pioneer cemetery at nearby Mist, as was Laura, who lived with the youngsters in that hidden land until her death in 1930.

The homestead was sold to a timber company in 1945 and has since then been part of a sprawling tree farm in Oregon's northern Coast Range. The house collapsed into its earthen basement years ago but its ruins are still visible, bounded by the silver skeletons of several large fruit trees; and it can be located on topographical maps by virtue of a symbol that indicates the existence of graves. These are the resting places of Lily and perhaps of Lily's husband George and of Frank Haycox's infant daughter Eleanor, who died in 1908. It is still remembered by locals as the Haycox place, mostly because they associate it with the grandson. Some believe Erny lived there as an older man and, while this is myth, WJ and his second wife were residents in the early 1930s; and if others assumed that the tall, slender fellow who tramped down to the main road to buy groceries and pick up the mail was the well-known western writer, it is not at all certain WJ would have clarified matters.

— 2 —

Stropped on Hard Stones

ON A SUNDAY DRIVE IN THE EARLY 1940S, IT OCCURRED TO the writer that his wife and children might like to see his birthplace. The building was, or at least had been, on lower Caruthers, a street of about half a dozen blocks bounded at one end by steep green hills and at its lower limit by railroad tracks and the Willamette River. He searched along this route for several minutes, stopping at intervals to stare out at various peaked-roof houses, but he found nothing that resembled the place that had been known to him from some earlier time. "Well," he said finally, "maybe they tore it down."

It hadn't been home for long. Bertha and WJ were gone from Caruthers well before their son's first birthday, moving in with Tom and Laura in another set of rented rooms. Then they left Portland with Erny in tow and for several years were simply drifting from one place to the next, for the most part mill towns and lumber camps and ranches scattered all about Oregon and Washington. WJ still stoked fireboxes occasionally; he worked in and perhaps managed a shingle mill for a spell, held jobs in various logging operations, was from time to time a woodcutter and a farm hand, and at one point was herding 2,200 sheep along Murderer's Creek in central Oregon. Bertha, the more practical of the pair and possibly the better provider, found employment with some regularity in restaurants and logging-camp dining halls, occasionally in a managerial capacity. Her son tagged along on some of these assignments and he learned his first trade in the back end of some eating establishment at an early age. He was, he said, a pearl diver, an occupation better known to most as dishwashing.

He never faulted his parents for this meandering. Indeed, he seemed to remember all the knocking about as an entertaining and instructive experience; and given time, he would have constructed a novel about it. It would have begun with a boy

> ... full of memories of moving around. His father, restless and touche, will quit any job at the drop of a hat. Many times they pack their possessions in suitcases and bundles, go down to the railroad shanty, light a bonfire in the track to stop the train, and go on to the next town. The boy's people have no sense of the future, no sense of thrift, no fear of tomorrow. They mirror the working people of their time—that is, the outdoor working people of the West. There's always another job around the corner; it has always been like that in the past. Many times the boy's people leave their trunk in some cheap country hotel and just walk away from the board bill, having no money; they've got such trunks scattered . . . throughout the northwest.

On one occasion, WJ left Bertha and young Erny and their bundled assets in one of these establishments and went away, telling his wife he would return when he had found a new position. Bertha waited some time and it was the landlady, who was observant in such matters, who finally told her that her husband wasn't coming back. "If you want him, you'll have to go looking for him," the woman said. Bertha said she did this and found her husband in the next town.

It is uncertain when the couple parted or what specific events led to the dissolution, or where they were when things flew apart. One of the last dependable sightings, by another branch of the Haycox family, occurred in the Puget Sound area, possibly about 1907. Those relatives remember that WJ worked for a sheet-metal company in Olympia, and some had the impression that he owned the enterprise. Bertha doesn't appear in this recollection, but Erny does. Marion Grace Haycox remembered hating her unruly cousin because he sat behind her in class and fiddled the tips of her long braids in his inkwell. Most likely, the young lady's torment didn't last long. WJ later claimed to have been "in charge of logging operations" at several locales in Washington, including Grays Harbor and Shelton. They lived in a lumber camp near Enumclaw east of Tacoma at one point; Erny remembered fleeing a forest fire there in a passenger coach attached to the end of a logging train, its occupants forced by the heat and smoke to lie flat in the aisles.

In later times, Erny would reveal small scenes of this early life to his children. One story involved a miniature sawmill he built somewhere in the woods, complete with buildings fashioned from boxes and a railroad line and a revolving saw blade manufactured from the top of a tin can. His trees were fern stalks. There was also a real freight car on some lumber-camp rail spur that with pride and considerable effort he filled full with beer bottles collected from around the bunkhouses and the community's trash dump; and for which he would later receive payment that must have been passed through the hands of several honest trainmen to reach him. And there was one of those silent, juvenile love affairs in which one party is uninformed as to other's blinding devotion. His family was moving from one rooming house to another and his task was to carry a suitcase back and forth until all the clothing had been transported to the new quarters. Unfortunately, the direct route led in front of a young lady's house and he could not bear the thought of her seeing him and discovering the truth of his circumstances. He thus devised another route, several blocks longer, to avoid the disclosure.

In these recollections, the old times were mostly good times. He told of being rolled into a buggy and taken to a schoolhouse dance—probably at Natal on the Nehalem River, from which the homestead was about four miles distant. The children slept on benches while their elders danced and howled, coyotes serenaded them on the way home, and when they got there, they would know that skunks had been investigating the chicken coop. His parents lived a few miles east of Portland one winter and so close to the railroad tracks that the rotary snowplow threw gravel down on their roof and punctured it in a hundred places. But it wasn't all that bad. "When the bitter wind howled down from the Columbia Gorge and ice clogged the river," Erny would recall, "the stove stayed red-hot all night long. There was always fresh bread baking in the kitchen oven, currant jam in the cupboard, a bin of apples in the basement—and the mail order catalog to round out a swell evening."

He saw his father occasionally after the family broke up but, for the next several years, not often. WJ continued to wander in the Northwest and, though he may have pled inability to give his son a proper home, it was mostly a matter of not wanting to be bothered with the child. Bertha moved to San Francisco after the separation. The boy heard from her sporadically but probably did not see his mother again for seven years. She sent her son a photograph in 1911, showing her and a female companion standing on the deck of the steamer *Harvard*, which operated between San Francisco and Los Angeles. It was a "bum" picture, she wrote on the back. Did her dear son recognize her?

Relatives assumed degrees of responsibility for Erny over the next several years, although there were gaps in that coverage. These were tough times. He was lonely and missed his mother greatly and must have had difficulty accepting what everybody else in the family knew, that Bertha and WJ had simply dumped him. Reluctant in later years to explain candidly what had happened, he would prepare short autobiographical sketches for his publishers in which his early knock-about times were condensed in a single phrase: "I was early on my own," he would say, with no further explanation. ◆

In 1910, when Erny was with the Haycox grandparents in Seaside for the fifth grade, he was under the supervision of eighteen-year-old cousin Georgie, who was by all accounts a businesslike young lady (Seaside's newest telephone operator) and pretty enough for the city's annual beauty contest. Even with Tom glowering in the background, the stay must have had its pleasant moments, for Georgie's beau and later husband, Earl Smith, managed the local ice cream parlor. The boy missed only three days of school that year and was tardy but once, and his grades averaged 89.

He was in Portland in 1911 and a woman named Harriet Stephens, perhaps a widow who rented a room or two, signed his fifth-grade report card. However, the few stories from this period suggest that Erny was at times unsupervised and substantially self-supporting, and sometimes hungry. He washed dishes in restaurants for meals and change but starting about now his major occupation was selling newspapers, and much later he pointed out to his son a street corner he had used for this purpose. It was a marginal location; there would have been a trolley at the intersection but it was several blocks south of the business district and a good many of the evening commuters would have already made their purchase. At least, that is how it seemed to son Jim, who asked why he hadn't moved closer to the center of things. It was the best he could do at the time, his father explained. "You had to fight for your corner."

Erny also sold newspapers in Lonsdale Square, part of a two-block park near Portland's city hall and court buildings, and would continue to do so when he was in Portland or in reach of it until about 1915. He worked here both early and late, for there were three dailies and he sold them all and, in addition, hawked the great radical sheet, the *Appeal to Reason,* on a weekly basis. The latter was a national publication obsessed with the evils of wealth and political power and was respected as no other by those who had neither. He would describe to his friend Stewart Holbrook the almost "religious" manner in which its faithful grasped and folded the *Appeal* or spread it on a park bench to read. He read the paper himself, he said, and believed every word of it: "I saw nothing in the system of free enterprise which was going to do me very much good."

He remembered this interval in his life less fondly, though not without humor.

> When I was in funds I used to have dinner at the Chicago restaurant on Second and Madison. For fifteen cents you got a hamburger, mashed potatoes, bread and coffee. The butter was painted on the plate with a camel's hair brush and the dessert was something out of this world. I never could eat it but one day, just for curiosity, I cut a small nick from one corner of it for purposes of identification. Sure enough, three days later, there it was again.
>
> On other occasions, when not in funds, I used to hang around the park blocks in front of the courthouse, and in the mornings I always watched

> the old men line up at the corner of the courthouse and wait for the garbage cans to come down from the jail. That's the way they got their breakfast and sometimes I wished I had had nerve enough to go over and do a little rustling for myself.

He needed to sell ten newspapers to make meal money. When slight surpluses developed, he would occasionally treat himself to a bottle of cough medicine, though he did not know why the codeine-laced tonic so appealed to him.

In early 1912, having been promoted to the seventh grade after a half-year's schooling in Portland, Erny was taken in by uncle Frank Haycox, who was then living in Clatskanie, a mill town thirty miles upriver from Astoria. This family included three closely spaced sons near Erny's age and a girl who was two years older; and Mary Elizabeth would remember that her cousin was a curious and bustling lad and, though of small stature, not in the least reluctant to represent himself. She said Uncle Frank found it necessary on several occasions to haul him up short for scrapping, not indicating whether it was the boy's deportment or his survival that most concerned her father. It may be assumed that some of the confrontations were unavoidable. Erny was, after all, a newcomer in a raw little town in which saloons far outnumbered all other forms of community commerce and his peers were the fractious sons of mill hands and loggers. The boy in the book he didn't live to write was a loner like that, "never staying in one place long enough to become part of a group . . . [and] always on the outside, fighting his way in."

Erny lived with Bertha's now-married sister Emma Himler near Oregon City during his final year of elementary education in 1912–13; Parkplace was the ninth grade school he had attended since 1906. He had by this time decided to become a farmer and was collecting agricultural bulletins and, for reasons undisclosed, committed himself to read every book in the Parkplace school library. "There were two hundred and fifty some volumes," he said. "I checked them off as I read them. The last book was Lord's *Oregon Birds.* I wasn't much interested in it, but I had to go through it to complete the project." There was a nearby streetcar connection to Portland, but it is remembered that Erny frequently walked to the big city, which was several miles distant, and that he carried a notepad with him and was thought to be scribbling things down on his journey. It was probably a diary; he would mention later that he left a couple of them in a trunk somewhere.

His grade school marks were on the whole acceptable—mostly 80s and 90s, the highest of these always associated with reading and spelling. History and geography and writing were somewhat more variable but produced mostly good marks. Arithmetic and grammar were his weaknesses and thirty years after the fact he would say, with somewhat more modesty than required, that the latter remained a lifelong opponent.

> To this day grammar is a mystery to me; and when, in writing, I come to a difficult construction, my invariable policy is to back up and go around. I am not alone in this. The average writer is a poor grammarian; and the average writer excuses himself on the theory that his function is to create melody and color and rhythm—not to conjugate verbs. ◆

Erny enrolled in Portland's Lincoln High School in the fall of 1913. He had found a job as a bellhop at a boarding hotel to supplement his newspaper selling and, early on, hadn't given much thought to further schooling. However, the state agricultural college was offering courses to young people with two years of high school and that, he decided, was too good a bargain to pass up. The attic of the Norton was storage space and here he found a bicycle; and dodging around crates and trunks, and rather later than most, he mastered its art. He exchanged pictures with his mother that Christmas and his was tendered with great affection, "with oceans and oceans of love from your loving son." She was then working at a restaurant in Imlay, Nevada.

WJ was in Portland again, clerking for a furniture company and later getting into the employment agency business, which would be his line of work until about 1930. There were a good many such offices in Portland, particularly specializing in sawmill and logging camp labor. WJ hopped from one to another until he had found every last one of them deficient in some capacity.* He remarried in 1913 to a Norwegian girl, Elinda Vog, eleven years his junior. Bertha would return to Portland about 1916, now as Mrs. William L. Pond. Both she and Billy waited tables but the ones he preferred had playing cards on them and he must have been good at the game. A roly-poly sort—Bertha towered over him—he dressed well, sported jewelry, and at least in the 1920s, drove nice cars.

Erny lived with his father and stepmother at times during high school and probably occupied some spare corner of the Norton occasionally. WJ signed his report cards but the signatures are shaky and one might conclude some of them, or all of them, to be forgeries. He did not attend Oregon Agricultural College (now Oregon State University) after his sophomore year; to his great annoyance, the school first stiffened its entrance requirement for the agricultural course to three years of high school and then dropped the program. In 1915, at the end of his sophomore year, he spent the summer in San Francisco, living alone in a flophouse. To support himself on this vacation, he first obtained a job selling magazine subscriptions and boarded the ferry one morning loaded with literature and application forms. On reaching Oakland, he said later, he lacked the courage to knock on a single door and the magazines were discarded under a bush. He also briefly worked as a delivery boy for a hat factory, but recalled that the boxes were so large that often he couldn't squeeze onto a streetcar with them and he soon tired of walking up and down hills. His principal occupation that summer was as a peanut butcher—a news vendor—on the Oakland, Antioch and Eastern Railway, an electrified passenger line operating between Oakland and Sacramento.

The job went something like this. First, you passed up and down the passenger cars selling peanuts and pretzels and other salty tidbits. A bit later you came back, this time with soft drinks to slack the thirst

* Some of WJ's resignations were probably of mutual consent, for on at least one occasion Erny was urgently called upon by his father to cover a petty-cash deficit at the office. There is nothing in family lore to suggest that WJ's job-placement career was tainted by anything more serious than imperious behavior or the occasional lapse of cash-management skills. However, some agency operators were unscrupulous, operating fee-kickback schemes that encouraged mill managers and logging bosses to accelerate employee turnover.

nurtured on the first passage. Then, particularly on warm days, you returned once more with ice cream treats and other cooling delicacies. He purchased his inventory in advance from a principal concessionaire and, to make any margin at all, had to march back and forth without much pause.

There was, of course, some opportunity for a sharp fellow to fatten the take a bit. He found a place in San Francisco where he could buy three packs of gum for a dime, and they could be sold on board for a nickel each. Crackerjack boxes were often discarded in fair condition, sometimes with a scrap of two of the carameled content remaining. He would reclaim these and take them to the baggage car, where there was a stove and a kettle. By steaming open the fresh boxes and transferring a bit of their inventory to the recovered containers, and then resealing the lot, a fellow could create some merchandise on which the return was infinite. And there was an even darker art, in which he was instructed by some of the older "butchers."

> Say that the customer would give me a fifty-cent piece for a five-cent newspaper. I'd assume it was a quarter he had given me, and return him twenty cents in change, meanwhile, however, retaining a quarter in the palm of my hand. If the customer noted the discrepancy, why, I was quick to drop the quarter into his hand and say, 'Sorry!' But half the time, at least, the customer didn't notice, and I was twenty-five cents ahead.

Even then, however, the job was never much of a money-maker and was hardly worth showing up for on holidays, when the OA&E ran excursions to a park in the hills behind Oakland. These were much favored by Italian families, who brought plenteous supplies of bread and sausage and cheese and wine, all infused with or surrounded by quantities of garlic which, he said, were powerful enough to caste a terrible spell on vanilla ice cream.

He would remember his summer in San Francisco with both pleasure and irritation. Of the latter, there is a passionate diary entry written two years later, which is introduced as "the vow of an insolent youth to an arrogant city. You'll hear from me again some day . . . [because] you didn't treat me right last time. You will the next time I come back in 'civilians.' Don't you like it? Neither did I when I walked up to the top of one of your darned old hills and disillusioned myself as to your hospitality." The affront was never revealed but more than likely involved a physical confrontation, for it is known that, somewhere and somehow in 1915, he broke his right wrist—or somebody broke it for him.

Shortly before leaving Portland that summer, Erny enlisted in the Oregon National Guard, joining Company B, Third Infantry Regiment, which was headquartered in Portland's armory not many blocks from the Norton. He had a serious, mature look about him, a high forehead and no birth certificate, and he told them he was an eighteen-year-old student. First Sergeant Adolphus A. Schwarz probably didn't believe him, but, then again, the sergeant probably wouldn't have said much had he known recruit Haycox was only fifteen because Co. B was barely half strength. What motivated Erny was the guard's annual summer camp, which sounded like a swell vacation. Given his California adventures that summer, however, he had little time for soldiering before fall. ◆

Scenes and characters from Erny's early life were reproduced occasionally in his fiction. Somewhere during his youthful wanderings, in some freewheeling mill town, he had looked upon the colorless face of a prostitute who had taken laudanum. This was Rose—much elaborated by his imagination, of course—who in the serial novel *Trouble Shooter* (1936) slips a locket with her photograph into the hardcase hero's pocket on Christmas Eve and, later that evening, commits suicide.

Earlier, in 1927, in the short story "Ambushed," Erny created a plucky frontier wife, Helen Chavez, in whom Bertha Haycox's trials and virtues are unmistakable. Helen's husband, a lazy man drawn to shady enterprise, runs off, leaving her with a run-down ranch, an overdue mortgage and two children. Then the cattle are rustled and that, it seems, is the last straw—but it's not. An organizer and accomplisher and rather fearless in grim circumstances, Helen fights back, charming her creditors and turning the ranch into a neat and freshly painted stopover that quickly attracts hungry travelers and hunters. She requires a man's help to ward off a land-grabbing neighbor, and at that point the story degrades to the predictable and forgettable conclusion of pulp western tradition. Helen Chavez, however, endures as a plausible personality—she is far removed from the decorous and generally helpless ranch maiden of that tradition—and is further notable as the writer's first female lead.

Erny also utilized recollections from his fragmented boyhood to describe young men who had observed a good deal at an early age. First among these characters was young Tod—his family name is never offered—who is the narrator of events in New Hope, an 1880 Nebraska river town in which the prudish values of its orderly citizens and those of a crude and carelessly violent frontier often mingle. The several New Hope stories, written between 1933 and 1937, are curious accounts in some ways, sufficiently different in manner from conventional sagebrush drama as to suggest an entirely different writer, and almost the only material Erny would ever produce employing first-person narration. The boy isn't Erny; Tod's father is one of New Hope's quietly powerful businessmen and his home is somewhere across that boundary street which teamsters and dockmen and other customers of the Beauty Belle Saloon and its surrounding community accepted as beyond their sphere. However, Tod may have been the young man that his creator, in his youth, wished to be; and some of Tod's encounters probably weren't far removed from Clatskanie or another logtown of the writer's residence in early years. This one, perhaps:

> Their talk went on, very even, very sure; and in a little while I slipped away, crossed a vacant block westward, and came upon the margin of corral and barn and open space where were outfitted the freighters and freighting teams. I meant to cut past this to gain the quarter of town in which my particular band of boyhood friends usually foregathered; but, as I ran between corrals, I arrived at a wide circle of men, standing about a fire, and across and about this area two teamsters were wickedly fighting. I could see them very plainly—two huge, gaunt men bare to the waist, all muscles coiling and swelling in that crimson light, blood dripping down their bare chests; and I could hear the dull sound of their fists, the

> crush of bone into flesh. It was not the first fight I had seen, but all this red savagery chilled me; and, when I looked around the circle of bystanders and discovered the lust shining in their eyes, and the lips drawn back over heavy, yellow teeth, it was like coming upon a circle of wolves, and I pivoted and ran home.

There was one boy, at a later time, of undeniable likeness to the writer. This was fourteen-year-old Billy Gattis, a parentless lad who supports himself selling newspapers and running errands in *Long Storm,* a novel of Portland in the 1860s in which the principal villain is secessionist Floyd Ringrose.

> A boy—an undersized boy with a solemn and sharp face—came through the crowd in a ducking, turning way and squeezed a place for himself beside Ringrose. The boy caught a barkeep's eye and said, "A bottle of brandy, two lemons, and a cup of loaf sugar."
>
> "That game still going on in Number Nine, Billy?"
>
> "Yes," said the boy.
>
> Ringrose stared down at this Billy and found nothing on the lad's face that he liked. "You're damned young to be in here," he said.
>
> The boy had the liquor, the lemons and the sugar in his hands. He gave back to Ringrose a stare which was as pointed and cool as the one Ringrose gave him, and slipped through the crowd. The barkeep observed this small scene with amusement. "You got a match there, friend. That kid's the best businessman in town."
>
> "Brash," said Ringrose.
>
> "He's stropped his wits on some mighty hard stones," said the barkeep.

—3—

Border Patrol and the Wobbly War

ERNY DID NOT MERGE EASILY INTO HIS FRESHMAN CLASS AT Lincoln High School. Wearing a suit and a tie every day may have been burdensome, but the greater problem was adjusting to a student society in which he was, or at least perceived himself to be, representing the lowest possible order. His classmates included the sons and daughters of common folk, but a good many of them were the offspring of merchants and professionals and others of high standing in Portland. He was an unpedigreed outsider, a baggage-hauler, a newsboy. Thirty years later, he would remember being "at that stage of adolescence which is a terrible thing to live through, and a frightful thing to behold. I was something formless and highly egotistical; I was a barbarian from the wrong side of the tracks, rude and bumptious and painfully embarrassed by turns."

But for the first time he would be in one place long enough to mix into a crowd and it did not take him long to reflect this civilizing process. In his sophomore year, he was accepted into one of the school clubs. Later, he was in the glee club and on the debating team and, had war not interfered, he would have been assistant manager of the school play in 1917. In his senior year, he was also a member of the Safety League, a somewhat mysterious association of seven young men whose carefully inscribed charter and rules of conduct must have been buried in a coffee can in somebody's backyard. What beyond friendship bound these boys together is unknown; perhaps friendship was enough.

The rough edges were substantially smoothed, though not eradicated. In school pictures of young men in white shirts standing straight and looking pleasant, he was ever the fellow at the end of the line, slouched gloomily against a post or some other object, in a dark shirt. He wore his National Guard uniform to class occasionally; it was another means of establishing separate identity and admirable if not heroic stature. Just fitting in probably never was the goal; he wished to be a pillar among his peers. A few months past graduation, he would look back at these times and bemoan his lack of accomplishment.

> During my last year at High I came to the conclusion that I had been too far apart from school activities. That I had not mixed enough with my classmates and had not got into the atmosphere of the school. So I began to play politics in my club and class—making myself conspicuous at opportune moments. That way EJH became conspicuous as a leader—yet in an election for president of [my] club I got defeated . . . due, as somebody told me, to politics injected in the campaign. I felt more badly over this charge than anything else during the school year. It wasn't true. [It was!] In class, I was given the majority of committee chairmanships and of the various class activities I was in most all. But much quantity, little quality. I was rushed for time and couldn't give justice to all. So though friends said I was "fine" and a "go-getter" I knew that their praise was hastily given and not the result of mature thought. I knew then that I was only 50% efficient.
>
> It must be corrected. And I will correct it. Nothing shall stand in the way of my success. *I will* shall be my motto.

Although this critical self-appraisal did not extend to scholastic performance, it certainly could have. His grades held up well into his sophomore year—those for the term ending February 1915 ranging from 87 to 91, a Very Good performance overall. Thereafter, as the man of affairs blossomed, the student withered. C's and D's began to appear with some frequency and in the winter term of his senior year he flunked final examinations in math and English and very nearly failed in deportment. The Third Oregon was called to active duty in the spring of 1917 and the Portland School Board would later allow that, based on the record, the young man probably would have earned passing marks had he been permitted to finish his final year. He attended his graduation on pass from Camp Withycombe, which was some miles east of Portland, and lost the diploma from his pocket while walking back to the train depot. Retracing his steps, he found the document in the street. It was hardly worth retrieving, having been crushed and dampened by a street-cleaning wagon. ◆

That was the beginning of his second tour of duty. The first had occurred the previous summer when the Third was rushed to the Mexican border below San Diego, there to guard against possible incursion by the bandit Pancho Villa. Erny joined his regiment on June 20, 1916, and, nine days later, boarded a San Diego–bound troop train at Camp Withycombe. The journey was detailed in a letter to cousin Mary by a patriotic and moralistic young man who was thoroughly cheered by travel and the prospect of military adventure. "We expect to march in a big preparedness parade [in San Diego] on the Fourth," he reported, "and then like as not will pull out for the border. If we do go we will surely see action for we form part of the first battalion, and the first battalion . . . will be the center of operations for the entire regiment."

There had been no young lady to see him off at Camp Withycombe and that was fine, he said, although "having a girl to think of causes a man to think twice before doing something that he believes his girl wouldn't approve of. It keeps his ideals brighter and makes him plan and look forward. . . ."

An incident in southern Oregon stirred him. The troop train stopped briefly at Roseburg and, within a minute or two, the station was alive with young ladies.

> At first they merely went to the car windows and shook hands with the boys, but as the time grew near for departure some of the fellows managed to get off the car, and just before the train left . . . [the mingled soldiers and damsels] were kissing each other right and left. One fellow . . . had been introduced to a girl by another, and he had been talking to her quite steadily. When the bell rang and the engine began to start up slowly, he leaned over and said something to the girl and in another minute she was in his arms. It seemed as if the girl was giving her very

> soul up to the man. I didn't fancy the man's part because I had seen him bidding good-bye to some other girl at Clackamas . . . and it seemed to me he acted a despicable part. But the girl was young and didn't realize, and she put all of the force of her nature behind the kiss she gave him. I sure wish I had a girl that would kiss me that way. I'd want nothing more.

He still wanted to be a farmer, he told Mary, but was beginning to refine the concept: "At times, farming seems too tame, and does not offer enough travel. But then the line of action that I have mapped out will keep me going. For if you must know, I don't intend to be a hayseed and never get beyond my farm. Nothing like it. I have a much wider idea."

Company B passed through San Diego in regimental parade and was posted to the border in mid-July, taking up a position immediately opposite Tijuana. It spent the next weeks there occupying lookouts during the day and manning "Cossack posts," roadblocks established after dark to intercept smugglers and discourage those tempted to loiter about the company's camp. There was a single incident of alarm, when Mexican soldiers were observed constructing fortifications and bringing in heavy artillery immediately across the border. A day or so later, the guns were determined to be construction timbers and over what had seemed at first to be a shallow, rectangular breastwork, a structure closely resembling a horse barn had begun to rise. The only other excitement on this particular front line, Private Haycox said, was bug collecting and rattlesnake hunting. The latter task was pursued with some vigor as he and his buddies were sleeping on the ground in pup tents, and warm bodies and blankets attracted visitors. You woke up carefully, he said.

Otherwise, it was singularly pleasant duty. Discipline was casual; the young soldiers ranged through surrounding hills when not on duty and were warmly welcomed by the residents of San Ysidro, the closest American community. Many boys ventured south to an iron-fenced monument that marked the border for an obligatory photograph. The crossing itself was wide open and busy; Tijuana's attractions, among others, included a racetrack and casino.

In August, Company B surrendered its position to another Third Oregon unit and moved to better quarters several miles north at Imperial

Beach. Hard by the surf and ventilated by a cool Pacific wind, it was in Erny's opinion the finest military station a man could want. There was a YMCA hut and a covered mess, and the squad tents were promised electricity. The camp was in easy reach of San Diego and, better yet, proximate to watermelon fields. Best of all, there were friendly young women in the area. Erny fell hard for one of them, a stylish Hispanic girl named Julia. Third Oregon prepared for a long stay and Erny among others was rather looking forward to it when, unexpectedly, the regiment was returned home and demobilized in September 1916.

The Mexican expedition was every bit the swell summer vacation he'd hoped for when he joined the guard. It had also provided color and stimulation and given a young man who had discovered the pleasure in putting words on paper a measure of confidence. Back at Lincoln High, just turned seventeen, he became a contributor to the *Cardinal*, the school's monthly literary magazine. Erny vigorously memorialized the passing of Jack London, that son of battle "who girded his armor and fared forth to exact from the world that which it owed him—and which it owes every man—and that which it will yield to every man who ventures." He made several attempts to improve the moral fiber of his classmates, a goal shared by any number of the magazine's correspondents. And there were as well Haycox articles devoted to soldiering. He analyzed the benefit of military service, described his experiences on the border, and produced a piece of virtuous fiction, "The Princess of Happy Valley," in which a dispirited young recruit is restored by his love for a child.

The sentimental and right-minded themes of teenage writers do not as a rule produce memorable literature, and few would quarrel with the writer's later assessment of this first work as "pretty terrible stuff." But that aside, this was where the joy of composition became known to him. Two of his Safety League companions, Ira Berkey and Bill Misson, seemed to have similar compulsion and there was talk between the three of reuniting in some kind of collaborative literary effort after graduation. Ira would write to him during the summer of 1917: "Seriously, I think your stuff ought to find an open market. It is free from that impression of being labored." ◆

When the Third Oregon mobilized again in March 1917, Company B was initially detailed to guard bridges and power plants and other vital installations in and around Portland. The armies of the Triple Entente did not present much of a threat to the Far Northwest but there was trouble, the worst in the way of labor turmoil the region would ever see, from the radical and angry membership of the Industrial Workers of the World. The Wobblies, as they were universally identified, had already drawn blood in Puget Sound and stirred fear and violent reprisal in many other parts of the West, and were at the peak of their brief power that summer of 1917. Logging operations and sawmills were crippled throughout Oregon and Washington and agricultural labor waned. According to some reports, apocalyptic events loomed with Wobbly firebrands flooding into the region on freight trains, recruiting on the fly and forcibly disembarking those gentlemen disinclined to carry the small red membership booklet.

Erny was promoted to corporal on April 17 and on or about that day found himself quarantined at Camp Withycombe; someone in the ranks displayed symptoms of meningitis. There would follow a training regime that made border service look quite tame—long days of drill and combat instruction with almost no free time. And then in early July, as the Wobbly threat grew more calamitous by the moment, a half-dozen Third Oregon companies were ordered to various parts of the Northwest to provide security. Company B was assigned to eastern Washington's Yakima Valley, where it mounted a hundred-mile-long picket line of sorts stretching north from the city of Yakima through Ellensburg and Cle Elum and finally to Wenatchee. Corporal Haycox's platoon of eighteen men, commanded by now Lieutenant A. A. Schwarz, arrived in the latter town at the end of a freight train on the evening of July 10, set up camp in a vacant lot near the Columbia Ice and Cold Storage plant, and marched to J. A. Schiscoff's cafe for a complimentary steak dinner. Next day, Chelan County Sheriff McManus helped the lieutenant identify facilities that seemed to require security, these including irrigation pipelines and ditches, power houses, bridges, and a highway tunnel. The platoon's role expanded a few days later to searching trains and detaining those scruffy riders who could not provide evidence of a paid fare.

It was hot as hell in Wenatchee, well above 100 degrees in the afternoons, but the countryside was much admired by the prospective farmer and his companions. The Columbia River rushed by "swift and threatening" in those damless days, and farms and orchards spread from the edges of the town and climbed the lower slopes of a narrow surrounding valley. A mile or so north, the Wenatchee River joined the Columbia and formed a separate, fertile watershed in which apples were cultivated in prodigious quantities.

A reassured local populace made its appreciation immediately and bountifully apparent. "The people are very hospitable and generous," Erny recorded in his diary. "We have been treated royally. Cherries and other fruits have been given to us in unlimited quantities since we arrived—we are taken for auto rides—and everything has been done to make us feel at home. . . . The irrigation system is our chief concern. A careful guard is kept over it. For if it were destroyed, the Valley would be ruined."

Uncle Sam's men had arrived none too soon. A week on, logging camps and sawmills and fruit-box factories in the area were crippled by IWW pickets, some shut tight. The situation was close at Leavenworth, at the head of the Wenatchee Valley, where more than half of the loggers and millhands walked off and, said the sheriff, pickets were aggressively discouraging those independent souls "who stayed with their jobs . . . [or] showed a disposition to go to work."

> Wednesday night, July 17, we got a hurried call from Leavenworth, 33 miles north of us. Thirteen of the men piled into two machines and away we went. There is a speed limit in Chelan county but we never worried about it—rather, I would say, we excited it considerably. I think we must have averaged 40 miles an hour. As for turns, most of them were made on one wheel, and I think that wheel was the steering wheel.
>
> Could there be anything more unusual—out of the ordinary rut of human occurrences—than rushing thru the black night, tearing around curves, clinging precariously to the side of a two-by-four road with a yawning canyon below? I think not. Such are the things that change a man's life, from the prosaic to the romantic. Romance lies all about us if we would but open our eyes to it. People decry the dull, commonplace

> modern life. But the life hasn't changed. Only man's imagination and responsiveness to the unusual has been dulled. There are more perils for the modern Lochinvar than in the Medieval age. The trouble is that the supply of Lochinvars is lacking.
>
> We got into Leavenworth about 2 a.m. and went to the police headquarters—then started our roundup. Very quiet and orderly we picked them up. In the early morning we raided their hall and took about 15. We rode across the river to their community house and took 15 more. After that, we toured the town, playing hide and seek from one street to another and by four o'clock had 11 more including 3 leaders. This just about cleaned the town up, so we took the train back with the last bunch. All told we got 42.
>
> What impressed me was the lack of violence. No resistance was offered at all. It was "pick up thy bed and walk" and they walked. It seems that they are disregarding their tenets by not resisting. But flesh is weaker than a violent Constitution, especially when that Constitution was probably written by men safe from the real vicissitudes of a labor struggle . . . [and] the business end of a .30 calibre gun looks very big and is a powerful argument for peace.

Corporal Haycox liberated a good supply of Wobbly literature at Leavenworth and from this and the local press gained a rather grim view of the enemy: "Up here they have discussed the easiest way to kill the growth of fruit trees—to burn grain—destroy bridges and the like. Summarizing, their creed is [that] *violence* is necessary—not to be used only as a last resort—but violence whenever practicable—to intimidate and defeat."* And yet, after spending a fair amount of time talking to his cap-

* Thirty years later, Stewart Holbrook, whose lumber-camp background and natural curiosity made him a nonpareil source of Wobbly lore, presented Erny with his own red card and "a very rare Job Report, printed to aid the homemade reporters of the Industrial Worker [a union publication]. And they were pretty damned good reporters, who never let a fact stand in the way of a good story" (letter, March 28, 1947). The flaming preamble printed in the card—actually, a pint-size booklet in which membership stamps were periodically affixed—mandated class warfare "until the workers of the world organize as a class, take possession of the earth and the machinery of production, and abolish the wage system."

tives in later days, he found them neither revolutionary by nature nor inclined to mayhem.

Were the IWW's objectives altogether valid? Were his captives true believers in labor justice at almost any price? Erny wasn't sure.

> The situation seems to be different here. The men, or at least the leaders, are demanding certain concessions from logging and mill employers, such as improvements in housing, shorter hours, more pay and other things that the Labor Unions have for years been advocating.
>
> Whether their requests are just or not I do not know. Some camps are pretty bad, I know from experience. But from what I hear the camps around here have very good arrangements for living and the "grub" is good.
>
> Most of the IWW's are men of little education. I doubt if some of them know why they possess the red card, excepting that they are with the "bunch." Man loves company and I suppose some of them figure that "Harry and Tom joined, so I'll join."
>
> The men in jail don't mind being there. They are getting lodging free and they know that they will be looked on as martyrs by their fellow comrades. One fellow boasted that he hadn't missed his winter quarters for 10 years.

The two Wenatchee jails—city and county—were shortly overflowing and a separate compound was constructed for the Wobblies, a 150-by-200-foot enclosure with watchtowers and a large bunkhouse that the Wenatchee newspaper said resembled an open-air pavilion. The prisoners would not have to worry "about the ventilation of their bed chambers." Nor much else, for that matter. They were held incommunicado—gifts of tobacco and blankets were accepted but visitors, even wives, were turned away. A local lawyer hired to represent the incarcerated was not allowed to speak to his clients and agreeably said he would not press the matter until the procedures of his appointment were delineated by some higher authority.

The Leavenworth expedition was, to the corporal's mind, the single worthwhile event in a summer made intolerable by ample servings of heat and guard duty. He studied books he had purchased on the fundamentals of military service and trench warfare and the Lewis machine gun, and an officer's manual borrowed from his company commander, but these were not designed to brighten anybody's spirit. Company B was lost in the hinterlands while the rest of the American army was on the move; Pershing was in Europe and the first formations of the American Expeditionary Force joined him in early July. Wenatchee, meanwhile, was raising its own legions—a cavalry troop was assembled for national service and a National Guard unit recruited; and Lt. Schwarz's command, which became a regular army unit on August 5, was left in largely unreported gloom. The corporal was grim when he set about composing his *War Diary* in a wirebound stenographic pad in late July. "I can't conceive of any lasting good resulting from my enlisting," he penned. "I'm not grumbling or whining. That's not my style. I hate a grouch or a slacker. But I think I'm in the wrong stall. *Dammit,* I wish the decisive stage were reached and I could get one good lick in, at least. Lord Gosh, how I hate to wait—stall around—mark time. *It gets on my nerves.*"

He had been a guardsman now for two years and two months. It had been a valuable education "but a little too complete for happiness."

Erny and a few others were posted twenty miles north of Wenatchee later that summer and lived miserably in a sun-blistered board shed. He thought about applying for officer's training, obtaining from one of his high school teachers—surely not his math instructor—a letter of recommendation. As on the border, the local residents were friendly and sympathetic, particularly pretty Jenny Windham. He bathed occasionally in a rushing stream, smoked cigars, grew a mustache, and prayed it would all end soon.

There had been a steady correspondence with high school friends and some of his scattered B Company buddies, and the news he received from other parts did nothing to lighten his mood. A couple of the Safety League crew were in uniform, but most of his Portland pals were working in the shipyards, making a great deal of money and finding ways to spend it. And then there was Corporal Leslie O. McLaughlin, Erny's closest army friend, stationed forty miles south at Ellensburg with Company B headquarters. Mac was not suffering one bit.

"Well, I get to go up town about once or twice a week in the evenings—that is, officially," Mac wrote, "and there are other times (ahem)... and say, talk about your dames. Well, you know, there is a normal school here and they're having a summer term and Oh! my boy, there sure are some kids up there. I know about twenty of them and they wanted us to come up some night and meet them all. They sure have some opinion of the 'rubes' in this town. Won't look at any of them and you should see the way they fall for us."

A few weeks later, Mac was a gone goose. "Well, I think I will do quite a bit of studying from now on. My 'wife' is in Spokane. Some girlie, boy. She sure is some kid, about as big as a minute and Oh! those eyes, and boy is she a blonde. But hell, she is engaged. Dammit, maybe I can beat his time. . . . I'd marry her in a minute but, hell, why rave? You don't know her."

The corporal was by now somewhat tested in matters of this kind. He and the beautiful Julia had corresponded for a time after he returned to Portland and then "she told me something I had never known before and shortly afterwards she stopped writing."* The *War Diary* concluded with a mawkish tribute to another lady, this one named Ruth, to whom the corporal pledged lifelong fidelity. He had "found Her, only to lose her again [and] please put it to my credit that I did not destroy the ideal." Ruth might have been a Portland sweetheart—Ira Berkey had asked him in a letter how affairs were proceeding with some young lady: "Do you think the party of the second part will acquiesce in that little proposition you outlined to me . . . ?" She evidently did not, for, a month later, Ira was offering consoling advice to a friend who lately had been spurned.

He saved one letter from a young lady, perhaps a cousin, who did not think the army had done him a great deal of good. "You never cursed nor smoked nor gambled before you joined . . . and what's more you said you never would—but you did and are doing it now." Perhaps that was overstating things a bit. Erny had firmly sworn off card-playing, composing

* The nature of Julia's disclosure is unknown. At a guess, however, she may have discovered that the amorous private was, at the time of their liaison, all of sixteen years old.

a self-addressed diatribe on that perversion that would have satisfied any sensible young lady. "My bluest moments arise when I think of the hours carelessly thrown away and what I might have done with them," said he. "When one comes stumbling away from a table after a night's game . . . he wonders what insane impulse led him onward and he curses himself for being the greatest died-in-the-wool, six-barrel fool."

One demon had been deposed—at least he said it had. As to profanity, his case never was acute and did not last much beyond his army service, if that long. Tobacco was another matter. He was smoking cigars at fifteen and did so for the rest of his life. He produced countless condemnations of nicotine and ignored them all.

Nowhere in the *War Diary* did Erny consider the path of his future life or express interest in writing as a possible undertaking. It is, however, reasonable to suspect that he thought about the latter occasionally. Though military service was momentarily a deadly bore, it had been entertaining and provoking at times, perhaps background for something beyond. It had inspired him to write in high school and, if he bothered to reread his Wenatchee work, he might have noted a few passages of faint professional promise. There was, for example, that surge of romanticism revealed on the midnight dash to Leavenworth. There was additionally in many *War Diary* passages a pronounced inclination to stand away from the conflict and to observe events unemotionally, as a writer might, so that they could be better understood and described. One might have expected a sympathetic reaction to the plight of the Wobbly prisoners, for he was the descendant of one like them and had known many more in earlier years. But he was more interested in the phenomena of industrial upheaval than in taking sides; there wasn't an ounce of kinship apparent. A snippet from his description of army life in the June 1917 issue of the *Cardinal* displays the critical mind at labor.

> . . . I enlisted with visions of—heaven only knows what—stirring my imagination to action. I was not utterly ignorant of what was before me, but at the same time, to me, then, the soldier's life was one great, grand and glorious dream. Today my respect and love of the military profession

> is greater than it was two years ago. But in what a different light do I regard it. Months of drills and campaigning have taken the rosy, impractical dreams away. In their stead has come the liking for the life that makes a man a wholly developed physical being and develops in him a stronger moral and mental character. Of course, if a jellyfish should by chance enlist, it is probable he will remain a jellyfish. The military life does not supply strong wills or high moral ideas, but it does strengthen and intensify those traits. It does not create; it builds up and reinforces.

This, to be sure, was pre-Wenatchee sentiment. The *War Diary*, while of interest as to Erny's state of mind and for its possible display of nascent creativity, contains precious few encomiums to military service. But most conditions are relative and one is inclined to suspect that, a few months hence, he would remember his central Washington summer as a pleasantly pastoral interlude. What came next was not.

—4—

St. Agony

THERE HAD BEEN RUMORS SINCE MID-JULY THAT B COMPANY would be recalled from its Wobbly war on short notice and sent with the regiment to a training base near San Francisco to prepare for combat in France. It was a prospect welcomed throughout the discomfited and impoverished ranks—they had missed a payday at Wenatchee—and as speculation became near certainty, Corporal Haycox made plans: "If I can get an occasional pass, I'll go to 'Frisco' and visit some of the scenes of my 1915 explorations. Familiar ground! The blue haze of the bay—the busy Embarcadero—Market Street, the mother of all the side streets and by-lanes leading to Barbary Coast and Chinatown. . . ."

It was too good to be true, of course. The expected destination, Camp Fremont near Palo Alto, had irreconcilable sewage problems and could not manage a large population. The Third Infantry, less those formations sent to the hinterlands, continued to train at Camp Withycombe and entrained for the East Coast on September 24. The guard-duty units struggled back to the camp in late summer as the IWW menace diminished and the corporal and his mates boarded an eastbound troop train on October 26. By November 2, the regiment was in one piece again at Camp Mills on Long Island. And as the regular army already contained a Third Infantry, the Oregon guard unit was renumbered, becoming the 162nd Infantry Regiment of the Forty-first Infantry Division.

Military staging and replacement depots—sometimes referred to as concentration camps in those innocent days—are not as a rule pleasant establishments. Even granting that, Camp Mills was by universal recollection detestable and Erny's first night there, hellish.

> When we arrived. . . it was to find a fifty-mile wind whooping it up across from the sound and no tents arranged for us. Our packs, in which our blankets were, had been put on a baggage car, the baggage car got lost, and there we were without shelter as the night came along. Somebody tore off a piece of the messhouse and started a fire which was promptly put out by an orderly from the brigade commander. As for food, there wasn't a trace, and so we stood and cursed while the most miserable night in the history of the world wore on and on.

The corporal found a cot somewhere and tried to sleep on it, but the frigid air passing underneath made that impossible. At length, he turned the cot upside down and wiggled under it, that protection reducing the night's deadly chill by perhaps one degree.

The 162nd was at Camp Mills for a miserable month. Even the regiment's unofficial history, focused on the nobility of military service, could not make the interlude pleasant. "The weather was severe and interspersed with chilly rain storms, sleet and snow," it acknowledged. "All troops in camp, however, were speedily reequipped with winter clothing . . . and even though the winter elements made drill almost impossible, the men were warmed by a fever of excitement and expectancy, so that there was little complaint over the camp conditions."

Among this document's many citations of virtuous soldierly behavior, those observations rank among its most egregious. In fact, the cursing and bellyaching was loud and continuous. The men were quartered in leaky canvas squad tents in which the floor boards, in those tents that had them, were mudslick and foul. These enclosures were heated by wood stoves that were far too small for the task. Beyond that, there was a shortage of fuel and the gathering of it was a trial. Work detachments were collected randomly each day and marched several miles through the sprawling camp to unload cordwood from flatcars. It was, Erny said, a dreary task lightened only by ingenuity.

> All the other companies had sent out their wood details and so here would be several hundred buck privates going through the motions of grinding labor while some officer looked on. Actually, we got to be geniuses at simulating effort without straining a muscle. One fellow stood

> on the car and pushed a stick of wood off with his foot. One man lifted the front end [of the stick] and one man took the hind end. And one man went along to do the grunting.

The food was also miserable and there wasn't enough of it. Quite possibly the only pleasurable moment at Camp Mills was the final one, when the 162nd took leave. The regiment was transported to the troopship *Susquehanna* at Hoboken on or about December 12, 1917.

> There was the usual delay—something blocked the loading and the young embarkation officers were nervously moving about. . . [and] then down the pier came a huge figure bundled in one of those old-issue overcoats . . . reaching almost to the ground. This one had no ornaments save for two black broad stripes encircling each cuff, between which were the stars of a Major-General. The embarkation officers came up on the trot. . . . I saw him check them with a gesture and explode a word or two . . . [and] shortly we were moving forward again. A gesture, a grunt, and five thousand men were in motion.
>
> I remember, after gaining the deck of the boat, turning back to get a last glimpse of this embodiment of power . . . towering above the group of subordinates clustered around. Then as I turned and ran after my company down the companionway, I still felt that man's will shoving me on. I never felt so insignificant in all my life.

They were at sea for about two weeks, during which time they were fed but twice daily: "We came charging down the stairs in six or seven long lines, all converging around the serving tables, having our coffee and rolls thrown at us as we crowded past. . . . At four we had dinner. The same lines charging down the same stairs. An unmentionable stew, a bit of bread, a cup of bitter tea, and an unfilled yearning for seconds."

The entrepreneurs among them located the ship's bakery and food-storage lockers and stole anything within reach: "We would crawl to the forward grating behind which were kept the vegetables, and prod through the bars with infinite patience, coming off after interminable lengths of time with a potato or an onion or a woody rutabaga, and we would crouch between the tiers of bunks below . . . and eat like a pack of furtive rats."

The *Susquehanna* was a German liner that had been seized and minimally refurbished after sustaining some fire damage on a prior crossing. On this voyage, it narrowly missed colliding with an ammunition ship after leaving Hoboken and subsequently lost power for a time off Sandy Hook. Even at full power, Erny said, it was the slowest ship in the convoy, the unenvied straggler most likely to attract the interest of a German submarine. The trip was fortunately smooth and uneventful, however, until the convoy entered the Bay of Biscay. That was where the Kaiser's navy waited for American troop transports; in this instance, it had anticipated the approach with estimable precision. Erny was on an upper deck, one of many soldiers detailed to line the railings and augment the ship's regular lookouts, and had a bird's-eye view of the action. It was about noon.

> Someone cried the alarm, gongs chimed deep in the ship, a siren wailed, and hundreds of soldiers lounging in unusual sunlit warmth for a December day swarmed below decks. The naval gun crew sprang into action, ripped off the canvas cover of the ammunition case, and swung the piece around. The breach block opened, a shell passed in, the block closed with a metallic 'plock'.
>
> The convoy had been swinging around and now was in a semi-circle. The subs were to starboard. I noticed the pennants hanging limp on the halyards of the transports behind us, bright splotches of color in the hot, still day; I saw the dazzling green water, the azure blue of the horizon, and in the center of the picture a dull gray-black snout, half awash.

The *Susquehanna*'s gun crew put a shell near the submarine and the escorts rushed forward.

> In from the right side of the picture streamed a subchaser, throwing spray high on her bow as she streaked straight across the scene, over the spot where the sub had gone down, straight on and out of my concentrated vision. Then a huge jet of water rose up, larger, taller than the one

> thrown up by the shell; poised a moment in glistening, jagged whiteness, and cascaded back. The water boiled and seethed, was calm. A film of oil slowly spread on the surface.
>
> The subchasers ranged back and forth like terriers on a hunt and spread out once more to their accustomed places. Our convoy ship led on; we fell in and with a fresh groaning of engines followed. The pageant was over. It had faded as quickly as it had started.
>
> Midnight came as we floated up the Loire channel. The boat was asleep save for the watch and a few communing spirits leaning against the railing. A sailor stood out from the ship's side and swung his sounding lead, singing the fathoms in a half-suppressed voice. A green and red and white light floated out of space.
>
> We entered the locks, threw out our lines and rose with the flooding waters. I could see a street lead away to the center of the town, marked by a statue. Paralleling the lock was a dark quay, along which was a row of shops, the buildings fitting into each other snugly and of the same uniform height. Through blurred windows came an occasional feeble light. I could make out strange names on the glass fronts by the half-hearted flicker of the gas lamps, Cafe Chene Vert; M. Goraud, Patisserie; Cafe des Marins; Le Cheval d'Or; Charcuterie. As I viewed them they seemed to lack perspective and appeared built up in one plane only—nothing but front . . . a street scene painted on the drop curtain of a theatre.

It was the port of St. Nazaire, on Christmas Eve 1917. A fellow traveler, Private Elmer Johnson of Company A, said the holiday was celebrated by the issuance of one bottle of soda pop to each of the *Susquehanna*'s passengers. ◆

St. Nazaire would be home for five months. The 162nd was a comparatively well trained fighting force, far better prepared for front-line service than the conscript army coming on behind. However, the American Expeditionary Force had other needs and, for that reason, the regiment would never fight as a unified command. The 162nd was piecemealed out, its privates becoming replacements for understrength divisions already deploying against the Hun while noncoms and officers were posted to training and supply bases. Company B was left intact for the moment and, relieving marine personnel, its troopers became St. Nazaire's military policeman.

> With red brassards on our sleeves, we were given the military policing power of a city of about 40,000 Frenchmen which contained at the same time at least 80,000 American troops. Down at the docks great gangs of American stevedores worked the tons of cargo pouring in; here disembarked division after division of fighting troops; and here, when a convoy dropped anchor, was the starting point for thousands of sailors bound for an evening's catch-as-catch-can pleasure. [And] at certain momentous times when payday came, there would be the spectacle of thousands of [army] men converging on the town square of St. Nazaire with the one idea of proceeding about their evening's entertaiment and exterminating, en route, as many military policemen as possible. And I think I should say at this point that nobody in the army considered it an unchristian or immoral act to take an MP apart and see what made him breathe.

There were about one hundred MPs on shift at peak hours to control this uniformed and occasionally troublesome host, and they did not always succeed. The black and red MP armband did indeed identify a fellow who, particularly if found alone on a roiling night, deserved a bad time, sometimes a beating. Erny would have benefitted from a towering presence such as he had observed on the dock at Hoboken. But now at eighteen, he was as big as he would ever be, five feet seven and one-half inches tall and probably less than 140 pounds. Even with the mustache, he had none of the major general's forbidding aspect

He was hospitalized at St. Nazaire for a couple of weeks that winter, having contracted mumps, and was briefly assigned to independent surveillance work when he returned to duty. The job seemed to involve wandering about alone near the waterfront, looking for signs of pilfering from the military warehouses in that quarter. While on this assignment one night, he discovered that several gentlemen were following him. He said that he picked up the pace and that they matched stride and, shortly, everybody was running. He considered pulling out his service revolver but suspected that they were armed as well and, in any event, there were too many targets. He turned into a black and narrow passage to elude his pursuers and was stopped by a high fence, the top of which he could neither see nor touch. But he could hear his opponents pressing forward in the alley. Somehow he cleared the fence—which he swore was ten feet tall—and did not stop running until he had located a particularly bright streetlight in the center of town.

There were variations of this tale. In one, he had been detailed by a mysterious Major Uri to gather evidence of criminal activity and had been set upon by some very tough-looking Frenchmen. This account was given in one of a series of 1931 radio talks in which he described various characters he had known in the service and his beginning as a writer in New York, and in which a degree of literary license is evident. In another and perhaps more accurate version that Erny related to family and friends, the pursuers were a group of angry black longshoremen. The MPs in St. Nazaire frequently interdicted card and dice games on the wharves and made a practice of confiscating the visible cash. The dockmen considered this to be plain theft.

About June 1, Company B was relieved of its policing duties and boarded a train. Some hours later "we were neatly dropped in the asparagus fields of central France, honored, they said, with the distinction of being the First Depot Brigade." They were near the villages of Contres and St. Aignan, at a massive compound where draftees newly arrived in Europe, some with only a few days of drill and weapons practice, were sharpened and polished into fighting men. The base, about sixty kilometers east of Tours, was a conglomeration of drill fields and rifle pits and great stretches of rough ground used for battle-simulated maneuvers. At its heart was a military city of wooden billets and tents and service buildings designed to accommodate up to six thousand men and frequently holding many more. St. Agony, as it was known, "surpassed man's wildest conception of bedlam. As it grew, the original streets turned to the right and to the left to fit the terrain; other tent cities sprang up . . . on the circumference and these in turn were used as the starting point for fresh building. A recruit coming into such a place—a great percentage of the new drafts passed through St. Agony—was soon stricken with a sense of bewilderment and confusion. Companies were jammed here and there, split in fragments and not infrequently lost to each other. . . ."

He said it was widely suspected that tucked away in some part of this jumble was a unit that had been utterly forgotten, "its existence buried beneath stacks of troop orders or [lost] through some slip of the pencil." Walking through the camp at night was disconcerting, he said, for it was not possible to do so without hearing lonely, frightened young men crying.

The noncoms of B Company became instructors at the base, teaching green recruits how to thrust bayonets and throw hand grenades and maneuver through barbed wire and, in Erny's case, how to shoot straight. He was a rifle instructor and this task, to the degree that the ranges and their instructors' billets were somewhat away from the main encampment, had the attraction of occasional solitude. Although there was slight risk associated with proximity to live ammunition and inexperienced marksmen, one did not have to worry about being blown up by accident, as occasionally happened elsewhere. But it was no Sunday stroll; none of St. Agony's six hundred or so cadre felt blessed as the troops poured through in increasing numbers and the training cycle, originally a month or more, fell to weeks and on one occasion had to be compressed into a single day. Of this time, he would later write:

> I think no body of men behind the front put in longer hours [than the camp's instructors]. The ships were always disgorging their thousands of rookies and some divisional commander up the line was always crying for replacements. We were the funnel, the transforming machine. We took'em in such a state they scarcely knew how to hold their feet and we were charged with teaching them a little something of the various pieces of lethal machinery, a little something of keeping in step with the other fellow. Maybe we had a month to do it—but not usually.
>
> So we had little time to lose when they piled off the trucks at our regimental HQ. From the moment they were billeted to the date of their

> traveling orders they never knew a minute's peace. Nor did we. It was up before daylight, rain or shine, and a fourteen-kilometer hike to the drill field. Maybe the whole distance in those infernal gas masks. Once on the field it was here to the bombing bays, elsewhere for bayonet or close-order drill. At every angle, activity. Snag'em along. Cuss'em out and keep'em moving. Another six-kilometer hike took them to the rifle range while back in town an old barn, plugged at the seams, was used for a tear gas chamber.
>
> It might have been a little easier if all had spoken a common tongue. But in a great democracy there are other languages than the English. Once, in a platoon, I had the following roll-call: three Poles from Wisconsin; five Mexicans from the old national guard of New Mexico; four Creoles from Louisiana; and twelve Italians from New York's east side. The combined English-speaking capacity of those fellows when written down with a large hand would have filled one small, brown cigarette paper. It took an interpreter to work with that platoon.

There is no diary associated with this period, but Erny scribbled occasional notes that he tucked in with his packet of letters from friends and family: "August 13. Finished running through over 1100 men on ranges in six days' time—giving complete instruction to practically raw recruits on rifle . . . 180 men a day." And: "October 13. Above entry looks tame now. We average 275–325 a day—seven days a week."

He managed a few days' leave that summer and went to Paris and found it uncomfortable because shells from Big Bertha, a German railway gun seventy-five miles distant, were falling on the City of Light. He made a stab at learning the language with the help of a French-English dictionary he acquired from a friend, and bought a better volume, the 1,664-page *Petit Larousse Illustre*, and a text of verb conjugations in Paris. He read Teddy Roosevelt's autobiography and copied down some of the ex-president's pronouncements on political life and patriotism. But there wasn't a great deal of time for independent study at St. Agony. In addition to the long days, the noncom instructors had classes three nights a week and when there was a slack moment between arriving levees, their brigade commander thought twenty-kilometer marches were good for morale and discipline. On such outings, they were required to sing their commander's favorite song, about Madelon, who served wine and provided other refreshments at a woodsy tavern. The colonel was Old Army, Erny said, given to prowling the camp late at night and when he found some delinquent from an after-lockdown card game scurrying homeward, would dress the man down for an unbuttoned tunic or a missing forage cap but then dismiss him without penalty.

Erny was promoted to sergeant on July 4, 1918. Like other "Old Third" men stuck behind the lines, he would have traded the new stripe for orders to the front. The regiment's privates had gotten to the real war and, as the year ran along, the noncoms began to hear stories of this friend and that who had been wounded or captured or killed. Some of the casualties were drifting back, reassigned to their original unit from hospitals or just passing through on leave and full of stories about life on the front line. Oddly, it wasn't easy for a training-command soldier to obtain a battlefield transfer. The only certain route was appointment to an officer training school, after which front-line service was automatic, but that seemed to take inordinate time.* He and others had been pushing this option for some time and—you might know—Sgt. Leslie O. McLaughlin got there first, and was snatched away so quickly that there had not even been time for comradely farewells. Mac would write, of course.

> Well boy, for speed, you're the nuts. I waited until the truck passed and then ran for it. We rode to the station . . . [and] hit some of those downhill curves at about 80 miles per. Well, I'll say the wife was nearer to that insurance money than she will be for some time.
>
> Well, old boy, it's whichever way the dice fall from now on, and here's hoping that you'll follow me soon and with lots of luck Anyway I hereby appoint you as service of the rear while this half of the firm is at the

* Erny evidently gave his immediate commanding officer and friend, Lieutenant Joe Reddick, a bit of heat over the snail's pace of his appointment for, after the war, Reddick was moved to furnish evidence that he had tried. His recommending letter—the proof—said Haycox was "one of the best sergeants I have . . . [and] has studied constantly in hopes of making the officer's school." All this puzzled son Jim, who some years later wondered why anybody would volunteer to get shot at; was his father really serious about it? "Yes," father replied to son, "I would have liked to have gotten my German."

front. . . . You remember I told you about the chest and barracks bag of things I had at my quarters; and here's a list of names of those fellows that want the fox wraps—you get the rest. . . .

A bit later:

Well, have you managed to get back to the outfit yet? I suppose I was the only lucky one. I don't know how long the school will last, but I hope to hear that you make it either here or Langres soon. And from what Lt. Manning said I'm quite sure of it. Just keep hitting the ball hard.

And finally:

I have before me your last and only letter since we parted and Erny it makes me shudder to think of the depths that you have allowed yourself to sink into as an NCO in the service of the USA. I honestly think the you're not worth a damn. What's wrong, anyway—has your favorite game of African Golf played out or is that old wing on the bum? Any man that can't even keep himself supplied with the necessaries in times like these—well, I can imagine that mug of yours without a cigar in it but that doesn't excuse you from writing. How in the hell do you think I stand it up here? Of course, we spend our weekends in Lyon and all that stuff, but I feel I'm lost or strayed since leaving the old bunch and a little note now and then would sure be good.

Erny heard from several high school friends in the final months of 1918. Ira Berkey and Ray Williams had gotten to France, and Ray's unit, a coast artillery battalion with 9.2-inch howitzers, took casualties at Verdun. Bill Misson was at Oregon Agricultural College in the Students' Army Training Corps; if the grades held up and he survived three months of officers' training, he was going "over there" to lay sewer pipe.

Bertha and WJ wrote more or less monthly. Their initial concern was that their only child hadn't applied for the $10,000 of war risk insurance available to servicemen. "Sonnie," she complained, "I had a talk with your dad and he tells me that he has never got those insurance papers of yours. So he wrote to Washington, D.C. and they write back telling him that they haven't any record there of any insurance policy for you.

Now, baby, you had better attend to that right away. Don't think me mercenary. . . ."

WJ had a new job on his son's nineteenth birthday. "I start today as Employment Manager with the Eastern-Western Lumber Co. This concern is one of the largest mills in Portland, daily capacity two hundred and fifty thousand [board feet] per 8 hours . . . [and] they are operating two shifts at present. The Logging Camp is . . . 60 miles down the Columbia River. They operate five sides and employ two hundred and fifty men. My business is to keep this Mill and Camp supplied with a crew. I receive in return for my services one hundred and seventy five per month. The position is permanent. The private offices are not in a flourishing condition, in fact they will soon be a thing of the past. The employment problem will be solved when each large Concern operate their own Labor department."

Portland was a festive city on Armistice Day. "I wish you could see the people today," Bertha wrote breathlessly. "They have gone wild over the Glad news. . . . Victory is Ours. . . . They have been at it since early morning. All the stores are closed and everyone is in the Grand parade. But this is nothing, I know, to what the day will be when you all come home again. Dear, when you arrive, come to Mother's place first, Please won't you? Be sure to bring me a Keep Sake from the Battle Field."

The sergeant recorded the moment cheerlessly. "It has created no great relief or happiness in me. Mostly because I have been trying for the last year to get to the front and didn't succeed. Peace. A blessing to *man* but nothing to me. Home has never been a strong desire in me. I am not the hearthstone species of man."

That mood departed, replaced by impatience. "Nov. 28. Rumors! Rumors! A million of them. The feeling is contagious but I doubt it's fulfillment very soon. Where there is an army there must be a Depot Division and 'that's us.'"

And then by joy.

> Soings, France. Christmas—and we are going home! After a year—the greatest and best news of all for an American—to return to that blessed country—I wish Mac were here to go with me.

Jan. 8. They said sometime between now and the middle of the month. I'll be mighty glad when we do. Mighty glad. Theodore Roosevelt died today at his home—Oyster Bay—thus passed away one of our greatest American citizens of all time.

I've much to do when I get back to civil life. Much to do.

The 162nd reassembled at Brest on February 4, 1919, boarded the *Canopic* four days later, and arrived in New York on February 19. It was likewise a calm voyage, although, the sergeant said, somebody left a large bar of laundry soap on a steam pipe over the soup kettles in the mess. It was a testimony to shipboard cuisine that no one found the soup distinguishably worse (or better) than that offered at any other meal on any other day. However, several hundred diners were made violently ill by the unintended ingredient. The troop train arrived at Camp Lewis, Washington, on March 4, and Erny was discharged a week later. He somehow managed to bring home his .45-caliber service revolver and a lethal, triangular-bladed entrenching tool. He wandered the streets of downtown Portland in uniform for a few days, feeling disconnected and directionless. He could walk into a theater without paying and people were friendly and deferential, but then, during one of these meanders, someone gave him a hard stare and he thought the message was clear enough. He bought some clothes and packed the uniform away.

—5—

"He would let nothing interfere . . ."

When asked at later times what got him started writing, Erny would say that "an inclination in that direction" had been revealed in high school but that it had also been the product of several happy accidents and that getting himself into college had been one of those fortunate occurrences. He learned a great deal about writing as a collegian, but the decision to become a writer had been made sometime earlier, most likely in France. A month after discharge, he wrote to the University of Oregon, inquiring as to a course of study "that will enable me to produce readable and salable material. Always considering of course the amount of ability necessary to undertake this as a vocation."

There had not been time for composition at St. Nazaire or St. Aignan, but Erny had mentally catalogued a number of wartime characters and incidents for later use. For the most part, these episodes didn't pan out, for soldier stories (his, anyway) weren't of great interest to the publications he approached over the next several years. But that didn't greatly matter; if they didn't sell, something else might. He had made up his mind and the only question now was whether he had the right stuff. That was what college would reveal. His vagueness on the issue is understandable; he would have thought an honest account of his decision—that he had thrown down the gauntlet as a teenage warrior in far country—unnecessarily dramatic.

He would also say at a later time that, once decided, he never wanted to do anything else and it is probably accurate to say that he never did.

There was an interval after college when he was a police-beat reporter, and journalism is arguably a separate discipline, limited to a presentation of facts. However, reporting standards in those days were flexible and common acts of skullduggery in the hands of an imaginative recorder routinely transcended reality. It was not much of a detour, if one at all.

At this beginning point, he probably had a conventionally romantic vision of authorship. He did not say much about his high school reading preferences, but they surely extended to the writings of expatriates and adventurers and these authors included Robert Louis Stevenson and Joseph Conrad, as well as Jack London. The much-admired Teddy Roosevelt's robust recollections had made a strong impression on the soldier and other literary or journalistic activists were known to him. Among the revealing scraps of paper he carried back from France was a newspaper clipping, the obituary of Captain E. W. Bonnyman. A onetime *New York Herald* staffer in Paris, the captain had wangled his way into the British army despite poor eyesight and a bad leg. By various evasions, he had twice gotten himself to the front lines, first to be wounded, then to die. The obituary praised Bonnyman's patriotism but Erny suspected something else. Perhaps, he scrawled, the fellow was simply "anxious to fight for the love of 'scrapping.'"

In the summer of 1919, Erny found employment as a warehouseman, moving monstrous bales of burlap about with an iron-wheeled hand truck for fifty cents an hour. He was substantially outweighed in this contest and, while he enjoyed physical activity, he remembered nothing pleasant about the interlude. He may have taken time off occasionally, sightseeing along those routes frequented by boxcars and gondolas. He had learned the customs of the "slide-door Pullman" much earlier, no doubt instructed by his accomplished father. That's probably how he made it to San Francisco and back in 1915.

In the fall, lacking funds to attend Oregon, he enrolled at Reed College, a small, newish liberal arts institution in Portland. His purpose in attending, he explained in his application, was "to equip myself for fiction writing." He applied himself diligently, receiving top grades in English and European history and a B+ in government. His instructor in the latter recalled him as "a superior student who grasped readily and well the material of the course." Still, said Professor Charles McKinley, "he was not particularly interested in the problems of American government nor my own orientation to them . . . [and there was] a slight aloofness from the rest of the class, whether from his greater maturity or from some other cause I know not."*

At Reed, he acquired the first of many rejection notices from the commercial press but was greatly encouraged when one of his classroom writing assignments was read aloud and discussed. He joined the staff of the school newspaper, the *Reed College Quest*, and produced several long critiques of athletes and fraternity men and other forms of frivolous life. As Prof. McKinley noted, the independent streak was visible; the year-end picture of the *Quest*'s staff found him in his usual place and mood, far to the left and scowling. Some of his disquiet may have reflected a rapidly receding hairline, which he attempted to conceal by wearing a hat—a fedora—whenever possible.

He worked the summer of 1920 in Alaska as a deckhand on a seventy-foot purse seiner which called in Ketchikan occasionally. It was filthy, smelly work, particularly for the fellow who had to stand down in the locker, knee-deep in salmon slime, and pitchfork the catch back up to the deck. He had once—just once—stripped and jumped off a boat or a dock to cleanse himself and, he said, very nearly expired in the North Pacific Ocean's stunning cold. It was marginally dangerous business at times; there were submerged rocks and treacherous eddies about, fog on occasion, and at least one wild storm that made a good story later. On almost any night, there was some chance of encounter with an armed stranger stealing from his employer's fish traps. A navy subchaser patrolled the

* Professor McKinley wasn't Erny's favorite instructor. Three decades later, when the writer sought a speaker with some understanding of government and political affairs to address his business club, McKinley was suggested. Erny demurred: "I don't think he intends it so, but somehow, with no leaven of humor, his remarks convey a certain innocent malice. From experience I find that it is often better to use the farmer's daughter as a human instance to drive home a point . . . [but] with McKinley, the audience gets to wondering if he ever knew a farmer's daughter; and such lack of moral frailty suffocates his listeners." (EH to President A. L. Strand, Oregon State College, October 6, 1949)

area but countless islands and inlets made surveillance difficult and the thieves were old hands at the business and skillful navigators.

When he returned home in the fall of 1920, he transferred to the University of Oregon at Eugene, his original choice, entering a school of journalism in which a subdepartment of creative writing existed. The accumulated summer paychecks helped at the start and, more important, he had uncovered a source of sustaining financial assistance. It was a federal program created for disabled servicemen and, he explained to that organization, he was among them. On his Reed College application, he mentioned being treated "for nervous condition and heart strain due to improper care of body in Army; it is a temporary condition." More likely, it was Graves' disease, an overactive thyroid gland that was surgically modified or removed in 1920. Whatever the malady, the Federal Board of Vocational Education accepted the theory that it was service-related and it would modestly and somewhat reluctantly contribute to his welfare for the next three years.

The program's inspectors came to the university periodically to audit the progress of its participants. Their interest leaned toward academic achievement in practical courses that might actually qualify a student veteran for gainful employment. Creative writing wasn't one of them, and they directed the young man to make better use of his academic time and the government's money. It was politic to agree with their suggestions, which he always did, and then ignored. He said the periodic reviews were unpleasant but, because "it was never the same guy twice," quite toothless. In 1923, he received two diplomas, the second of which—from the FBVE—pronounced him cured.

At Oregon, Erny quickly bubbled to the surface as a columnist for the school's daily paper, the *Oregon Daily Emerald*. He was The Campus Cynic and in this role found many aspects of university life worthy of comment, which, as the nom de plume implied, was generally not laudatory. He took issue with the way young ladies and gentlemen acted, with professorial pretensions and administrative foibles and, when sufficiently exercised, even the color of buildings and the deprived state of the university's landscaping. He advised on classroom deportment and delighted in campus politics and was invariably confounded and contorted by the opposite sex. He didn't understand their smiles, which he clumsily mistook as meaningful; or their hairdos, which he found impaling battlements of netting and hairpins; or their hats. He wrote:

> The early spring hanging gardens are with us once again. We drab male nonentities may now see more kinds of fruit, vegetables and flowers than Burbank and the seed catalogues together are able to fabricate, by watching the main avenues of promenade and observing the little gardens go floating by, five feet or more above the ground. After viewing some of these floral and faunal exhibits we are led to echo the words of that famous experimenter who first ate a green apple. In the midst of his suffering, he turned to little Eva and said with a sad, sad smile: "Ain't nature wonderful!" Yes, Adam, old scout, quite wonderful, but its creations are not to be classed with Easter bonnets. Not at all.

He found seniors wanting.

> A senior can be told as far as you can see his pants flop and flutter and stream out in the breeze that he manufacturers as he goes along. (I am not prepared to fully authenticate this statement. It may be that the senior makes the breeze, or it may be that the breeze already exists, is there ipso facto. The question that arises in this connection is: Does a senior at any time walk fast enough to create a breeze?).

And he battled pretension wherever he chose to find it.

> I am truly cosmopolitan. I wear Boston garters, Paris suspenders, occasionally a Panama hat, smoke Havana cigars, enjoy African golf, once in while take French leave, and swear by undergarments made in lower East New York. Isn't that cosmopolitan? Further, I read the Atlantic Monthly and think the advertisements are just awfully pretty. Further, when an eastern visitor disparages the West and the Westerners, I heartily agree and try to disparage myself more—in his presence. . . . Isn't that the very acme of cosmopolitanism—of culture?

George Turnbull, an assistant professor of journalism at the time and the school's dean for many years following, said Cynic was entertaining but, if intended to reflect the disillusion of a Lost Generation, unconvincing. The column appeared less frequently in Erny's junior year but was now supplemented by imaginative reportage of school events that, on their own merit, did not loom large—band recitals and sorority fund-raisers and other such pastel pleasures. He had become the *Emerald*'s most visible contributor, his initials frequently appearing in the headlines of his articles as if he were part of the event itself. This method worked well enough as long as nobody took him seriously. When they did, things went less well, as happened in January 1922 when he and the *Emerald*'s editors jointly declared war on the university's Reserve Officers Training Corps, demanding its removal from the campus.

At a great and liberal university, they said, the study and practice of war no longer had a place. Mandatory military training defied the spirit of disarmament and the ROTC was, in fact, one of those jingoistic institutions from whence the poisonous fumes of professional soldiery sought to overwhelm a public desire for a universal peace. The veteran sergeant could not resist a commentary on the university's own officers-to-be, whom he found comically dressed and incompetent. "Our little standing army (or reclining army—as it seems it is from observation of the drill grounds and barracks during drill hour) is about as valuable as a pewter beer mug in a church," said he. "The University is apparently oblivious of the spectacle of inconsistency it presents in allowing it to remain at the side of its regular curriculum."

The campaign disappeared a few days later. Erny said that he and the *Emerald*'s editor, together with a student editorial board that had been hastily appointed under the safety-in-numbers theory of defense, were bundled off to a meeting with the president of the university. He said that this high and mighty and very angry administrator (Prince Lucien Campbell by name) left no question at all about who was leaving the campus if one more unsympathetic word about the ROTC appeared.

Professor Turnbull said many assumed that Erny would become the newspaper's editor in his senior year, but he declined to compete for the position, accepting instead the editorship of a weekend literary offshoot, the *Oregon Sunday Emerald*. A once-a-week effort was about all he could manage, for he was busy on several other fronts, cluttering his time with campus and extramural projects which were unified only to the degree that they required pounding a typewriter. He was a steady contributor to *Lemon Punch*, a humor magazine, and likewise produced comic material for the student yearbook in each of his three years at Oregon. Also in 1922, mostly while attending summer session, he wrote a dozen longish book reviews for a Eugene newspaper, the *Morning Register*.

This would seem to have been sufficient collateral activity for one who was obliged to devote reasonable effort in studious pursuit. But, in fact, much more of his time was committed elsewhere, writing adventure fiction. He had come to the university to learn that trade and found the academic offerings dealing with composition immensely valuable. They were the only classes he cared much about or in which his grades reflected sufficient concentration, and he would forever credit his instructor in creative writing, Professor W. F. G. Thatcher, with revealing the mysteries of the business. Fiction writing is a profession learned or at least perfected by most of its practitioners through persistent labor, and he began producing short stories almost immediately on arrival at the university and never stopped. He did not much care for the merriment and ritual of fraternity life but he joined Delta Tau Delta, most likely because he was attracted to a small building adjacent to the fraternity house—a two-room shed used occasionally as housing for the fraternity's cook. He quickly appropriated it as his office.

It was a rough accommodation and furnishings were no doubt Spartan—probably a table or homemade typing stand, odd bits of shelving, a couple of chairs, and some sort of heating device to resist the moist and chill of western Oregon winters. But it was ideal for his purposes and its walls would be decorated with an ever-expanding collection of rejection notices from national magazines that found Erny's work, impressive though it was, unsuited to their needs. By the end of his school stay, in June 1923, he had pinned up fifty or more of these messages. On more than one occasion, he explained that, while acceptances were pleasant, his real goal was to cover every inch of every vertical surface of his rustic study with rejections from every magazine in America.

He kept no close record of this three-year creative effort and could only guess at it later—maybe three dozen stories, he said; maybe a couple more than that. Some of the manuscripts probably were abandoned after repeated denials, although it was not his habit to give up on them easily; a bad effort might be salvaged with a bit of a rewrite, perhaps a fresh lead. He demonstrated no particular attachment to western adventure; themes were as varied as the magazines he sent them to, his output ranging from wilderness sagas and seafaring tales to sports and detective yarns. Specialization might come in time but, he said, a writer's first objective was simply to sell something to somebody. He eschewed only the more lurid periodicals, which he disdained as destructive to the artist's mind. "No self–respecting wielder of the pen ought to cater to Uncle Billy's Sheet, True Confessions, et al.," he pronounced. "There is no glory, nor respect, nor money, to be found in writing sex literature. Once having dabbled in it, the pen is often weakened and blunted for more accepted and catholic types [of literature]."

He often had several manuscripts in motion simultaneously and he kept them moving, one magazine's reluctance simply becoming another's opportunity. While the refusals mounted, there would be from time to time modest evidence of progress in the returning envelope—an editor's scribble on the margin of the form-letter rejection or a typewritten note telling him that he was getting close. "We were hard put to in rejecting this," said the *Liberator*, returning an unidentified work: "Something very fine about it but just slightly wanting." Passing on "Jungle Gods", *People's Popular Monthly* explained: "This story is exceedingly well written, but it is not a story of success, and we make it a rule to print no stories of failure, or any stories that are in any way depressing." The editor of *Yachting* Magazine read "Crossing the Straits" twice before returning it. "The story is good and I would like to ask if it is founded on fact, or if it embodies an actual experience. If you don't dispose of the story elsewhere and can return it to me next summer, I will then be able to use it in one of the fall issues."

His first acceptance was "The Corporal's Story," which appeared in *Overland Monthly*, a San Francisco literary magazine best remembered because Bret Harte was its first editor, in June 1921. It told of a young national guardsman on the Mexican border and of his love for a flirtatious and unfortunately soiled cantina girl. *Overland* printed a second short, "The Three Wise Men," a rather quiet western, four months later. And though eschewing violence, the author was instructed by *Overland*'s editor to "tone it down some as certain expressions . . . would shock sensitive female readers." The compensation in each case was a subscription to the magazine or extra copies "in lieu of money which the Overland does not possess." Further honor arrived at the close of his sophomore year when he was awarded the $25 Edison Marshall Prize in his short-story class for a work, "The Veil," of which only the title survives.

Eddie Marshall, Erny's first contact with a living, breathing producer of popular adventure fiction, was a story himself. He had tired of student life at the University of Oregon after two years, concluding in 1915 that the world at large was a better classroom. In his case, it proved to be, for he sold a fistful of shorts and novels in his first years and in 1921 won the O. Henry short story prize for "The Heart of Little Shikara." Eddie was also a Delt who returned to the fraternity house periodically with cigars and songs and wonderful stories of his adventurous life, which over time described travels to the far ends of the earth that were occasionally illustrated by photographs of a husky, mustached fellow in a pith helmet crouched by some large, reclining beast. Erny responded opportunistically to the award, praising Marshall's talent and industry in a short article published in late 1922 by a thin writer's magazine in Boston.

> Quite the best thing about Eddie Marshall is that he has no false standards about "art." Still, each story and each novel brings with it a surer sense of touch, a more rounded and matured view of life, a better and more original choice of phrasing and wording.
>
> It's a treat to watch him at a reunion. He's the life of the party. Excess vitality bubbles continually to the surface. He's boisterous, eager to share the hilarity and be in on the fun. And yet he's always looking about, catching people's expressions, snaring their queer or fresh phrases, always pumping them on certain things they seem to know best. Now is that not the attitude of the artist?
>
> And he works—"to beat the devil."

So did Erny, who, in mid-1922, finally acquired fully professional standing, selling "The Trap Lifters," a yarn about fish piracy in Alaska, to a pulp magazine specializing in nautical adventure. *Sea Stories* paid him $30 and ran the piece that October. Erny quickly sold three more Alaska shorts to *Sea Stories* and cracked two other pulps, *Ace-High* and *Top-Notch*, in early 1923. And if this were not sufficient, the daily *Emerald* and the Sunday edition each published a Haycox short story in 1923, unquestionably two of those works that the professional trade had found of great but unsuitable merit. ◆

The shanty office provided that solitude required for deep thought and labored composition. Its separation from the fraternity house was equally useful because Erny often worked into early morning hours and, within the walls of Delta Tau Delta, the clatter of a nocturnal typewriter would have disturbed the slumbering brotherhood. The shanty also reinforced the fraternity's view of their literary member as a man apart, one who seems to have been admired for his energy and ambition but otherwise put down as a reclusive sort with occasionally bizarre habits and few close friends. It is uncertain whether he made any progress at all as to female companionship while at the university. Later, his wife thought that he had been briefly engaged to a young lady whose dominant personality and spirited ways soon frightened him away. Others say he scarcely ever dated.

Jim Case, who was a Delta Tau Delta freshman in Erny's senior year, remembered the "slightly built but wiry . . . [and] almost bald" upperclassman forty years later in a happily-mixed metaphor. "He reminded me of an eagle looking for a fat bird—hooked nosed, piercing eyes and impatient with trivial conversation." Case found him friendly, though "a little indulgent or faintly condescending . . . [and lacking] that easy-going suavity that marked some of the boys who came from wealthy homes and had plenty of pocket-money."

Case observed: "He would let nothing interfere with his writing . . . [and] drove himself unmercifully, and I used to wonder how long he could keep up such a pace without breaking down. His only recreations, as far as I could learn, were hiking over the hills around Eugene and playing tennis." Case came to associate his fraternity brother with the central character in "Jungle Gods," which Erny had asked him to read. "It centered around a strong, driving explorer who pitched his terrific strength against the horrors of the African jungle . . . never doubting his ability to bend all enemies to his will."

Erny continued to fret about his loss of hair, Case said, and when he had sold a couple of stories "he hired one of the frosh to give him a thorough scalp massage every other night." This was done in front of the fraternity's fireplace where all could witness the performance, and was an event of constant interest and comment. Case assumed the bold approach was meant to suggest to the brothers that their literary member didn't give a damn what they thought.

In fact, on many evenings, the masseur was Arthur "Ole" Larson, a fellow Delt and journalism-school classmate who also yearned to write and was Erny's closest friend at the university. Easygoing Ole, who was a sprinter and captain of the Oregon track team in 1923, may have been the only fraternity member who was both welcome and comfortable within the Delt's writing annex. He was Erny's critic and sounding board when called upon and, as he had spent the war on a subchaser, technical adviser on the pieces sold to *Sea Stories*. Erny paid Ole one cent a minute, though never more than a dime, in the futile attempt to restore some form of life to his scalp.

The University of Oregon's J-school class of 1923 produced its share of qualified press professionals. Edwin Palmer (Ep) Hoyt, a close friend then and ever after, wrote adventure fiction early in his career but did too well at newspapering. He rose quickly through the ranks at the state's principal newspaper, becoming the *Oregonian*'s managing editor in 1933 and publisher in 1939; and he was later editor and publisher of the *Denver Post*. Jessie Thompson (later, Scott) worked for three Portland newspapers and was a published novelist, short-story writer, and poet. The class of '23 also produced an editorial-page editor for the *Oakland Tribune* and a copy-desk chief at a major Los Angeles daily and several (Ole being one) who made a good living in advertising and promotion.

Graduate Haycox probably would have succeeded as a newspaperman, though his brief encounter with the real thing offered no assurance of that. He completed courses in editing and publishing because he had to but avoided the reporting class, which normally is obligatory for a journalism degree. The short-story and magazine-writing classes, together with excursions into drama and criticism and writing style, substituted in his odd case. Still, the university demanded some balance in his scholarship and his final year was darkened by three successive terms of animal biology, a deadly lab course that no doubt was offered at the earliest possible hour. ◆

Erny probably was recalling his own early attempts at adventure fiction when, in a 1941 magazine article, he talked about the problems of the novice writer. "Sometimes in reaching his key points he finds himself hard put to create sufficient pressure and tension in the scene and bring the whole story to its climax; therefore, in a mood of bitter desperation he flexes his muscles and tries to strong-arm the scene with adjectives, exclamation points and sounds of fury. This is the good old grunt-and-groan method. Mr. Max Wilkinson of Collier's calls it the 'He-bled-freely' technique."

Early Haycox was of the muscular school occasionally. The short story that *Yachting* Magazine wanted to see again arguably was a work in which adjectival and metaphoric excesses were present. Yet, florid or no, as the writer would have further noted, it had accomplished its primary purpose. Some editor liked it, bought it, and printed it. In the case of "Crossing the Straits," in fact, two editors found it acceptable and, with a modest change of title ("Over the Straits"), it ran in *Sea Stories* in January 1923. The story probably is based on an actual incident from the writer's story-inspiring Alaska summer job in 1920. It describes the stormy passage of the tender *Star* from Ketchikan to a cannery on Prince of Wales Island, a dangerous expedition necessitated by the *Star*'s fast-ripening cargo of sockeye salmon. There is a sudden explosion of wind and wave, the violence of which temporarily stills conversation in the wheelhouse.

Another dizzy roll, sending us far to the side, interrupted the sentence. The shriek of the wind crept up a note. I could just make out, directly in front of us, the twisting, contorting water. Now it would pile up to a sharp peak and the jagged edges would be whipped off by the wind, driving against the front of the pilot house with the sharp rattle of machine-gun bullets. Now we would meet a huge wave head on and the boat would stagger back while the spray went flying high into the air. Now we went plunging into a trough with the sickening drop of an express elevator, while the foredeck completely disappeared from sight, buried under the seething, boiling eddies of water. Then we would labor to the surface in time to meet another onslaught.

We were struck from the side and went reeling, careening over with our bottom half out of the water and the runway on our under side completely submerged. I clutched the wheel tightly to keep from smashing against the wall, while time and again Bob hung suspended, head and shoulders over me for a long breathless instant, his body standing out in shadowy silhouette against the side windows. Then we righted ourselves, shipping a load of water that went sweeping, sliding over the deck and came spurting into the wheelhouse, under the doorsill. Now and then we would stand on our stern, bow completely out of water, like an angry bear on its haunches, and the next instant we would be slammed violently against the front of the house, stern boosted up, nose deeply buried, while I twirled the wheel vainly and prayed for speedy recovery.

"Must be wilder'n all-get-out outside the islands," remarked Ed, as we went hurtling down into a giant hollow.

"Must be," returned Bob, eyes glued to the pane. "Good blow here in the straits." We came out of the trough with a leap—high into the air we went.

"Wish I had a good hot cup of coffee," I said after a century or so.

"Huh! There ain't nothin' stickin' to that stove 'ceptin' th' polish. Chew of t'bacco help?"

I could hear nothing from the galley; evidently there wasn't anything left to fall from the shelves.

The beginning writer, Erny said, could be forgiven for all manner of literary sins, provided he or she understood this one thing. "There seems only one way for the novice to go about it, which is to take paper and write, and to repeat this time upon time until he achieves some precision at it. In a sense it is a good deal like juggling—and nobody learns juggling out of book. For the young writer, or for any writer, the eight hour day is better than six, and if the young writer should get indigestion from the process it is probably caused by what he eats rather than by his hours; for with the exception of Sir Walter Scott I never heard of a writer who died as a direct result of overwork."

— 6 —

The Gift of Prospect Park

"The rum runners," the last of the college-written stories, appeared in two issues of *Sea Stories* in July 1923. It would be a half-year or more before the next sale, and, in this dry period, Erny's comfortable survival back in Portland required securing other employment. This he did, obtaining a position on the reporting staff of the *Oregonian* at $30 a week after a couple of idle months. He was assigned to the night police beat, a 6 pm to 2:30 am shift spent in the press room at police headquarters with companions from the city's three other dailies. He filed stories by telephone or by messenger if there was time, and tagged along when officers were summoned to a promising crime scene or when the police ambulance raced to the aid of accident victims. Later, he was recalled as an inquisitive beginner and himself admitted to poking around in odd corners. He was, for example, fascinated by a small holding cell where suspects were sometimes quartered for a short time before interrogation. If a couple of fellows needed a minute or two of privacy to concoct an alibi, it was a God-sent haven—provided, of course, they didn't give much thought to a boxlike structure against one wall of the cell that would have been just big enough to conceal a crouching officer, and did. Jessie Thompson, also a brand new *Oregonian* reporter, said Erny seemed to like the job, even if temporary, caring enough to search carefully through each evening's first edition to see if he'd made the paper that day.

She would also recall from him "one piece of awfully workable rule-of-thumb advice nobody in the School of Journalism's newswriting courses had produced. I was doing all sorts of general assignments, and confided to Erny that direct quotes worried me a lot—sometimes a person expressed himself so clumsily. Erny said: 'You don't say what the person said: you say what he was *trying* to say.' For a fiction writer that is the perfect answer; and even for a newswriter, it's damn good." Having avoided the reporting class in J-school, reporter Haycox was unburdened of all those nitpicking rules that restrained poor Jessie.

He said he rather quickly learned that getting a story printed in the *Oregonian* without substantial alteration was aided by some knowledge of each of the half-dozen characters who rotated at the copy desk. One had been a seafaring man, another had studied for the ministry, a third was a reformed alcoholic, and so forth. It was tough to do in a short piece, he recalled, but you improved your chances of easy passage immeasurably if you worked a nautical term into your story, extolled the Good Lord, and cursed Demon Rum. These were Prohibition times, of course, and the last required no great effort. But his intuitive skills didn't fool everybody. One of the old pressroom hands, reviewing the prospects of several police-beat youngsters one quiet evening, told him he wouldn't make the grade. The judgment may have been influenced by knowledge that reporter Haycox used his spare moments in the pressroom and off-hours back at the newspaper, often into breaking dawn, to continue his assault on the fiction market.

Bylined news stories were uncommon in those days, so only one of his reporting contributions can be identified. He told relatives that he was assigned to investigate a speed trap in Kalama, Washington, got himself arrested without much difficulty, and exposed mild corruption. The story disclosed that the town marshal was hauling large numbers of motorists to a special police court and splitting fines, sometimes running $40 to $50 an hour, with the judge and city. There was some speeding, it was acknowledged, and one miscreant was unapologetic—he either said, or in the reporter's view was trying to say: "What does it matter if I kill a man or two in these small joints?" Still, the practice of incentive pay for traffic cops contravened Washington state law, the apparent leakage of monies into other willing hands offended public sentiment, and the mayor resigned.

Erny also contributed to the *Sunday Oregonian*'s large book column and here at least got his name or initials recorded. An eclectic and generally friendly critic, he plowed through sea stories and histories and various personal narratives with the confidence and verbal dash of a seasoned literary observer. His selections included two works about R. L. Stevenson, both of which he recommended with comfortable knowledge, and one which sampled the writings of his beloved Teddy Roosevelt. In the president's energetic prose, Erny observed, "the swing and the vigor of the man's character shines through the printed word. Perhaps in the future this may be one final aspect of his greatness; that his desire and his seeking always cut away impeding barriers; that he never knowingly hid behind false poses. He had no time in his life to assume an idea or a station that did not fit him. Either he changed the idea and station or he abandoned it." A travelogue produced by British press baron Lord Northcliff revealed a man "with the zeal of a good police reporter"—high praise indeed. Roy F. Dibble's *Strenuous Americans* was mildly entertaining. "There is, however, a surplusage of Dibble."

Portland's criminal environment was at that time a convergence of bootlegging, gambling, prostitution, and conventional thuggery, a good deal of which played out in waterfront dives and Chinatown dens. It made better copy if "prominent and influential" citizens were involved in its episodes, as they often were, and if the criminals themselves possessed unusual physical or psychological attributes. Many met this test, among them nervous, ragged, and freckled-faced holdup men; a "praying burglar"; and unscrupulous Zona Dale, who was "tough as an eight-minute egg." There was "Irish Mary" Stevens, who got the police department's morals squad temporarily discharged for graft and undue intimacy, and the swindler Milan Sajatovich, "the daddy of them all, the arch-master of the box trick." Other promising arrests included those of "Seattle Shorty" and "The Jew," who were fond of robbing motorists; and somebody who claimed to be Prince Albert Sichofsky and ran his confidence game in

Portland's high places; and Leo "One Arm" Burke and a friend, found sitting in a car near a crime scene—good enough for a pinch back then. Best of all was Nettie L. Lindley, who "sat in the office of United States Marshall Hotchkiss last night worrying over the lack of a needle to darn a pair of her husband's socks, but not at all concerned over the fact that she faces indictments charging her with sending poisoned candy through the mails to a rival in love. . . ."

The reporters got much of their material from sociable detectives who frequented the press room, and they almost always took the department's side of things. When a "moonshine-demented veteran" burned to death in a padded cell (someone had given the addled and liquor-soaked prisoner a cigarette), the reporter quickly noted that it was an unavoidable accident. Police actions were generally described as swift and efficient, sometimes bold, occasionally spectacular; and when one portly officer overpowered two assailants and sat on them until help arrived, the *Oregonian*'s writer called it one of the greatest acts of courage in police annals. There must have been occasional misunderstandings between reporters and officers for, in late 1923, the morals squad raided the city's press club and found bottled beer. But these things worked out; the case was dropped when the evidence disappeared.

Still, some incidents overwhelmed the press room's cynical humor. Erny found himself in a skid road basement during a police investigation one night. "The man who ran the place had built up duckboards above the water. He had a counter and a coffee urn. For five cents you got the worst coffee that could possibly have been brewed. But if you bought a cup of coffee, you had the right to lie down on these duckboards, without mattress or quilt, and sleep out the night. I counted more than three hundred men packed like cordwood . . . in this damp, cold, evil place, lighted by a single fifty-watt light bulb." ◆

Erny resigned from the newspaper after six months, in early 1924. He had a bundle of manuscripts and had recently sold three stories, one of which involved a young reporter who found rural life and a farmer's daughter more appealing than Portland. In his case, the decision was that of an aspiring and mildly successful author who felt the need to "get closer to the market" and that place, where all the magazines and editors could be found and cultivated, was New York City.

He had accumulated a war chest of about $400, although, subtracting train fare and incidentals, probably had half of that by the time he had settled in the big city at the end of March. He rented a fourth-floor walk-up room in the Village, bought a typewriter on time, and began writing in his small chamber and calling on editorial offices. The process of creation, he said, was often fertilized on long walks through Manhattan or around Prospect Park in Brooklyn, during which he would try to cobble up some kind of plot and, if that worked, begin to insert characters and incidents. He sometimes returned as empty-headed as he'd started, but it was on one of these excursions, which sometimes covered eight miles, that he concocted the rotund master of Burnt Creek, Oregon, storekeeper David Budd. This generous, wise, courageous, lethargic, and meddlesome character would be the centerpiece of four of the ten short stories that *Western Story* magazine bought from him in 1924 and, all told, Old Dave lasted through nine installments.

Erny started a monthly record of income and expense in June, when cash on hand was a discouraging $43. July 1 found him with $185, thanks to three sales. August 1 was dismal, back down to $50, but the tide turned the next day—three checks arrived, totaling $276—and by year-end he was $704 to the good. This was mostly due to the generosity of editor F. E. Blackwell at *Western Story,* a Street & Smith publication that was one of the largest and longest running of a hundred or so "pulpers" devoted to western melodrama in the early twentieth century. Blackwell liked the young man's work and encouraged him, though Erny said it was in a somewhat despairing manner, and bumped the rate on the Budd stories from $110 apiece to $130.

In the back of another ledger, Erny logged his daily progress from November 13 to December 18, 1924. His purpose, set down at the beginning of the record, was "to check up on daily work performed. Time is to be kept account of as well as money. Time is the original form of money." He had just completed the plotting of a novelette, *Valley of the*

Rogue, and averaging a bit less than two thousand words a day, he would finish it in two weeks.

There were, of course, distractions and dry spells.

Nov. 14. Over to Weehawken to see Burr/Hamilton dueling ground . . . home and wrote Ch. I . . . read 20 pages of Coman's *Economic Beginnings of the Far West.*

Nov. 17. Wisdom tooth out this morning. 1600 words . . . and revision of Ch. II. Wrote letters to dad, Bob Case, Arthur and Lawrence. In this record is to go only a list of each day's practical achievements. No hot air. Washed some clothes.

Nov. 18. Very worthless day; copied chapter 2 . . . [and] typed off a synopsis of some Coman. Have made two permanent habits in last three months—daily shave and morning shower. Next will be 7 o'clock rising, starting in the morning.

Nov. 24. 1600 words on "Valley;" some work on the map [of the early West]. It looks very nice. Aim to have it show the posts, forts, rendezvous and trade trails of the Western Country between 1800–1850.

Nov. 29. "Valley" to Western Story; saw A. R. Wetjen off to London on Cameronia; to Cadmus Bookshop and priced some early Western history. Home and wrote 300-word prologue for "The Road to Danger Town." This is to be an experiment. I can't see beyond Ch. I. The trick worked before.

Dec. 1. 3200 words on "Danger." If I can keep up plot and suspense, it will be a good story. Went downtown and bought Chittenden's *The American Fur Trade of the Far West.* $40. Lot of money, but believe I shall eventually get full profit.

Dec. 3. Tooth out and jaw scraped. It was badly infected. *Valley of the Rogue* accepted, which means $440. This about crystallizes a notion of mine: No more short stories. Hereafter to write novelettes and to tackle the full-sized novel length. Have the beginning of a good field in Early Oregon.

Dec. 4. Bought a couple of book review magazines. I presume it is necessary to keep abreast of current literature, but it seems a waste of time and money. Follow my own furrow. I need only more sober, technical knowledge, greater industry, greater patience. We shall get as far as we shall get.

Dec. 6. 2800 words on "Danger." I dunno—I dunno!

Dec. 8. It looks pretty good at this particular stage.

Dec. 11. 800 words. Very poor. Have not smoked for 6 days. Very restless.

Dec. 12. Story finished; to WS in the morning; walked 4 miles. This a part of the routine hereafter: bath; some reading; to bed.

Dec. 16. Studying Chittenden; mind zigzagging between some plots. Fallow period. Shortly I aim to do a story of the Missouri river during the fur era. But next one will possibly be another Oregon novelette.

The inclination to write longer stories wasn't difficult to understand—novels were, after all, the métier of the giants of his profession. He had produced one fairly long piece that fall and quickly sold *Red Knives*—which at 35,000 words was equal to four or five shorts—to the *Frontier*. That magazine paid him $500 for the effort, a stupendous endorsement of voluminous prose in its own right. The problem was that longer stories took longer to write and uncomfortably extended the interval between paydays. Still, it was worth trying. The "Danger Town" experiment was unsuccessful, at least in the eyes of editor Blackwell, and it is not known to have appeared elsewhere. His next story was another lengthy one, *Roll Along, Missouri!*, the fur-trading piece. In early 1925, before it sold, cash on hand had withered to almost nothing.

He had made every penny work. The few books he bought were a necessary resource and he purchased a $42 suit to appear presentable in editorial offices; but aside from these items and the unavoidable dental services, he was the soul of parsimony. He stayed in a cheapest possible accommodations and, when he had somewhere to go in the city, he walked. His meal allowance was about $2 a day, so he frequented the Village's hole-in-the-wall eating establishments, which he would recall as "temples dedicated to mangling food beyond taste or recognition." These were, he added, typically operated by failed poets and painters, usually in a cellar or two flights up, the upper level featuring "a broken skylight through which came a young cloudburst of New York soot; and invariably, too, these places were infested with a variety of high-diving spiders, trained . . . to light in your soup or water glass."

For entertainment, there was the Village itself, in full Bohemian bloom. He was invited to parties now and again or at least tagged along to a couple of them—it didn't seem to matter much whether you were invited or not, nor did anyone much care when you got there. These gatherings were generally bedlam, he said: lots of people talking and nobody listening; perhaps a soprano voice and a misused piano beating against the din; a plate of sandwiches if you were lucky; and women in the strangest get-ups a Portland boy had ever seen. One of his hostesses was reprising Sarah Bernhardt or Helen of Troy; he could not decide which. Her costume "was batiked in nine odd colors and profusely illustrated. A rising sun burst over the hills by her left shoulder; to the right of this was a bed of dahlias and, in serial order, reading downward, I made out a more or less pictorial history of our country beginning with Johnny Appleseed . . . and ending with Admiral Peary planting a flag at the North Pole."

His first room was an attic cubicle under a tarpaper roof and, depending on weather or time of day, it was either an oven or an icebox. After selling a few stories, he moved. "Once [a writer] began to get along in the world, once he survived the cheese and dill pickle period of semi-starvation, he went away from there, without regret," he would recall. "If he carried off any memories it was usually memories of money he had lent to one or another of the artistic bums who remained forever behind to live on hot air and borrowed sandwiches."

Those first months would contribute to a grim view of the city and its residents, and he would never establish great rapport with either. The lower edge of the Village was a rough, crime-ridden neighborhood and patrolmen on nearby lower Broadway, a safer venue, were quick to "boost along" any solitary male stroller. The New York City police force was composed of thirteen thousand surly Irishmen, he said, and while he could not forgive their bad manners, he understood the cause: "There is a tension in New York nowhere else met with; a banging and ramming and jamming and roaring of traffic and people; people snarling and running and crowding, all utterly and absolutely without manners. And a great percentage of them foreign, especially Jewish and Italian. Now, an Italian may have manners but a Jew has no concept of personal dignity and none of the privacy of personal affairs."

In March 1925, Erny decided to go home for a while. He was tired and felt awful and was certain the cause was the terrible food he was eating. As he periodically skipped meals when things were tight, lack of nutrition may have been as much to blame. He had enough money left to buy a Pullman berth and to allot $25 for meals on the train. He closed out the cash book on April 1, at which time the balance was $40. He had sold nothing since *Valley of the Rogue* in December.

To be sure, he intended coming back after a few months of Oregon restoratives. The first session in New York had gone reasonably well; he had averaged one sale a month between June and December, which amounted to just over $1,700, considerably better than reporter's wages. It made sense to give it another try, for he'd come across some interesting local story material; there was, he found, an Old East as well as an Old West. And there was another, even better reason for returning. On March 4, 1925, just before departing, he'd gotten married at the Little Church Around the Corner. She had a job and a career in the making and was going to stay in the big city. ◆

Her name was Jill Marie Chord and he had known her for just a year. They had, in fact, met on the eastbound train—she was headed for New York to attend art school. He commenced the courtship immediately and one late night the club car attendant begged them to part so he could go to bed. By journey's end, Erny had heard a good deal about the Chords and Jill's seven maternal uncles, the Sullivan brothers, all of whom had settled in eastern Oregon and were miners and ranchers and saloon keepers and, very likely, the collective inspiration for the Dave Budd character. Erny also knew about Jill's indefatigable mother, Mary, who had held the family together in Baker City, Oregon, by taking in boarders after husband James died in 1911; had since then built a career in department store sales in Portland; and had just now been promoted by the J. C. Penney Company to the post of buyer at the firm's head office in New York. Jill, then twenty-two, probably wouldn't have been on that train without knowledge that Mary and Jack, Jill's twin brother, would be coming along shortly.

She was a pretty, petite girl, just two inches over five feet tall with auburn hair and an impish, adventurous spirit. Her idea of a good time was camping in the Cascades with her Portland pals, or trailing horses somewhere, or climbing Mt. Hood. She liked good times but was steady and sensible. Knowing that Erny would want to take her out when the train stopped in Chicago, and aware that he couldn't afford to, she pulled down the blinds of her compartment and locked the door and hid from him that day.

Jill first stayed at a residential hotel near Central Park and she and Erny would meet at a subway station nearby. He would greet her with the thought, until she rather tired of hearing it, that "great oaks from little acorns grow." When he sold a story, they rode through the park in a hansom cab while, at other times, the romance was propelled less expensively in a rented rowboat from which the two could admire the Plaza Hotel and speculate on the pleasant lives of those who could afford such a place. When Mary and Jack arrived, Jill moved with them to an apartment on Martense Street in Brooklyn, where Erny was almost a fixture. He got along well with his prospective in-laws but Mary may not have realized how quickly the romance was moving along, and Jill knew her mother would have objected to matrimonial plans—for the time, at least. Her daughter had some prospects as a commercial artist if she kept at it; there had even been a suggestion from Fashion Art Academy, where Jill was enrolled, that the young lady's talent was sufficient to consider European training.

Jill did not wish to disappoint her mother, nor did she want to abandon her art courses or leave a position she had obtained with Mary's help as an illustrator in the J. C. Penney advertising department. The marital arrangement was thus more complex than most, and was to have been accomplished in secret. The couple agreed that Jill would keep working and studying in New York. Erny would say nothing of the affair back in Oregon and return east as soon as he felt better, and they would manufacture some story about a later marriage at a later date. It occurred to neither of the conspirators that statistical columns devoted to newly issued marriage licenses appeared daily in New York newspapers. Mary quickly learned and, back in Oregon, Erny confided to a few close friends whose assurances of privacy were quite worthless. Despite this, these two would publicly maintain for some years that they were married in New York on June 28, 1926. Mary joined the conspiracy with printed announcements to family and friends and, in a final touch of deception, Jill and Erny drove to Washington D. C. and Philadelphia after the phantom ceremony. This was advertised as their honeymoon. ◆

All that walking around New York City, through all those statue- and monument-adorned greens and parks, had drawn Erny close to the War of the Revolution; and before leaving the city in 1925, he had begun to search libraries and bookstores for biographical material on its principals and for descriptions of specific engagements. He traced maps and dug into such other details as nourish the curiosity of a writer drawn to history: what were the weapons and how were they handled; what did the uniforms look like, when such were available; how did the fortifications on Breed's Hill appear from the slightly higher elevation of Bunker Hill; between frequent bouts of near starvation, what did the Continental soldier eat for supper?

He would over the next eighteen months produce ten short stories and one novelette, *Winds of Rebellion*, set in the turmoil of the American Revolution—a good third of his total production in that period. These were probably the best of his early work, lacking the contrivance and exaggerated characterization common to the pulp western. He found a simple dignity in the colonial period and its stalwarts, and this seemed to steady and balance his authorial hand, to repress restless action to some degree in favor of mood and scene.

Had he persisted on this course, he perhaps would have achieved a degree of recognition in the trade, as a writer of some capacity, sooner than he did. However, he didn't, dropping the colonial theme in 1927 to concentrate fully on westerns. It was a practical decision. The western-story market and the financial opportunities associated with it in the 1920s were larger, and he was in no position to ignore those relative economics; and his background inclined him to go in that direction anyway.* Still, it had been a useful interlude. In New York, he discovered the pleasure and stimulation of research as an adjunct to his imagination; and he also found in himself a capacity to utilize gritty, factually founded material to good effect. Neither revelation had substantial immediate impact. In later times, however, he would be perceived by some—and probably saw himself—as both storyteller and historian.

"With Grape and Bayonet," one of the Revolutionary War pieces, featured a surly enlistee and an ailing sergeant at the Battle of Trenton. It was war in all its detestable glory.

> Housegger bowed his head and tried to cover up his free hand. The fingers holding the gun butt ached miserably; his feet were beginning to chill despite the steady motion. And for all of his solid body, he began to tremble. There was no withstanding the steady onslaught of that wind. Of a sudden it seemed to redouble its fury and deadliness; the head of the column surmounted a roll of ground and slid down a slope. The rending and crashing of ice swelled on the eardrums. They had reached McKenky's Ferry. The column flinched and came to a stop.
>
> The night rolled inward and Housegger, looking sidewise at the sergeant with a hostile vision, saw him as a man might see a ghost, with deep, staring eyes and a face all white. The latter spoke:
>
> "You see, my boy, that to fight a battle there must be first some preliminary torture. Ah that wind! But the battle itself is but a momentary interruption of the strategy. We don't win campaigns by battles. We win

* Of the ten Revolutionary War shorts Erny wrote, four didn't sell, perhaps suggesting a thin market for this kind of work and further explaining why he stopped trying. He got occasional turndowns on his western stories, but sold nine out of ten.

by marching around the enemy until he is drunk with bewilderment. This, no doubt, is some of the fun you came to share with us."

George Washington is an incidental character in the story, as he was in several of these pieces. But he is a bit player looming large.*

Housegger was not of that breed endowed with acute perceptions and strong imagination; but the setting which surrounded this figure [General Washington] was one which was likely to strike the dullest with a certain impact. The crying and howling of the wind; the enveloping storm clouds in the brooding sky; the weaving patterns of snow in the air; all these things tended to make a vivid impression. The lantern guttered and the general's cloak flung itself about his neck. Housegger watched him finish the note and hand it to an aide.

In that instant the youth had a clear, definitive picture of a face: a square, almost massive face, ruddied by the wind. There was a reflected glint of the lantern light in blue eyes and a revealing of a generous mouth set in calm, deliberate lines. Patience was written on the features of this man more clearly than it could have been in cold letters in a book. Housegger, slipping by, heard a sonorous, level voice.

"How did you find us so quickly, Major Wilkinson?"

"It was not difficult, sir. I followed bloody footprints in the snow."

Among the writer's few unfinished manuscripts was a long Revolutionary War piece, *Black David*, which was discontinued after four chapters. He also considered, but never undertook, a biography of the period's most curious and conflicted personality, Benedict Arnold. Early American history remained a passion—although he stopped writing about those times, he never did stop buying books on the subject.

* The author thought GW a remarkable man although, like other notable Americans, adulated to unreality. "We began this process of distortion in our earliest days as a country and our greatest victim was George Washington. Here was a heavy-blooded, robust, reserved and fairly uncomplicated Virginia country squire. He was a good general, a competent statesman, and possessed a character which commanded the respect of his countrymen; but when a succession of foolish, incapable biographers had gotten through with him, his follies, his warmth, his human qualities were gone and he came to be one more ten-foot statue in our gallery." (Address before the Oregon State Legislature, February 12, 1945.)

—7—

"Have you read those stories?"

REHABILITATING IN OREGON, ERNY STAYED INTERMITTENTLY with WJ and Linda at Silverton, a Willamette Valley mill town where his father was a recruiter and safety officer for a lumber company. But the son was in and out, visiting friends thirty miles away in Portland and, for the last time in his life, riding freight trains and feeling the recuperative powers of that "free and easy" existence. He was writing too and he received several checks from New York; *Roll Along, Missouri!* finally sold, as did three short stories, which added up to about $1,000. With a part of this bounty, he made a down payment on a used Willys-Knight automobile and, feeling immeasurably better, drove back to New York in August 1925, recording in several letters the scenes and rutty passages of this journey. He often slept in the machine, which he ditched several times; Wyoming and Nebraska roads, he observed, had changed little from stage and wagon days. He had company, including several door-to-door book salesmen and "one dud from Detroit who wanted to get rough." The best of the fellow travelers were two young ladies who fixed meals and didn't object to getting out and pushing.

He located in Brooklyn, on Linden Boulevard. Jill must have found the apartment, which was three blocks from the Chord place on Martense, and she lived there with her husband at least some of the time. However, nothing about their convoluted first year together is easily assumed. The writing went well enough; over this final period of eastern residency, he made about $400 a month from story sales, which included the Oregon epic he had talked about, "Frontier Blood." He resolved to account for every penny of his income and to establish a "sinking fund" for emergencies and a second account for stock and bond investments, both to be nurtured by rigorous savings. It did not work quite that way, of course. He would put the occasional windfall into a corporate or municipal bond but, a month or two later, would have to borrow against it and was never much ahead of the game. It was all too pleasant to have a few dollars spare for once in his life and all too easy to distribute them. Gradually, he would convince himself that he actually worked best when pressed by financial obligation.

He searched bookstores and acquired a pile of ancient New England newspapers, continued a law course he had started earlier, and took piano lessons. In December 1925, the Willys-Knight was swapped for a 1923 Cadillac touring car on which monthly carrying costs put to rest any hope of constructing a financial buffer. When the weather was suitable, he and Jill, Mary, and Jack spent windblown weekends motoring through the countryside, inspecting old towns and battlegrounds. He wrote frequently to Ole Larson in Portland in this final New York interlude. The letters included a good deal of outrageous western vernacular, fraternity gossip, general nonsense—and, occasionally, indifferently structured reports of his progress or state of mind.

> . . . feeling better than for a long time. I walk eight miles every morning around Prospect Park and write 5,000 words every day that I write—which is pretty close to five times a week. I expect someday to write yarns that will be mighty popular. Meanwhile, I do like money. Next year I want to return with sufficient of this said money to look me up the farm I've wished to have for many years.

> My desire is to hit both SEP [*Saturday Evening Post*] and *Collier's* before leaving here. . . [but] that remains to be seen. *Frontier* is good to me in putting my name out. Some of the stories are good, too. Others are not so satisfactory.

> I give you two years to read me in the anthologies, and one year to peruse my first novel, a slash and dash thing of the Southern swamps in 1780. It will be about the first time in my personal history that I'll feel settled.

As to writing, he had justified his unapologetic romanticism.

> I don't like realism so very much and couldn't achieve any great success writing it. . . . When the blade swishes and the trap doors open and the Kentucky rifle cracks in the nick of time, you must [of course] agree to the fundamentals of this kind of thing before you can enjoy it. You must have the ability to call out the love of uncertainty, the acceptance of the derring-do idea, the appetite and the ear and the eye for all the sensations and sounds that go to make up romance. To be a kid again, in other words; or else to have carried over into age the zest of playing. . . .
>
> I think most people make the mistake of believing realism the only method in which real character is drawn. That's error. Some of literature's most graphic and profound and enduring men and women—mostly men—are purely romantic creations.

At the same time, he was in his twenty-sixth year an empirical philosopher.

> . . . did you follow Luther Burbank's exposition of his religion? Best idea I've ever heard a man publicly declare. "Let us say that there is some great force moving the universe, something which man knows nothing about, but which it is good for him to believe. . . . Not a God of wrath . . . no heaven or hell in the scriptural sense or any literal sense. . . ." And, so far as I can figure it, not a God with a card index of every one of us creatures. But for us, we have our day, do our bit and then—all is darkness and everlasting oblivion. Not much hope, as far as I can see, for E. J. Haycox in any other existence or any other planet, with or without tail or wings. But he has, let's hope, left some bit of work behind, and a few kids. His ashes may then push up the daisies and that's resurrection, isn't it? And of course no man dies who has left an original idea or concept behind.

A recurring theme in the letters to Larson was getting back to Oregon.

> Speaking of coming home there's considerable pressure here in some quarters for me to stay on another year. The argument waxes and wanes. I hold out like a good and faithful soldier.

> I do not deny it is profitable and pleasant to meet your editors.... And yet insofar as writing is concerned, I say once more that actual contact hasn't any more virtue than the United States mail. [New York] is a pretty cold place, a busy place and likewise a place where friendship is practically always based on financial advantage. I have fretted for want of elbow room and green country ever since I came here; I never feel half ways physically fit in the town—and you bet your bottom dollar I'll never come back again to stay for more than a month.

The "considerable pressure" came from both Jill and mother Mary. Neither thought it reasonable for Jill to abandon her career, which was going nicely. She had now done a couple of national advertising layouts for Penney's and a few freelance assignments. She and brother Jack had business cards printed that transformed the apartment on Martense into an artist's studio offering both fashion illustration and theatrical design services. Jack, who was also working for Penney's, helping create a retail display department, had high hopes but no credits for the latter. Erny, however, did not wish to remain in New York for a minute longer than necessary. He could not convincingly refute the argument that it was possible to write adventure fiction in the big city, as that is precisely what he was doing, nor could he lightly dismiss his wife's career prospects. He may have suggested that there would be opportunities for her in Portland, if that is what she truly wished. In fact, the idea of a working wife probably unsettled him, as it would have many 1926 husbands. He wanted a fertile homemaker and helpmate and Jill was reluctant (and Mary too diplomatic) to make a large issue of the matter.

In August 1926, they left New York for Portland, the Cadillac piled high with luggage, his typewriter and an easy chair (he intended to read and write in comfort on the road), his books, and a remarkable assemblage of camping equipment. The latter included an eight-by-eight-foot umbrella tent, a cold box, a gas campstove, a metal table and chairs, two cots, kapok mattresses, and a "dingus" that connected to the Cadillac's battery and provided light in the tent. There was also an Airedale puppy purchased from a breeder on Long Island. They were prepared for anything but bad weather for, with all that paraphernalia, the car's convertible top was difficult to raise.

Erny was thinking they might spend a couple of months on the road and, had they observed the original itinerary, which swept through the Midwest, veered north to Glacier Park and then south through Wyoming and Colorado to desert country and southern California, they well might have. However, by the time they reached the Grand Canyon, where it was snowing, the desire to finish the trip quickly was uppermost. It was that kind of journey on which a thoughtful man and a reasonable woman might well have formed disparate views. She tended to remember the rustic accommodations—one was an abandoned construction camp—and the sight of her husband attempting to erect that bulky umbrella tent in a Nebraska windstorm. On that particular night, the farmer who had allowed them to occupy his orchard was moved at length to call them inside.

Back in Portland, they rented a small house in a neighborhood of small houses on the east side of town, in which one room was set aside as his office. They bought furniture on credit and settled in. In June 1927, Jill wrote somewhat breathlessly to her mother that she was pregnant and expecting in January. They drove to Baker City later that summer on the first of several trips they would take in these years to see her cousins, during which she could introduce a husband who was now an established writer and, in the undiscerning eyes of Portland and Baker City journalists, already a famous one. He executed his first formal speaking engagement in front of Baker City's Kiwanis Club. It was, after a few jokes about his profession, a discourse about the individualism and enterprise of American character.

They returned to Portland to discover that WJ and Linda had moved in, pitching a tent in their backyard. Jill was mortified by the labor-camp appearance of things and the tent was struck, but at the cost of sharing cramped quarters with two people who were in no hurry to leave and whom the mistress of the house began to dislike fervently. Linda wanted to learn how to drive the family car and said she'd be glad to help when the baby came. When she entertained her Norwegian-speaking relatives at the house, Jill was certain they were talking about her. As for WJ, there was a wallpapering project he said he could handle; however, he actually didn't know much about the business and it had to be redone professionally. As this hot summer wore on, Jill became less and less tolerant of the arrangement and at length she told her husband that she was leaving. "If I have to live with relatives before the baby comes, I'd rather have it be my mother and Jack."

When she woke the following morning, the in-laws were gone. She would say later that she never knew how her husband arranged the disappearance and perhaps he was relieved not to discuss it with her. Of course, he had given his father money to relocate elsewhere. WJ was still working occasionally but frequently required subsidy and was not shy about seeking it. One of his methods involved taking out loans, which he would ask his son to co-sign and on which, some months later, his son would be required to cure default. Direct cash contributions were best, of course, but Erny couldn't always oblige. At times in 1927 and 1928, he needed the finance company himself to smooth out an unpredictable cash flow.

Erny and Jill were renting a slightly larger place two blocks away when Mary Ann was born in January 1928. She was a small, perfect baby, soon to be red-haired like her mother and from the first hour smothered with attention. The child deserved a home of her own and it was purchased in September 1928, a shingled, two-bedroom house on Sacramento Street overlooking Portland's Rose City Golf Course, with a small room in the front that made a fine writer's study. It cost $12,500 and as the purchaser had neither a sufficient down payment nor a predictable income, the seller demonstrated some courage in agreeing to take back a $5,000 second mortgage on top of a $7,000 first.

Financial progress had been slow at first; Erny was essentially broke at the beginning of 1927 and not much better off a year later, having earned and spent about $6,000. Thereafter, conditions improved, his income rising to $9,600 in 1928 and from 1929 through 1934 ranging from $10,000 to $12,000 annually—sums that, in current dollars, increase roughly tenfold. There was enough in 1930 to finance occasional stock and bond trades and to make a down payment on another of those rolling symbols of achievement, this one a $2,900 Studebaker roadster with tire wells in the fenders and, in the words of one of the writer's youthful cousins, "the largest hood ornament I had ever seen." The family took its first ambitious vacation that year, a voyage to Alaska; and half the cost of the trip appeared on his 1930 tax return as a "strict business expenditure." Deducted too were his twice daily trips to the post office, his office-at-home costs, his book purchases, and virtually anything else that might be construed as instrumental to the creative process. The Internal Revenue Service was not always sympathetic, ever suspicious that a story sale recorded in January had really taken place in December and opining in 1929 that the family car, though occasionally used for business, was not a depreciable asset.

About 1931, the family began vacationing at Cannon Beach on the Oregon coast, renting an oceanfront house to which they would return annually for a dozen summers. These were lengthy sojourns, often running six weeks, although Erny didn't permit himself that much leisure. Until mid-August, he often spent weekdays in Portland, driving the hundred-odd miles each way for weekend clam-digging and huckleberry harvesting and horseback riding on the beach. When he did stay over, the typewriter came along.

He took on a New York–based agent in 1930 and began hiring typists to produce finished manuscripts. In 1931 he moved his desk and typewriter from home to an office on an eastside Portland artery, Sandy Boulevard, where he would share quarters and full-time secretarial help with attorney Paul Sayre until 1940. The area, called the Hollywood District, was principally known to the rest of Portland as the location of an ornate motion picture theater and of Yaw's Top Notch, a legendary purveyor of hamburgers and cream pies in its time. Deciding where to go for lunch was never a problem.

Erny worked with his office door closed and a window open because he consumed a dozen or more cigars over a day's time. His workroom furnishings were modest, and fortunately so, for he was an absent-minded smoker as well as a persistent one, and his desk and homemade typing stand were frequently seared or stained. Things upon the desk suffered as well, the occasionally smoldering page of copy being retyped if too badly used. His secretary, Ruth Pearson, quickly learned to remain alert in her employer's composing room. On one occasion, reaching over his desk to retrieve something, she felt a sharp sting and had to have her skirt rewoven to eliminate the damage done by a casually placed corona.

A son was born in May 1931, a noisy and rather homely tyke who was named for his father and would be called Jim. Erny would have welcomed more but the boy put up a struggle before presenting himself and, for that and other reasons, Jill said that two youngsters were sufficient. The marriage had by this time become a bumpy affair. Jill could be emotional and abusive, telling her husband on one occasion, after Mary Ann took a tumble, that he could not be trusted to look out for the child. She had begun to interpret his professional dedication as dismissive of her. There were other irritants—his family, of course, and as his star rose, a good many of his business and social contacts. Among his college-educated friends and their sorority-refined wives, her twelfth-grade education was a quiet embarrassment. She also began to question her husband's fidelity, suggesting that those summer trips back to Portland were not sufficiently explained by a need to work.

Robert Ormond Case, who was two years older than Erny and at that moment a writer of approximately equal standing, was a good friend with some knowledge of his associate's marital situation. Affiliated by school and fraternity, both former *Oregonian* staffers and *Western Story* contributors, and now Portland's two leading producers of adventure fiction, they talked and traded ideas a good deal and with their wives were frequently at the same bridge table or dinner party. Case was a tall and courtly man with a soft voice and a reserved manner, unfortunately epitomizing those refined qualities that, in her defensive and suspicious mood, Jill interpreted as patronizing. Case knew something about the relationship because Erny confided in him occasionally, and he considered his friend sorely put upon by a graceless, querulous woman; a fishwife, Bob called her.

Erny was at home the same cheerful, moderate soul that his friends saw abroad. He was attentive to his wife and probably loved her and was genuinely fond of mother Mary as well and did not ridicule brother-in-law Jack's artistic ambitions. He remembered birthdays and anniversaries, promoted family outings, was home punctually after work and almost never absent in the evening. An affair at that time, for him, would have been both temperamentally and logistically impossible. At the same time, he sought perfection in his mate as well as himself and either did not recognize or simply hoped to overcome her resistance to his initiatives. His gifts to her were frequently books of literary merit that she had little desire to read, but they kept coming. He was also inclined to correct her grammar and her spelling and punctuation, to the point that she became reluctant to show him letters she'd written. And he irritated her in small ways; not least for a diligent housekeeper was that trail of cigar ashes which often advertised his presence.

Emotionally as well as intellectually, they were miles apart. A gregarious fellow would have suited her better, and one without pretentious friends (truth be told, some of his were). A more emotive and romantic partner would have been a better match, one less devoted to a pursuit that was inevitably exclusionary. She would say later that she might have been happier married to a druggist or dentist back in Baker City; and she would also wonder from time to time what she might have accomplished as a commercial artist had her husband been at all supportive. They often slept apart on Sacramento Street. She told her mother it was the only way either one of them could get a night's rest. ◆

He was, as he boasted to Ole Larson, capable of producing five thousand words a day, but it was not for him a sustainable pace. In Portland, he seldom managed half of that over any long spell. Research and story plotting took time, the latter sometimes extending to several pages of typewritten outline. Occasionally, he also would rough out a map of his imaginary town or territory—the community of New Hope, Nebraska, for example, with all of its streets named and principal buildings identified. And he edited and redrafted extensively. He was at his best in the morning hours and a good day was four to five pages of new copy—more like two thousand words—out of a bulky Remington Standard equipped with elite type and a left-hand carriage return. Afternoons were reserved for revisions. Every Haycox story went through two or three typings and on those days when the morning words seemed to pour forth with unusual ease, brilliance, and abundance, he said, the afternoon reconstructions were unfailingly substantial.

In the late 1920s and early '30s, the net of this effort was 300,000 to 350,000 words of copy annually. It was a creditworthy performance, though hardly exceptional among pulp fiction's top producers. Zane Grey, the old man of the western-story mountain, averaged about 100,000 words a month in his prime; and Frederick Faust, among whose twenty or so pen names was Max Brand, was capable of two million a year. Perhaps spoiled by their success, which was immense, neither was known to devote great time to revisions and, in terms of their market's expectations, maybe rewriting would have been wasted time. But for them and many lesser composers who found pulp fiction an easy mark—several of whom had more than one hundred book-length works to their credit—hurried preparation was not particularly useful training. For some reason, and the "good-enough" theory has been advanced more than once, writing formula westerns was not often the stepping stone to higher achievement.

Careful constructionist Haycox, of course, hoped that it would be. Meantime, however, he was rustling cattle on starless nights and swapping lead in dusty towns with the best of them—to the point that, by about 1930, he was more frequently published and more generously compensated than most. Between 1927 and 1932, counting individual installments of longer pieces as well as short stories, Doubleday, Doran's *Short Stories* and *West* magazines alone carried his work more than seventy times. His plots were inventive, although, inevitably, somewhat repetitious—a particularly common one involving those independently minded young riders who stumbled into other people's grief or came back to the scene of some earlier indignity. One such principal, emblematic of many, was Hugh Kingmead, falsely accused of murder in *The Return of a Fighter* (1929). He reappears in Sun Ford after several years' absence to reclaim his name and the family ranch, a task requiring violent confrontation with the powerful rancher who has taken over the country and whose blackest deeds are performed by a typical Haycox villain of that time, a large, ignorant, fearless gunhand with a miserable disposition and a colorful name. In this instance, Kingmead's ample opponent is Ruby Lusk, a misproportioned bully with curiously short arms and legs.

> This shortness of limb helped accentuate the remarkable bulk and depth of his chest, the muscles of which ran upward and outward to his shoulder tips and seemed to double back along his arms, making them appear like great pistons coupled to an engine. Other series of muscles stood out on a neck that had once been measured in Gesher's store at nineteen inches around.
>
> Atop this unwieldy frame perched a head that apparently had been beaten out of copper. Such was the color and texture of it save where the white scars of conflict had been gouged in the surface. His nose was flattened, his lips were thick and sank against teeth as if they had at one time been crushed there. Down over an extraordinary narrow forehead fell a jet and oily cowlick, and beneath this were two almond-shaped eyes. . . .

Erny's pulp prose was now going for three to four cents a word, about double the 1924 rate. *West* paid him $2,800 in 1928 for *Free Grass*, which ran eighty thousand words over six installments and then, in February 1929, appeared as a two-dollar hardcover. That was his biggest earner so far, and royalties from this first honest-to-God book added another $500 to the pot. The story, built around a trail drive from Texas to Montana, was, to New York reviewer Will Cuppy's mind, "a typical example of the drop-that-gun school, with strange interludes of Thanatopsian prose." Erny wasn't troubled by Mr. Cuppy's dismissal, for he never held that writing for the pulps had much to do with substance or artistry. It was a training program, he said, and it paid the bills. True, he conceded to Ole, there was an alternative.

> There's two ways of getting into the swim—my way of starting with the half-centers and writing on up through the pulp field to the big fellows. The other way is for the man that can do only the best that's in

> him and keep writing that best until he whips himself into shape to thunder right through and join the top notchers with his first accepted stories. This last way isn't the way most men do it nowadays. Most of us prefer serving our apprenticeship with a little pay coming in.

But it was the very lowest rung on the ladder and he knew it. Ole remembered an incident about this time in which one of Erny's well-intended friends was particularly generous in praise of several recently published works. Ole said that Erny accepted the tribute quietly and then asked, pleasantly enough, "Have you read those stories?"

He sometimes diluted the obligatory mayhem of the pulp formula and the preposterous achievements of its heroes with humor. In 1928, in "Bound South," he invented two comrades whose adventures were routinely comedic. They were the equanimous Joe Breedlove, who loved mankind if given any opportunity to do so, and the dyspeptic, easily affronted Indigo Bowers. Their travels and troubles extended through eight episodes over three years—a couple of book lengths in total. There can't be much doubt that the writer was tired of pulp prose and reaching hard for the next rung. In 1930, he spend a good deal of time on a piece that he submitted to *Collier's*, the *Post*, and, before finally giving up on the thing, to five other slicks.* But the Breedlove-Bowers saga was neither overtly nor subliminally a rejection of the pulp western. Its creator was having fun.

In "Bound South," Indigo has experienced difficulty in a frontier town and, at the moment of his initial meeting with Joe, is principally concerned with avoiding a posse. The two discuss the problem in a western idiom that, while possibly an honest representation of the time, wouldn't have been acceptable to *Collier's* and its like. Also unacceptable was robust humor, outlandish behavior, and various other extremes of man and nature that the pulp magazines welcomed—and all such would shortly disappear from the Haycox western. But in "Bound South" they are still on display:

* The story, "Dr. Jim's Patient," remained in the author's reject file for thirty-five years. Jill sold it to *Shell Scott Mystery Magazine*, where it appeared in the May 1966 issue as "Death Rides the Trail."

"Was yuh ever in Canyon?" asked the stranger in a high pitched voice.

"No," admitted Breedlove, "I'm from the north. But I was rapidly vergin' tords that point."

The small one made expressive gesture with his hands. "Stay away, stay away, brother. Nineveh an' Tyre—they don't compete. Nossir, they don't nowise compete with Canyon. A sink o' iniquity, a stinkin' hog waller, a condemned blotch o' scurvy on nature's benign countenance." He looked at Breedlove almost meekly. "Amigo, I ain't tongue-tied, but I shore have to improvise on the English language to name an' classify that Siwash smellin', snake-belly crawlin', festerin' heap o' boards what—"

"Ample," interposed Breedlove. "Plumb ample. I gather Canyon had done you some great wrong."

The small man's voice had a way of breaking and rising to falsetto in anger or excitement. It squeaked now like a pair of rusty hinges. "Wrong? Did you say wrong, amigo? Huh, what it done to me was a-plenty." He kicked at the loose stones with his feet, adding somberly, "But I guess I did a few things m'self. Did yuh see a passel o' beetle-faced gents sashayin' acrost the landscape down yonder?"

"I saw tracks cuttin' westward about two miles."

The wiry one looked gloomily at his horse. "Uhuh. They're a follerin' a dead trail I laid down. Me. I'd been out of this stagnatin' country by now if the paint hoss hadn't struck a hole an' sent me to hell and gone on my coco." He squatted down and laid a brown hand on the animal's neck. "He shore was a good horse, too."

Something inside Breedlove grew warm and friendly. He announced, through a ring of smoke, "Name's Joe Breedlove. Bound south. Nothin' in p'ticular. Jes' a-travelin'."

"I dunno what they took me for," muttered the small one, rising on his haunches. "I was a-mindin' my own fool business, which ain't usual for me, but nev'less I was readin' my own hole cards. Thunder, but trouble jus' popped up like a gusher comin' in! Out goes the lights an' bang goes the furniture. Well, when a man ain't wanted he'd orter have sense enough to depart. Which was what I proceeded to do even if the dang' fools tried to impede my progress."

"Some towns is mos' unusually clannish thataway. It takes a can opener to get in an' a crowbar to get out." ◆

Erny began a diary in September 1930 that was, he said, the direct descendant of a dozen others he had at one time or another commenced and then abandoned. The timing was fortuitous, for, in this short period, his career suddenly turned a corner.

Sept. 5, 1930. I begin this point to keep some sort of a more or less permanent record of my own daily affairs for my own satisfaction.

A man never stands still. He goes forward or he goes back. But it is next to impossible for him to disassociate himself from his ego long enough to determine which way he happens to be tending. The record of daily achievements and failures is lost, the things he does soon are confused, soon fade and are forgotten. Even the passing urges, the hot feelings, the sudden convictions disappear . . . and when he does attempt to cast up the record, his imagination lies to him.

It is possible for every normal human being to be a hundred times greater than he is. But most of us just drift . . . never rising very high nor falling very low; but always, always dissipating that great reservoir of capabilities within us.

Sept. 9. A couple of weeks ago I had a nibble from a New York literary agent, who said he had been asked by *Collier's* to get one or two of my western stories. I sent one old one and later a fresh one written with *Collier's* in mind. The opportunity exists here for me to get out of the pulps where I have been so long and profitably.

Sept. 10. To date, for this year, I have taken in $8,800. In the succeeding three and a half months, I hope to write: a novelette, a short story, a novel of the building of the Union Pacific, two short stories, a novelette, and a novel—these listed in the order they are to be done. There is here about $9,000 worth of work. Now let us see how near we come to the fulfillment of the plan.

This was a preposterous objective, in practical terms condensing almost twelve months of normal effort into less than four. He closed the year at a good pace—seven more stories had rolled out, about 100,000 words, by Christmas. As to the greater goal, which was closer to 250,000 words, he must have quickly realized it was unattainable. Perhaps this helped explain why his mood of achievement was shortly reduced to a state of mild depression.

> Sept. 19. I find myself in one of those recurrent slumps which come to me each year regularly. I believe the root of the trouble is physical rather than mental. I have decided—this makes the hundredth time or more—to stop smoking.
>
> From Sanders, New York agent, a letter indicating . . . "The Manhunter" [is] a good yarn with the possible exception of being a trace overwritten. Wouldn't doubt it. But he thinks he will try it on the big boys.
>
> Oct. 1. Today thirty-one years old and Jill, as usual, made a ceremony of the event. In much better humor than last year when I left the twenties forever behind. Never say women alone regret age.
>
> It seems queer to reflect nowadays that older and older men are in places of responsibility. If we had another Constitutional Convention, how many men would be under forty?—very few if any at all. In 1787, one of the Pinckneys was 24; 32 was not even an uncommon age. Is [it] this specialized and complicated world . . . that takes a man from forty to fifty years to get established?
>
> Yesterday sold . . . a story to *Collier's* for $500—and to me this is advancing to another state entirely. Now the question becomes, can I repeat?

The diary's reaction to the first sale to a top magazine was oddly muted, this long-sought and vastly significant achievement being noted in one matter-of-fact sentence and then, in the next, qualified as to importance. He was now reasonably confident of his skills but never would be wholly certain of sustaining them or satisfied in all respects that they were sufficient. Coupled with the economic benefits of his craft, these doubts nagged and pressed and helped explain why he was a steady if not relentless toiler.

Oct. 10. Perhaps I am crowding the line too much; yet I work well under pressure and always have. And I sometimes doubt if there is one man in a thousand . . . pushing himself at too fast a pace. Of course it is impossible to put literary work on a machine basis, but I do not share the common fear that persistent, assiduous and sustained labor is harmful.

Oct. 18. Thursday night to the Press Club to see and meet and hear Clarence Darrow—and somewhat disappointed. Darrow is about seventy five and undoubtedly has a rather brilliant mind—but a destructive one. He has reduced life to an extraordinary simplicity. Nobody is responsible for being born, and nobody shapes his career. It all happens, willy-nilly. We are constantly outside ourselves. A criminal is not a criminal at all, but a man affected by differing circumstances . . . to be pitied, protected. He has no respect for the existing order, believing it a rather destructive combination of self interest and greed. I do not believe [Darrow] . . . a great liberal, for a true liberal is animated by basic ideals, and I doubt if the exigencies and the makeshift opportunism of Darrow's life [have] left him with any.

Dec. 10. I am up to my usual tricks—working rather hard to wind up in the usual burst of glory and make the record surpass last year's. It is queer how much this diary revolves around money. The emphasis on it makes me out a considerably avaricious fellow, which I am not. If I had an eye to posterity I'd probably dress this account with high ideals. But this is an honest account of my state, of what I labor for, and the satisfactions I get from that labor.

Dec. 31. Here comes a familiar evening and a time for familiar thoughts and regrets and self-promises. My financial shape is terrible, due to my own fault. I make plenty of money, and it dribbles like sand through the careless cracks of my fingers. There seems to be nothing of the Scotsman or the Jew in me.

There were a few more entries, the last written June 18, 1931. *Collier's* had now published his second short story and purchased two more. The night preceding, he had been master of ceremonies at another Press Club event—a new experience for him and great fun. He had the bit in his teeth now. "Half the battle is confidence... the feeling that one can place the pen stroke exactly where he wants to place it." ◆

It occurred to him one day in 1929 that he should produce a magazine devoted to the profession of writing, and he devoted odd moments to the project for a couple of years before letting it go. He solicited several articles for the venture, including one from Eddie Marshall, who sputtered back: "Two thousand words! You speak as though they grew on bushes." But Eddie said that answering the question—what was the single greatest element in fiction writing?—didn't require two thousand words. "The greatest thing of all is to devote to it every second of time, and every ampere of energy the writer can possibly spare from cradle to grave. Strip to the waist before you begin. Cast away all luxuries from your pack—you won't have time to eat them, and you won't have strength to carry them."

James Norman Hall, coauthor of *Mutiny on the Bounty*, apologized for the delay of his comment, explaining charmingly that mail service in Tahiti was a monthly thing "and as we have only two days between the arrival of the southbound steamer and the departure of the northbound one, I did not have sufficient time." He was a romantic, he explained, but inclined to Joseph Joubert's view that fiction, to be justified, had to be more beautiful than reality. "I don't, of course, mean that a writer should falsify his vision of life. I merely mean that, unless he can see beauty in life, and nobility in man's struggle against fate, then he had better not write at all."

Hall confessed a certain disregard for careful plot and structure. "I may fill a notebook with notations of situations, fragments of conversation and the like as reminders, but I let them find their proper place during the actual process of writing." This he tried to do every morning, he said, but not always successfully, and did not share Eddie's conviction that time off was evil. "Nevertheless, I am a great believer in regular habits of work. I write slowly, often painfully, and I have never yet written anything that has satisfied me."

Erny agreed with most of Hall's observations: he usually knew where his stories were headed but was lenient, as Hall counseled, if the story "decides otherwise when it is being written." But some of the Tahitian perspective was lost on him. He couldn't afford the recommended patience ("If a story is worth telling at all, it is worth brooding over at great length.") and perhaps wondered if he was being spoken to directly at one point: "As for writing for a living," Hall observed, "I heartily disapprove of it. Unless a man is a genius, when forced to earn his bread and butter by writing, he turns out an enormous amount of drivel that takes away whatever relish he may have had for the bread and butter." Worse yet, Hall "was not a lover of breathless action in a story."

Erny also wheedled an article for his pending periodical out of his college instructor, Professor Thatcher, and, at odd moments, made notes as to further content and other contributors. However, he had no time for the sustaining effort of magazine editorship and the *Serious Writer*, which would have been its title, did not progress beyond his imagination.

Bertha Haycox,
circa 1898.

William (WJ) Haycox,
circa 1914.

Bertha Haycox (right) with a friend aboard the steamship *Harvard* in 1911. "This is a bum photo of me. Would you know it as me?"

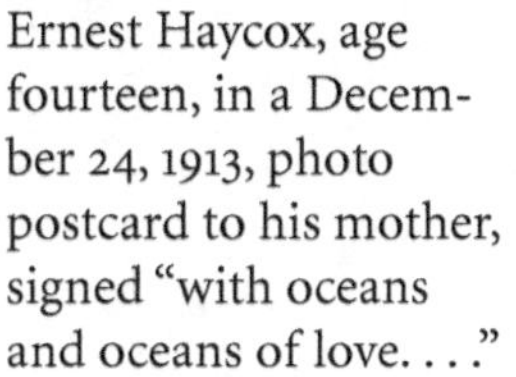

Ernest Haycox, age fourteen, in a December 24, 1913, photo postcard to his mother, signed "with oceans and oceans of love. . . ."

Erny with his cousin, seven-year-old Alvera Himler, at Parkplace in March 1913.

Erny at Lincoln High School, circa 1917.

“Cigar—and me,” as Ernest Haycox described this photograph, taken when his Third Infantry Regiment of the Oregon National Guard was posted on the border south of San Diego in summer 1916.

Haycox on the border with Julia, 1916. “Looks like I’m sick,” he wrote, “and I am—lovesick.”

Erny Haycox, soldier, in a photograph given to his parents as a Christmas present in 1917. It is dated 1919, but with only one service bar (Mexican border, most likely), no stripes, and a clean upper lip, that is doubtful.

Soldier Haycox at Wenatchee, 1917. "Things aren't quite as bad as my mug seems to indicate," he observed.

Corporal Leslie O. McLaughlin, or "Mac," "for whom I'd go thru hell, high water, and high prices," Haycox said.

Corporal Haycox in France, 1918. "Juenesse—mais—un bon soldat" (young—but—a good soldier), he wrote in the photo album under this picture.

Staff of the Reed College school newspaper, the *Reed College Quest*, shows a gloomy Erny Haycox at far left, 1920.

Deckhand Ernest Haycox aboard a fishing boat in Alaska, 1920.

Haycox stands with what probably was his first car, circa 1923, financed from his collegiate story sales.

Erny and Jill (Marie Chord), sometime after their marriage in spring 1925, in one of their first husband-and-wife snapshots, location unknown.

Erny and Jill encounter trials during early motorcar travels. This snapshot may be from an Idaho camping trip in 1927.

Erny, in a particularly arresting suit, poses circa 1929 with Jill and Mary Ann, born in January 1928.

Portland writer Stewart Holbrook, who combined history with humor in books and magazines, described friend Haycox's newspaper-selling days.

Ernest Haycox is pictured aboard the Alaska-bound *Dorothy Alexander* in 1930, on what was the family's first ambitious vacation.

Erny Haycox, at work in his office on Sandy Boulevard in 1929, one of the dozen or more cigars he smoked daily, in hand.

John T. (Jack) Chord, Jill's twin brother, in the early 1930s.

Haycox on skis in the early 1930s.

Erny Haycox, on the tee in the early 1930s, flanked by Bob Case on the right and Arthur B. Epperson, a close friend of both and, said Epperson, an occasional go-between for information neither Haycox nor Case was comfortable with soliciting directly from the other.

Oregonian publisher E. P. Hoyt, a college classmate and, like Bob Case, one of the writer's closest companions in the 1930s, encouraged Erny to seek political office.

Jill Haycox with daughter, Mary Ann, and son, Ernest Jr., in a photograph taken by Jill's brother, Jack, possibly in 1934.

Mary Ann and Jim (Ernest Jr.) at Cannon Beach in Oregon about 1936 with Duchess, the family's St. Bernard.

Jim Marshall, roving correspondent for *Collier's* whom Erny first met while in New York in 1937.

— 8 —

Old Voices

A NOTEWORTHY PORTLANDER BY ABOUT 1930, ERNY WAS ALSO becoming a visible one. His emergence began with invitations to speak at this gathering or that and, before long, extended to occasional radio appearances. Newspaper people, who considered him almost one of their own, came by his office now and again to examine this fellow whose latest book was circulating about the country to the city's apparent benefit. A local scribbler wasn't equivalent to a good baseball team or a new bridge but, still and all, he was a nice civic ornament.

He enjoyed the attention, finding it pleasant to see himself mentioned in print or to stand at the head of some gathering of businessmen or clubwomen. He had a comfortable manner of presenting his views, which frequently commenced with a deprecating reference, probably as old as Thucydides, to his own status or that of his profession generally. This old saw, for example: "The other day some neighboring lady asked my wife what I did for a living. My wife said that I was a writer, whereupon the lady, studying the answer in her mind for a moment, said: 'Oh, I thought he worked.'" Lamenting the hardship of his craft was always good for a laugh.

> Possibly you will wonder, if writing is such a drudging job, why we go on with it. I can only answer in the words of young Billy Malone, who came down off the high desert to the town of Painted Post, sat in a poker game and was stripped of all his earthly possessions. Coming out of the place, talking to himself, he was taken in hand by a friend.

> "You know that game was crooked," said the friend. "What made you sit in it and lose your shirt?"
>
> "Sure, I knew it was crooked," replied young Billy, "but I had to play poker someplace, didn't I, and that's the only game in town."

He conceded that many good citizens suspected the writer was "a long-haired, poetical-looking creature . . . who begins work after dark when he works at all . . . lives in Bohemian quarters and likes to disobey all the Ten Commandments. They have read of Shelley and Oscar Wilde and Edgar Allan Poe—who admittedly were queer ducks—and they think that all other writers must be like those three." But sliding toward more serious material, he would explain that those of this view were wrong to grossly generalize the image.

> . . . what I'd like to get over to you is that we writers as a class are no more and no less than American businessmen. The rank and file look like businessmen and act like businessmen. Their interests are those of businessmen—and they must be just as shrewd on details if they are going to get along. I know a great many writers. Of the number, I recall but one who works after dark and he only does it because he has another job for the daytime.

If his description erred at all, and perhaps it glossed over contemporaries like Fitzgerald and Dos Passos and some of their restless confreres, it was at least an honest account of himself. You could describe it in other and uplifting ways, but writing was a business enterprise—not plumbing or trucking or banking exactly but requiring parallel measures of sweat and perseverance if you planned to get ahead. In his case, there was also a significant kinship with the conservative philosophies of the business community. It followed that Erny was a solid Republican, supporting that party's nominees as quickly as he could (which, on the national level, would have been Warren G. Harding in 1920). He requested and obtained an autographed photograph of that gentleman, and also had one from Calvin Coolidge, Harding's successor in 1923. TR was the one he most admired, of course, and seemed to be most influenced by in his political thought.

In June 1933, Erny joined Rotary, a national service organization composed of business owners and managers in which many Portland enterprises, large and small, were represented; and almost immediately he began writing a weekly column for *Spokes*, the Portland chapter's newsletter. As the club would not have dared ask this busy man to grace their little four-pager, it can be assumed that he suggested the idea and that his weekly rumination, "On Reflection," was part of a grander scheme. It would provide visibility and recognition of another kind in the community, perhaps leading to other things in time. He had begun to think fairly seriously about some form of political activity, although he did not then, or ever, successfully reconcile that idea with the immense demands of authorship.

His motives weren't wholly selfish. The column was a place to be heard on an issue that deeply troubled him, which was the vast expansion of federal power associated with Franklin Roosevelt's New Deal. He did not dispute the need for radical action to cure some of the country's desperate financial problems; to lift the common man's burden, were that possible; to rescue twelve million unemployed. But what happened to individual rights and the traditions of local government if, as one proposal went, the power of Washington D. C. was extended through the creation of twelve regional federal capitals? What happened to the common man's savings if a policy of purposeful inflation were adopted? And what became of free enterprise if, as one of those "eager and intense and perfervid" intellectuals in Washington had declared, the country's capacity to overproduce required permanent production controls?

> Let us lay all the fancy words and arguments aside. It isn't so much a constitutional issue—for the constitution can cover almost any sort of government we want; it isn't a question of poor man versus rich man, or of property rights versus human rights . . . [or] even a straight political issue. Simply, it is the old, old question of how far this government or any government shall reach down into the lives of its citizens, how far it shall extend its arm through the shop door and the home door, how far it shall command people to obey its decrees, how far it shall depart from our original concept of democracy as expressed in the old town meeting.

In "The Course of the Blue Eagle," which appeared in Rotary's national magazine in December 1933, he supported the National Recovery Administration's attempt to "take the present cruelty out of competition" through a scheme of minimum wages and fixed selling hours and allocated production time. But it remained governmental intrusion and "a sort of socialism . . . which would have been so instantly and bitterly resisted by our fathers. . . ." The question now was whether business could finish the job of correcting inequitable free enterprise without further interference.

That was his concern, and he didn't think it had any business being labeled a conservative viewpoint. Was not the defense of individual liberties, he would ask, or of the rights of the small businessman against big business or big government, a fundamentally liberal concept? "I suppose I am some sort of Jeffersonian reactionary," he would say some years later. "I fear and distrust bigness in anything, government not excepted; and I have a great skepticism concerning the infallibility of my masters. Yet—and now we get to the root of the matter—I also know that private enterprise, for all its marvelous efficiencies in the things that flow from profit, has produced great wastage and break-up beyond the area of profit. If there were no national forests there wouldn't be a damned tree left along the crest of the Cascades."

Where Erny stood second to no conservative or Republican was in his dislike of Franklin Delano Roosevelt. He conceded the president's immense popularity and good intentions but found him nonetheless an aspiring despot. "And now Franklin Roosevelt," he wrote, "completely absorbed in his New Deal, angrily cries out to the world that those who oppose his beliefs are servants of greed and corruption, lackeys of great wealth and minions of autocracy. It has so familiar a sound; it is part of a story that is repeated so often. Men do not seem to change. Fighting for their beliefs, they come to feel that those who do not share these beliefs must be morally defective and mentally not very bright."

Erny was a featured speaker on the perils of federal encroachment at Rotary gatherings statewide during this period and was elected to the Portland chapter's board of directors in 1934. He also edited *Spokes* in 1934–35, during which time his column work declined and he recruited the family pediatrician, Dr. Morris Bridgeman, to fill the void with observations on family health. The Christmas issue of 1934 was a double-size edition that, in addition to hearty Rotarian greetings, included several scenic, snowy photographs, two of which were attributed to Jack Chord. ◆

Mary Chord, now a senior manager in Penney's buying operation, loved her job and was loath to miss a day, although she came to Oregon to see each of the babies. She was generous with her good fortune, helping nieces with school financing and lending money to other Depression-strapped members of the Sullivan clan. She was likewise supportive of her daughter and son-in-law—one of her first advances financed her daughter's engagement ring and she stood behind that shoestring purchase of the house by the golf course, telling them she was good for $1,000 if things got tough.

She had abandoned Catholicism in favor of Christian Science and, when her health began to fail, she did not seek medical help until her condition (probably heart trouble) was advanced. The illness ultimately forced her from the job and she moved to Cincinnati, where Jack had relocated, and where she died in late September 1932 in her fifty-fifth year. Jill had written to her mother almost every day that summer, begging her to come west and describing to her various small rural houses she and Erny had scouted, where Mary could live pleasantly with flowers and chickens and weekend visitors when she strengthened. Jack called near the end and Jill rushed east, too late.

Jack was a merchandise display manager for Penney's in New York and Cincinnati until about 1930, when he resigned to become editor of *Display World*, the trade publication of his profession. He had considerable talent as a visual marketer and would later hold senior positions in that discipline with Marshall Field and Montgomery Ward in Chicago. He wrote a textbook on the subject, probably the first. But he would have happily traded these professional accomplishments for another line of work, for what he really wanted to be was a lyricist, writer, and set designer for musical comedies. In New York, he joined United Scenic

Artists Local 829 and was involved in a couple of amateur theatre productions. He wrote book and lyrics for a stage musical, *Smiles*, which was produced by a college theatrical group in Cincinnati in 1927. He also composed lyrics for light, romantic ditties, some of which were copyrighted; and he would complain later that a George White Broadway production number was troublingly reminiscent of one of his works and that the lyrics of "Rhapsody in Blue" were suspiciously similar to another.

Not long after Mary's death, Jack abandoned his editorial position and became a permanent houseguest on Sacramento Street. There was an unfinished room upstairs that became his bedroom and studio, where he wrote two complete stage plays, one of which was *Chaffee*, adapted from his brother-in-law's second serial novel, *Chaffee of Roaring Horse.* Erny must have offered encouragement, as one artist might another, but would have had restless moments if he actually read the stuff—for example, *Chaffee*'s chorus warbling:

> You see be-fore you cow-boy hands
> Whose clothes are for the prair-ies;
> We much prefer the spa-ces than
> The crowd so filled with fair-ies.

Oh well. *Smiles* evidently was the only J. T. Chord play ever to reach the stage, and that but briefly; and though several of his lyric efforts were set to music by experienced hands, they do not appear to have produced even minimal royalty income. But that did not stop Jack from trying. Probably the last effort was his adaptation of Robert E. Sherwood's 1927 play, *The Road to Rome*, as a musical comedy in 1946. Mr. Sherwood, through an intermediary, expressed firm opposition to the project. Jack appealed the decision, submitting his material to composer Richard Rogers with the thought that, if they got something going, Sherwood might relent. Rogers did not reply.

Jack remained part of the family in Portland for about two years. Finding the household colorless, he redecorated; and he encouraged a contemporary lifestyle involving theatre and dining out and such social niceties as a cocktail hour before dinner. Unlike his sister, he was driven to elevate himself, studying self-help books on etiquette and proper grammar and pushing his own creative capabilities, which were substantial, in several directions. Later in Chicago, his avant-garde, occasionally minimalist window displays for Marshall Field were much noted in the trade, and the brownstone he occupied and decorated on the city's north side was featured in *Interior Design and Decoration* magazine. He was skilled at photographic composition, collecting several hundred awards for his stereoscopic work in the 1960s and '70s. He was also a clever and persistent acquirer of first and limited editions, focusing on contemporary American authors (Kerouac, Mailer, and Salinger, among others); and when he disposed of this collection in 1963, its 495 items were auctioned by Parke-Bernet Galleries in New York.

Jack was a handsome and mannerly six-footer who, though impossibly naive, easily attracted women and, to a degree, enjoyed their company. One of these admirers was a Mrs. L., the unhappily married operator of a Portland bookstore where he occasionally helped with window displays. She quickly fell for him and, while her advances were not altogether welcome, he was reluctant to discourage her, for she claimed to have Hollywood connections. When he showed her some of his work, she praised its brilliance and begged him to let her send the material to her close friend, motion picture mogul Irving Thalberg.

The relationship ran on for some months. She invited him to a hotel-room party in Portland to meet several actor friends who were passing through town, but while the room was appropriately disheveled, it was empty (they had gone to Longview, Washington to visit friends, she discovered; but why not spend the night?). A later meeting was similarly foiled (fog, she said; their plane had been grounded). And there was a proposed car trip with her friends that Jack couldn't make, having taken ill with mumps. The tangled affair covered fifty-seven numbered paragraphs in a notebook otherwise devoted to lyric compositions, and it ended with Jack preparing to leave for Vancouver, Canada, where MGM studio representatives were anxiously waiting to met him.

Jill said that about this time Jack confessed that he was in some kind of pickle, and her impression was that someone had tried to lure her brother and a female companion across the international boundary—perhaps succeeding at it—for purposes of fabricating a violation of the Mann antiprostitution act. An extortion attempt, perhaps; or was Mrs. L. simply casting her net one more time? Jack hid in his upstairs room for two weeks and then fled to Chicago. If it was a shakedown, the presumably ample resources of a sympathetic brother-in-law would have been the target. Mrs. L. couldn't have expected much from the primary victim; she had paid for too many drinks and dinners.

Jack's sudden departure from Portland was not unwelcome, for Jill had come rather quickly to view her brother as a jobless sponger. The accusation offended him, of course. "You seem to forget that I often paid the paper bills, the laundry, the garbage; that I bought quite a few things for the house," he would write several years later. "Should you still feel that I did not hold up my end of it. . . set a price for my stay there." In fact, money hardly began to explain her antipathy; they had been competitive since childhood and Jill could recite countless occasions from early years when her twin brother had been unjustly favored. Now she ridiculed his cosmopolitan airs, his lack of gainful employment, and his circle of Portland friends, both male and female. Jill and Jack never did settle their grievances and their one attempt at living together thirty years later was noisy failure. ◆

Pleased with the work of its new contributor, *Collier's* soon asked Erny's agent, Sydney Sanders, for first look at every new Haycox manuscript. This readily granted request was not a commitment to buy any particular number of stories, or any at all for that matter. In practice, however, it became a blanket purchase order. The magazine accepted almost everything he wrote, which included ten short stories in 1931 and half a dozen or more annually from then on. And their short-story rate for beginners—$500—moved up steadily, to $1,000 by 1936 and double that by 1940. Erny would become restive at times, suggesting to Syd that they should probably not have all their eggs in this one customer's basket, golden though it was. But there was really nothing much left for the obvious second source, the *Saturday Evening Post.* Or anyone else, for that matter.

The condition applied equally to the serial novels, which would shortly become Erny's dominant source of income. *Collier's* bought its first, *Starlight Rider* (his fourth), for $6,000 in 1932. They paid $8,000 for *The Silver Desert* in early 1935 and in that magnificent year also purchased *Trail Smoke* in May and *Trouble Shooter* in December, bumping the price $2,000 on each occasion. Between shorts and serial installments, he was in the magazine eighteen times in 1935, sharing space with Oregonians Bob Case, Dick Wetjen, and H. L Davis, fellow westerners James Warner Bellah and Alan LeMay; popular American romanticists Kathleen Norris and Clarence Buddington Kelland; and a redoubtable British quintet. These were mystery specialists Sax Rohmer (creator of the evil Dr. Fu Manchu) and E. Phillips Oppenheim and three of considerable talent elsewhere—G. K. Chesterton, H. G. Wells, and Winston Churchill.

His income in 1935 nearly tripled, to $30,000, and he was for the first time required to support a federal government he did not particularly approve of with what seemed to him unnecessary generosity. He therefore produced a tax return in which only half of his 1935 earnings appeared. The other half was reported separately by Jill, who, he explained, "works continuously with me in producing our stories." The idea would have reduced their joint tax burden by nearly $1,100 if Internal Revenue Service had believed him. However, it did not, transferring most of the money back to his return and assessing a $94 penalty.

While Syd handled a good deal of the back-and-forth with *Collier's*, relaying their queries and his interpretations of them to Portland, Erny and one magazine fiction editor, Ken Littauer, soon began to correspond directly. One of the earliest exchanges started with Littauer's observation that Charm Michelet, *The Silver Desert*'s secondary heroine, had slipped out of character at one point. "The Charm you created was not only too gallant to bear herself so, but too wise," he opined. The complaint was muted by a generous postscript about one of his recently published shorts: "'High Wind' has made many friends for you. In fact there are those who say it is up to Willa Cather."*

* "High Wind" is the story of a young lady from New England come west to marry, and greatly depressed by Abilene's rough manners and ceaseless, scouring gale.

Erny warily thanked him for the praise. "When any writer gets the hint that he may be writing near the edge of semi-permanent stuff, a kind of malarial germ gets into his system. It's a horrendous thing when it gets the upper hand . . . all his writing muscles get a bad case of cramps. I seem to have my most satisfactory days when I come to the office with a slight sinus attack and a knowledge that the rent is overdue. In this mood of low desperation I usually get something done."

A bit later, Littauer asked his thoughts about the illustration of *Trail Smoke* and received a detailed account of frontier fashion, right down to the ribbons.

> We're pretty close to the Gibson girl, yet you'd find that in the western country it was a modified thing—less of hair puff and not so strong on the big hats. A good hat, if the illustrator needs one, would be a stiff-brimmed black straw, moderately wide and flat-crowned. For riding, the women would be perfectly proper in a good buckskin split skirt . . . [though] in some sections it was a daring innovation and not quite nice. A man's hat will do . . . not the ten gallon thing, which is strictly a modern rodeo accessory, but a stockman's hat, soft-brimmed, moderately wide . . . that doesn't possess the exaggerated peak.

On his men, he continued, "guns should not be too universal, Some wore 'em and some didn't. It was a hell of a bother for a man to have that slapping his leg when he didn't need it. Dressed up for occasion this fellow wore a blue serge suit eight times out of ten with a stiff shirt and a very uncomfortable air . . . [and if] he wore a gun on those occasions, it was inside his coat. As for guns, no pearl-handled butts—nothing but the black handle of a .44, on the right side. And no two-gun men."

He had been researching the West for fifteen years now and knew a great deal about it. When there were missing pieces, he knew where to look for them. His own library on the subject—books, old magazines and newspapers, maps, photographs and the like—had grown from Chittenden's epic to hundreds of documents; he spent close to five percent of the household's gross on new library material in the early '30s. Some came from antiquarian dealers in New York and Boston, though he was known to booksellers in half a dozen other cities; and he found some things on his own, being disposed to investigate almost any establishment with a shelf or two of ancient work in the back. He pestered libraries and historical associations across the West with queries and requests and sent his secretary to the Oregon Historical Society so many times to retype excerpts from old files (these sheets then being assembled into research notebooks) that on one extended occasion they gave her a desk of her own.

Some of his best sources were the once wide-eyed children and restless young men who had seen the last quarter of the nineteenth century from a wagon bed or a saddle and could still remember the sign on a long-lost building or some western character's colorful irregularity. Most of these commentaries were unsolicited; it would be a letter, probably in a shaky hand, advising that a recent story had passed muster, generally agreeing with the correspondent's memory of that time or place, whereas some other writer didn't seem to know a lariat from a lodgepole. A few, particularly the old horse soldiers, tendered amplifications or polite corrections—as to the color of a particular company's horses, for example, or the precise wording of a drillfield command, or the manner in which a carbine was slung from the saddle, not that such details could be uniformly applied. The celebrated Seventh Cavalry was said to be notably aberrant in its customs but almost any frontier formation had stylistic eccentricities and might claim to be "a law unto itself"; and if you mentioned that unit, even in fiction, you were supposed to know these things. Perhaps the writer's most egregious misstep occurred when he thoughtlessly mounted one of his courageous young lieutenants on a mare. But his most noted distortion of fact seems to have been a story in which he placed his rider in sage desert a hundred or so miles east of where old-timers remembered that shrub first appeared on that trail. The number of postal protests convinced him that "they had formed clubs" to advise him that, hotshot western writer though he might be, he didn't know one damned thing about their particular corner of paradise. There were unsolicited manuscripts occasionally—a good story from times past, the sender would say (and sometimes he or she was right); maybe someone else could find the right words.

On occasion, he hunted down witnesses. In *Rim of the Desert* (1940), rancher Clay Morgan, learning late that a piece of government land adjoining his spread would be auctioned the following day in a far town, rode the 190-mile distance in eighteen hours. The feat was suggested by rancher Tom Overfelt's spectacular journey of about 1885, also to an auction, said to have covered two hundred miles between his Trout Creek ranch in central Oregon and Lakeview on the California border in less than twenty-four hours. The greatest achievement of man and horse in American history, some said. But was it possible? Erny located Maurice Fitzgerald, who had been with Tom for most of the trip, and Fitzgerald discounted the tale. They were long in the saddle, Fitzgerald said, but also slept two nights at ranches. "That famous ride . . . was a piece of fiction concocted to impress Henry Miller [Tom's boss] with the untiring vigilance of his subordinate. . . ." Overfelt, his onetime companion said, "was a natural boaster." Fitzgerald claimed the endurance title himself. He had scouted and carried dispatches for General O. O. Howard in the Bannock-Paiute uprising in 1878, on one occasion covering about 110 miles on a single mount in eighteen hours. "When it comes to long horse-back riding in Oregon, I think that your humble servant has easily the record."

In the end, Erny accepted the judgment of another long rider, North Dakotan Ben C. Bird, who had trailed a herd from Texas to Montana in 1884 and as a deputy sheriff in 1895 covered about 150 miles in sixteen hours, changing horses three times. Bird didn't say whether he'd caught up with the fellow he was chasing but the gentleman in the photograph enclosed (still a tall rider at seventy-three) didn't look like a quitter. On the former deputy's testimony, Morgan's ride in *Rim of the Desert* was allowed; and it wore out four horses.

Lew L. Callaway, a Montana lawyer and jurist who had known Virginia City as a boy, remembered it street by street for *Alder Gulch* (1941). He also advised on the stage routes and lonely rural stations frequented by road agents during the vigilante period. Erny asked him how a respectable and single young woman might have gotten on there in 1863 and Judge Callaway wasn't sure. There weren't any schools yet: perhaps as a waitress or a seamstress or a household servant. "I would not know what honorable vocation a lone woman could have followed except as stated." For the record, the heroine of *Alder Gulch*, Diana Castle, set up a restaurant in a tent.

Trouble Shooter, the Union Pacific novel long on his mind (and finally written in 1935), had been researched for a decade before he wrote it. It would incorporate the memories of Charles H. Sharman, who had helped build the country's first transcontinental rail link as a surveyor. In his eighty-eighth year, Sharman spent the best part of a month in 1929 composing for his curious friend in Portland an account of his life between 1866 and 1869, much of it spent in lonely tent camps miles west of end-of-track. Sharman swam the broad North Platte River to set the first survey stake for a 2,300-foot-long bridge, watched painted Indians run off his party's horses and mules, and in the final winter, when construction never stopped, saw tracks rushed ahead on temporary embankments raised with blocked ice and snow. He had been fortunate to survive the project, having been first assigned as a rodman in the party of senior surveyor Percy Browne and then bumped from that position by young Stephen Clarke, whose superior credentials were those of his uncle, New York politician Thurlow Weed. Both Clarke and Browne were butchered by Sioux warriors in 1867.

Lee Howard, who lived his last years in Portland, was a prized and persistent source on old times. His father had been a sheriff in Dakota Territory and in 1876, as a government inspector, had taken his boy along on his rounds of Indian agencies. They were in Fort Abraham Lincoln a few weeks before the Little Bighorn disaster and tawny-haired General Custer, with whom Lee's father was acquainted, would nod to the awestruck boy now and again. "I was highly honored when he would talk to me. Never trust any Indian, was his advice to me; and once he told me that he hoped to see me when the Indians were all killed off." For his friend Haycox, Howard produced page on page of detailed and graphic recollection.

Many other willing and sometimes garrulous ancients were known to the writer—some too fuzzy to be relied upon, others simply delusional.

One such, a tramp with a long beard, appeared at his home one spring afternoon, identifying himself as the brother of the Lone Ranger and demanding audience. Young Jim was snatched inside and Erny called and told to come home quickly. The visitor had a good deal to say but made no particular sense; he was fed and given a few dollars and, at his request, driven to a railroad yard where he said he had other important business.

Some of those who told tall tales, of course, were abiding by one of the great traditions of the frontier, and among them were more than a few horrendous liars. Reviewing a book on the life and times of "Arizona Bill" Gardner for the *New York Times* in 1944, Erny was confronted with a man who had witnessed virtually every noteworthy event in the post–Civil War West and knew most of its heroes. It was a remarkable story, but Arizona Bill would have required a time machine to cover all that ground. "Perhaps it is kindest to say that an old man, looking backward, sees visions and presently believes them to be real," Erny wrote. "There have been many hundreds of men who, picturesque and amiable, made a career of this sort of fakery; and if all men who claimed to have been with Custer actually had been there, Custer would have gone into battle with an army corps instead of a thin regiment." ◆

Gen. George Armstrong Custer has been examined frequently, sometimes to his credit, often not. Erny had heard the arguments, of course, but most likely arrived at his own conclusion. He'd been through a mass of literature and military documentation relating to the Little Bighorn debacle for his Seventh Cavalry novel, *Bugles in the Afternoon* (1943). In this process, as was his custom, he had also queried several long-retired cavalrymen as to what they knew and what they had heard on the subject. His Custer, a colorful character who is frequently displayed in moods of excess, is an insubordinate glory seeker—courageous, reckless, flawed. In part because of this unappreciative characterization of a mythic American figure, an editor wondered whether the *Bugles in the Afternoon* manuscript should be checked by an expert. Certainly wouldn't hurt, Erny replied, although finding such a fellow might be a task.

. . . almost all of the experts in this particular field [are] carrying torches, pro or con. I know of no other item in our history so completely unsullied by calm or detached judgment. Probably three generations ago the Burr episode was similarly placed, and probably three generations from now Roosevelt II will be still the source of perpetual controversy, although I have wistful hopes we'll settle his hash sooner than that. If I were to send the story to either [E. A.] Brininstool or [Fred] Dustin—both men who have given great amounts of time to the subject—they would instantly challenge my emphasis on Custer's leadership qualities, since neither man will admit any good at all in Custer. Probably both would insist Reno was a more positive force than I have indicated. There is much evidence to indicate Reno went to pieces in the fight, and on the hill. I skipped that, but I didn't give him much of a part; and Brininstool and Dustin probably would feel I should have played him up to better advantage. By contrast, Captain Luce, now superintendent of the Custer Battlefield and an ex-Seventh man, would blast everything I said, since Custer was God to him.

As to emphasis, I have tried to remember two particular things about Custer. One is that, regardless of the animus against him, no man can rise as he rose, so swiftly through the grades, purely by luck and chance. He had to have something. I made the attempt to credit him with courage, dash and a sort of leadership which carried men into action with a yell. The other thing is that no man can possibly create as much resentment as he created without having serious flaws in him. There is scarcely a question as to his latent capacity for insubordination. He demonstrated that several times. His expressed intent to break away from Terry, after Terry had helped him so much, is a full view of the scurvy side of his character.

. . . I [haven't] attempted to lay the blame for Little Bighorn on him wholly. It seems moderately clear that he wished to get ahead of the others and polish off the Indians before anybody else could share the credit. The one significant thing here is that he failed to send back [scout George] Herendeen to make liaison with Gibbon, as Terry intended he should. He did not take the extra troops offered him by Terry. In his own mind, he had it in the bag. By waiting a day longer, by not marching so rapidly, he would have given Gibbon a chance to swing up, and that might have saved so much loss of life. Even so, it is debatable. After all, it was Terry's campaign; and although Custer split his regiment into three pieces and so destroyed his attacking weight, it was Terry who previously had split the expedition into two wings and thus had destroyed *his* attacking weight. All this was in the best tradition of Indian fighting and might have been successful except for one thing: There were just too damned many Indians. All of them guessed wrong on that—though they had warning of it days before. And here was Crook, heaving back and forth with a strong column, a hundred miles south, intimidated by two lickings and never coming up. So it was a tragedy of errors compounded by all of them and capped by a concentrating of Sioux never seen before and never seen since.

The strongest impression I have of Custer is that of a man with a terrific energy hooked to a mind that was wholly adolescent. He seems pure extrovert; he is his own greatest drama. He was tender to his wife; he was also unconsciously harsh to his wife. He never seemed to know the full consequences of his own actions, never thought far ahead. He was at the mercy of his own wild gusts of energy . . . [which] could make him inordinately brutal to his own men under the guise of discipline. . . .

I took liberties in analyzing his character and now and then I went into his mind. All that, however, is permissible fictional license. And the longer I think of him the shabbier I see him as a man. I can't see in him those primary adult qualities of self-discipline, compassion, understanding, humility, the realization of a commander's heavy responsibility to his men, or an honest obedience to higher authority. There wasn't any spiritual depth to him. He would have bored me with his rank juvenile qualities, his playacting, his exhausting fits of energy which were dangerous because no man knew which way his energy would strike, his spells of moodiness, his egotism.

I shall stop before I write the story over again.

—9—

The Garden of Allah

IN JUNE 1936, AFTER A FOUR-YEAR ABSENCE FROM HIS DIARY, Erny returned to summarize intervening progress.

> We have gone through a depression and now seem to be coming out of it; and now must pay for it. We have had three years of Roosevelt, whom I despise as a man of no fixed and settled convictions and with a good many prejudices. As of this day it looks like he'll be reelected for another four years; though the tide of public opinion has swung violently through the last two years and may swing again sufficiently to throw him out. Our house is paid for. We have no serious debts. We have our small ranch, 25 acres, on the Willamette where Dad is living. Our desire is to find a nice piece of land in an excellent neighborhood and put up a really fine house—the last, we hope, we shall ever need. Next week we pack up and go to Cannon Beach for six weeks. I look forward to this more eagerly than any other thing. I have, since the last entry, sold six novels to Collier's and a good many shorts. The situation there is excellent—if I keep writing at the same level.

The beach trips involved safari-like preparations. The car was capable of holding the family, boxed groceries and suitcases, and a nervous St. Bernard. Camping equipment and many more bags and bundles of essential holiday gear followed in a trailer. Early departures were the rule; they could not wait to see and to hear the pounding Pacific surf. But the trip seldom was completed before noon. They would stop when Mary

Ann complained of illness and again when Duchess the dog began to twitch and groan and drool; she had a nervous stomach too. By 1938 or so, Erny and Jim made a project of collecting beer and soda pop bottles discarded along the roadside and, until Jill put her foot down, they would stop to inspect almost any glittering object—worth a penny, sometimes two, in the quart size.

The rented house fronted a long, wide, perfect beach with easy clamming at early morning low tides, a splendid surf for pleasure in the warmth of the day and just enough driftwood for evening fires; and it provided entertainment of many other kinds. Some fellow landed a small plane near the house one morning; a local businessman who was something of a drinker drove his delivery van into the waves; and Max Kalander, who was the swimming instructor at the Cannon Beach Natatorium, climbed towering, sea-swept Haystack Rock with Swiss mountaineering skill. There were guests at the beach house occasionally and, as often, Portland friends occupying nearby rentals who made fine sunbathing companions on the beach and huckleberry harvesters on Tillamook Head. There was a traditional camping expedition on the sand at Hug Point, several miles south, where Erny would pitch the old tent and cook over a fire for Mary Ann and Jim. Perhaps remembering earlier times, Jill avoided camping.

Duchess attended, of course, as she did most outings. When the family went into the water, she was always at hand, gaining some notice in the community as an animal that appeared to enjoy breasting the waves as much as any human. The spectacle of a surfing St. Bernard drew small crowds at times. But it was not what it seemed. Her sole purpose in participating was to rescue her family from danger, which she would accomplish by firmly securing a hand in her mouth and pulling it, and the pained individual attached to it, back to firm ground. On one occasion, she broke into the natatorium and tried to retrieve Jim from the pool. She had no use for water whatsoever.

In Portland, Erny and Jill belonged to the Rose City Dance Club and attended its functions at least monthly. They rented costumes for a club Gay Nineties party on one occasion; he added a toupee and mustache, entered by himself, and was unrecognized. They skied at Mt. Hood several times each winter; they were hardly skilled at the business but did not seem to care. He practiced the piano and also struck a golf ball from the left side, with a predictable inclination to hook or slice off the tee. He said the second shot, where something of an angled trajectory would have been useful, was always string straight. Their closest friends in the 1930s included Ep and Brownie Hoyt, Bob and Evelyn Case, Ole and Kay Larson, and several other college holdovers. This crowd played a good deal of bridge—at least the women did. The men were known to huddle in kitchens, concocting outlandish story plots. The social crowd also included the Sayres and Bridgemans, a few Rotary and dance-club acquaintances, and a couple of Sacramento Street neighbors, Edward Sinclair and Dr. George Armen and their wives. There were two Armen boys and the older of these was the titular head of the street's juvenile mob. When he proposed one afternoon that they secretly mount an expedition to Rocky Butte, which was a couple of miles east through mostly uninhabited brush, Jim and Mary Ann and several others readily agreed. By five o'clock that afternoon, there were frantic parents in almost every house on the block.

Erny and Jill were serious parents. Both youngsters were enrolled in kindergarten, badgered into piano lessons, and encouraged to read and to write letters and keep scrapbooks. The parents were not remotely religious, but the children were required to attend a Presbyterian Sunday school and Erny and Jill attended Christmas pageants and other juvenile liturgical events. In this, they unquestionably were influenced by Edith Brostrom, who was a part of the family for more than a decade and the only household retainer who ever met Jill's rigorous expectations, the mistress being as hard-working a homemaker as ever assumed that burden. Edith was a kind and devout widow of Swedish ancestry who was often the preparer of sturdy meals much favored by Erny, though Jill did some of the cooking. Dinner was offered promptly at 6 P.M. and, often as not, was pot roast or meat loaf or chicken, preceded by salad, accompanied by gravy and rolls and potatoes and another vegetable, and concluded with pie or some other ample sweet. Perhaps because he'd missed a good many meals earlier, Erny made much of this nightly event.

The Great Depression was hardly a factor in family life. There was a WPA crew near the house on one occasion; Jim watched the laborers build a rock wall along a side road leading to the golf course. People came to the door occasionally, looking for work. Jim tagged along with his father one day to get gas for the car. There was a very old vehicle at the station with a flat tire that evidently couldn't be fixed, the tube having been patched too many times. The occupants of the vehicle, a man in overalls with his wife and two children, seemed distressed. After a further attempt to repair the tube had produced a further explosion, Jim began to laugh. Erny startled him with sharp words. There was nothing funny about the scene, he lectured the boy. The fellow obviously couldn't afford a new tube. They drove back home in curious silence.

He produced a "schedule for season, 1938–1939," which dictated his daily routine and set some two dozen personal and professional tasks, several of which—speaking engagements, letter-writing, and making new acquaintances—reflected his fascination with political life. He ordered himself to walk to the office, which was a good two miles, and prescribed weekly swims and horseback rides for the family. He was to finish his ship model, edit his motion picture film, catalog his library, help Sister with her piano lessons every morning, and curb all wayward tendencies: "never more than one cigar morning and one cigar night." And he did most of these things at one time or another and, a year later, would sadly consider his lack of Prussian will and make another list.

There were Haycox relatives in Portland, WJ's older brother Frank, his boys Frank Jr. and Ray and daughter Mary Johnson, with whom there was almost no contact. They believed that Erny and Jill wanted nothing to do with them, and they were half-right. Supporting WJ and Linda was bad enough, Jill said; Frank and his two boys were no better off and, therefore, every bit as dangerous. Bertha had never been a problem that way. She returned to California after Billy Pond died and married again, this time to Joel Cartwright, the English-born seaman. Billy evidently was run down by a car about 1930; some who knew the man assumed his death was not accidental. Bertha would not claim the body, fearing that someone would step forward and demand payment of her husband's gaming debts, and it may be that the corpse wasn't identified. In Oregon, at least, there doesn't appear to be any record of this William Pond's demise.

As for WJ, who was living on the old Haycox homestead in the early 1930s, the farm on the Willamette River near Portland that Erny bought in 1935 offered the prospect of self-sustaining bliss. Everybody hoped for that. However, mainly due to his son's inability to properly visualize and support the enterprise, this agricultural interlude worked about as well as every other one of the father's endeavors. It was too wet for chickens and a bit dry for tomatoes unless, of course, one invested in a pump large enough to bring water from the river. Rainfall ruined the hay crop one year and the cherries and peaches produced bountifully but were not worth picking at the prices offered. The place really wasn't big enough to operate profitably and, anyhow, the doctors had advised WJ that he was working too hard. The letters from Butteville, which were never terribly friendly, became more and more accusatory. Erny's father finally washed his hands of the project.

He addressed his boy as "sonnie" and dealt with him much as one might a wayward adolescent. "Yourself and Jill done a very fine job in preparing this house for our benefit . . . but was it necessary to stay away for one year in the belief that you could not visit here and enjoy the benefits of that work? And when you did come, make it plainly evident that the result of that one year's work was a disappointment to you both? [The doctor] advised that I secure lighter employment with shorter hours . . . and that is exactly what I am going to set about to do. I expect to find it more difficult to reestablish myself than ever before and we are not leaving this place until a position is secured that will provide more of a future or security than is provided here." WJ said he would tidy a few things up and wouldn't leave the place unprotected, but Erny and Jill drove out to the farm one summer weekend and found it deserted.

They saw Jill's Baker City relations occasionally, some of whom now lived in or near Portland. Among the latter were Dorcas Brown and her daughter Ethel, they being the wife and daughter of Harvey Brown, the sheriff of Baker County who was killed by a bomb when, on the afternoon of September 30, 1907, he opened his front gate. Aging Alex and Mary Patton lived a few miles north, near Vancouver, Washington. By one account, he and brother Webster accompanied their sister Eliza, who was James Chord's mother, from Scotland to Baker City about 1872. Alex was said to have left a wife and children to come to the New World, planning either to send for them or return home after a period of wandering. However, he took up with Mary and did neither. Webster, meanwhile, is recorded as departing Newburgh for America in 1882, this date appearing on a silver snuffbox engraved with the good wishes and fond farewells of his Freemason brothers. So this was, perhaps, a second journey for Webster but, if so, no more pleasing than the first. He missed home and shortly returned to Newburgh and was its watermaster and sanitary inspector and the clerk of its city council for several decades following. Somehow, Jill wound up with the snuffbox.

In late 1936, the Haycox family heard from Jack, who, to their substantial surprise, announced wedding plans. He was married in January 1937 and the honeymoon was a several-month journey to Japan and China and the Philippines, accomplished on a series of tired tramp steamers, one of which nearly foundered. His written record of the honeymoon ran to 160 pages, all in verse. ◆

In March 1937, Erny took the train to New York, a place he hadn't seen since 1926. He had not yet met his agent, though Sydney Sanders had represented him for seven years, and he wanted to size up things at *Collier's* and see what other publishing opportunities might exist. He stayed at the Waldorf-Astoria Hotel, wandered through the old Brooklyn neighborhood, bought a sizable collection of bound nineteenth-century *Harper's Bazar* magazines and reported it all in a series of long letters to his wife. "Outside of a few more buildings that grow up nearer the sky, this town hasn't changed a particle," he reported. "Same canyons, same people, same subway rush, same smells, same funny t'oity t'oid street accent. If we lived here we'd be ducking around like natives inside of a day. But Lord forbid we'd ever have to live here. When I stepped out of the Waldorf I got the same feeling of loneliness—just a peanut rattling around in a monstrous hollow drum."

At *Collier's*, Littauer greeted him like favored kin, editor William Chenery took him home for dinner, and managing editor Charles Colebaugh attended him with eccentric charm. He had been worried about their reaction to his latest novel, *Sundown Jim*, on which all three had to sign off. They hadn't finished reviewing the new offering, but he got the clear impression there wouldn't be any objection and that his standing with the magazine could hardly be improved. Sydney Sanders passed muster easily. "Now there's a fellow you'd fall for," Erny told Jill. "English, with crinkly hair, a brown square face, white teeth, fine voice, slightly larger than I am, excellent build and fine clothes (which my ten percent helps pay for)." He was also taken by another transplanted Brit, Jim Marshall, a roving correspondent for *Collier's* he'd met at Chenery's house.

> Marshall had said something to me about not knowing just where his next assignment would be. He said it was just like Collier's (Chenery) to have him in New York for three or four days and then suddenly say, about five minutes before train time, "Oh, by the way, Jim, you're going to Africa."
>
> Sure enough, we were talking idly about England and Jim said the Coronation ceremonies in England reminded him of a possible good story. Immediately, Chenery said: "Well, Winston Churchill was to have written that story for us, but how would you like to go over and cover it?" Jim said, "yeah," and Chenery said, "I'll cable London tomorrow and we'll find out."

Marshall specialized in Asia and, as it turned out, was dispatched back there. In December 12, 1937, he was severely wounded when Japanese planes bombed the U.S. gunboat *Panay* in the Yangtze River and strafed the sinking vessel's lifeboats. Three were killed in that incident and ten others seriously hurt.

Erny's week in New York was littered with amusing restaurants and awesome gatherings. At one literary luncheon, he met cartoonist O. Soglow and gawked at illustrator James Montgomery Flagg and writer-adventurer Frank ("Bring'em back alive") Buck. A college friend and big-city lawyer, John MacGregor, showed him some of the fancy night life, including a French-themed place where the chorus girls wore next to nothing (but, Erny assured his wife, the fake waterfall was more interesting). MacGregor also wangled an invitation for him to the city's annual press club spoof where Mayor Fiorello La Guardia and New York Governor Herbert Lehman and national politicos Jim Farley, Harry Hopkins, and Al Smith and their ilk appeared to be having a great time. One evening he went to Martha Langguth's apartment for dinner—she had been close to the Chords in New York and was another of Jack's perplexed admirers. "Of course she wanted to know all about Jack, and Mrs. Jack, and I told her what I could, which was not very much. She said she thought the girl must be extremely good looking, an extra special wearer of clothes, and able to stand on her own feet—because this was the kind of a girl Jack always insisted was the only kind of girl. And she wondered just how Jack was going to adjust himself. I said I didn't know—and I guess that's what we're all wondering."

March 4 was Erny and Jill's twelfth anniversary. He sent her a cable and also expressed his fidelity by mail. "We have had a lot of luck and a lot of good times—and a few bad times. The bad times don't count, but I kind of looked back to see what had caused them—and I think that the few troubles we have had have all come about from a lack of understanding. I know I have not always put myself in your shoes and tried to see the thing from your viewpoint. Had I done so, a good many of our little differences would never have arisen. I do love you, and wish you were right here."

He may have known by now that Jill was interested in someone else. It was a long infatuation, stretching over several years. Her admirer was also married and for a time had been one of Erny's good friends; the couples played bridge occasionally and one summer, perhaps the fateful one, were close neighbors at Cannon Beach. The fellow was unspectacular as to personality or appearance, the kind one might meet and a few minutes later entirely lose from memory. But he had a gentle and sympathetic manner and a woman with marital problems, however imaginary some of them might have been, could easily have found in him those measures of understanding and respect perceived lacking at home. Some years later, Jill would tell Mary Ann that her paramour had at one point pressed her to run away with him to South America—that was how they did it in the 1930s—and that she had refused, being unwilling to leave her children.

Erny returned to New York in early 1938 for another round of business meetings and on this occasion devoted considerable time to the collection of literature from pricey furniture and fixture stores. He and Jill had recently purchased seven acres in hills west of Portland on which they would build (starting in 1939) that "really fine" house, and it would be—six bedrooms, six bathrooms, a grand entry with a circular stairway, a formal dining room with muraled walls, and a two-story office and library. The general layout of the office annex was suggested by Brigham Young's study-library, which they saw while visiting Salt Lake City in 1938. Jill had the last word on furnishings, though not on the structure itself. That was his dream and she would say many times that she never shared it.

He returned to the West Coast in 1938 via Los Angeles, stopping for a day in Tucson to scout scenery he would shortly describe in *The Border Trumpet*, completed that May. Jill declined to accompany him on the second trip east and demurred when he cabled her to meet him in California, pleading illness. "Perhaps I can get away after you return," she wired. ◆

The first motion picture sale was "Stage to Lordsburg," a short that appeared in *Collier's* in April 1937 and was bought by John Ford three months later. Then, in June 1938, Paramount Pictures acquired the motion picture rights to *Trouble Shooter*, which would be produced and directed in suitably epic proportions by Cecil B. De Mille. Both films were released in early 1939, as *Stagecoach* and *Union Pacific*, respectively, and Erny was suddenly a commodity of some interest in the high-octane world of the silver screen. It was a serendipitous turn of events, for he was working on a modern novel sited in Hollywood and felt the need of a bit more background; and Sam Goldwyn wanted fresh blood on a story for Gary Cooper, a cavalry piece that no writer thus far had managed to get right.

Syd Sanders negotiated the deal, which was for $2,000 a week for a month with various vague extensions possible. In April 1939, Erny and Jill and the kids moved into a bungalow at the fabled Garden of Allah on Sunset Boulevard

Sheilah Graham and Scott Fitzgerald had moved out of the Garden a few months earlier, but this assemblage of stuccoed, tile-roofed cottages —fronted on Sunset Boulevard by a small hotel and nourished at the center by a swimming pool large enough to influence weather—never lacked for famous customers. It was the home away for out-of-town actors and screenwriters and musicians with occasional motion picture assignments and some, among them the eccentric and often boisterous Robert Benchley, were nearly permanent residents. Like many others, humorist-actor-writer Benchley, nominally a New Yorker, was said to find considerable fault with Hollywood but not enough to reject its generosity. Some aspects of the Garden didn't entirely please him either, particularly Sunset Boulevard's rushing traffic. Benchley hailed cabs to get to a bar or restaurant within sight but on the other side of the damned speedway.

The Garden was reasonably priced compared to the better hotels and offered relative privacy if you had a relationship working or a serious hangover. Although the Haycox family remained unaware, a remarkable number of its guests suffered both maladies steadily. Schwab's Drug Store, an equally fabled landmark, was just a block away and, happily for guests in need, on the same side of the street. The Garden's management, imposing no moral code, tolerated nighttime revelry—nude bathing, too. But it was firmly against noise during daylight hours and Jim was frequently scolded by Ben the Bellhop (who, though not a landmark, was an institution) for chattering and creating small commotions with his sailboat in the pool. Jim never met Mr. Benchley but shared his awe of Sunset Boulevard. It rained one evening and, standing on the sidewalk in front of the Garden, the pleased lad witnessed three minor collisions in about fifteen minutes.

Erny put in long days at the Goldwyn studio on Santa Monica Boulevard but, otherwise, the family's two months of residence were a marvelous vacation, far removed from the dreary Oregon spring. The kids were enrolled in a private school a half-block away, where the classes were mostly outdoors. Jill cooked occasionally, but a variety of supper clubs in the neighborhood—the Players Club, the Trocadero, Ciro's, and Mocambo, to name the best-known—made eating out a nightly temptation. The children's dinner could not be long delayed, so the Haycoxes usually arrived when the establishment had barely unlocked its door and there were no other customers at table. The family would dawdle over the meal in hopes of catching the early show which, if it appeared on schedule, might be one of the popular dance bands or the Andrews Sisters. On weekends, they were vigorous sightseers, investigating the La Brea tar pits and the Mt. Wilson observatory and, on one occasion, flying to Catalina Island. And, of course, there was a studio tour. They saw a piece of *The Greater Glory* in the making on a sound stage, a scene in which Gary Cooper and several others were doing something with a boat in a pounding surf. With Hollywood magic, the entire episode—wind, waves, struggling bodies, and the boat—was contained in a pool about the size of a backyard fishpond.

Sam Goldwyn was reputedly tough on writers, quick to fire or reassign a man or a brace of scribblers if things weren't going well, but he evidently found Erny's motion picture treatment of *Seventh Cavalry* for actor Cooper satisfactory, or at least superior to those that had gone before. There was a studio dinner one evening at which Goldwyn effusively praised and thoroughly embarrassed his Portland employee, concluding the elegy with the startling observation that, with all the man's creative talent, "he's not even one of us." That remark has several possible interpretations, almost any one of which would have accurately described the situation. Erny was fascinated by Hollywood but not particularly comfortable with it, as he explained in a long letter to Ken Littauer, written while he was still on the studio payroll.

> I lay down two premises. A business as big as this one has, by the laws of average, a hell of a lot of able men in it. Secondly, it is show business, which is not a business susceptible to rational method, since it deals in an intangible. Third, the law of averages also indicates a tremendous

number of odd fish, mentally, physiologically and spiritually. Fourth, all the nickels and dimes of an extremely large country collect here to make every kind of value abnormal. Fifth. There are not enough first rate actors, directors, writers or general talent to go around, since it is so ceaseless and voracious a thing. Six. According to what I hear, there is more plain lack of intellect among the chiefs of this business than in any other. Seventh. The technical end is a marvel and has outdistanced all other ends. Eighth. The chief trouble with the story angle of this business is that a story has to pass, necessarily, through too many hands before it emerges as a picture. It runs a terrible gauntlet. The first man's original conception frequently goes on the screen as thirty-seven men's composite hopelessness. Ninth. I don't know much about it, having only been here six weeks.

And those are my two premises.

I have been lucky in that Syd drew a contract that made them leave me strictly alone until I had done my particular job. But otherwise my view of the processes by which a story is arrived at is not approving. Those processes respond to the laws of neither man, beast nor vegetable. In my business I write a story . . . [and] it is thoroughly mine. When it is done, it is then a simple matter of whether you like it or whether you don't. But down here somebody sells somebody a title and somebody else is put to work on a treatment and the treatment is no go, and another man does another treatment, and these treatments pile up like the snowy drifts of Bridgeport during a hard winter. There were five before me on this job and but for the kindness of Providence, there might have been another five after me. It just goes on like this.

The story of *Wuthering Heights* is typical. [Ben] Hecht and [Charles] MacArthur did the screen story from the novel and sold it to Goldwyn. Hecht and MacArthur are the high-priced babies of this industry. I'm told Hecht gets from $3,000 to $9,000 a week, depending on his mood. Goldwyn then put two men on the Hecht story to adapt it. No go. Two more men to readapt the adaptation. No go. Somebody else to re-readapt the readaption. Still snake eyes. So they put the son of Walter Huston on it and he went back to the Hecht script, which by this time was at the bottom of a hell of a pile of mss., and decided that was the story all the time. So he followed it, and the story was good.

This place is, insofar as types of people are concerned, a veritable country store. You can find anything and everything in some pigeonhole or on some shelf. There are excellent writers here, and writers who are only such by self–designation. There are also writers of national reputation who come here on contract with a flourish, and turn out indifferent performances, and leave—thereafter to write clever satire on the town. There are old-time script men who are lovely to witness. One came into the office today. Somebody had just finished a treatment—which is anything or nothing, but is a sort of glorified synopsis—and this new man's job was to write the script, to break it down in terms of camera shots. He sat down at his desk, with his hat on, laid out two packs of cigarettes, rang for a typewriter and a typist, picked up the treatment and began to read it; this afternoon he'll start dictating. He's been here twenty years, has an ambition to write fiction for magazines, is a ruddy, impulsive Irishman, matter-of-fact outwardly, inwardly shy; but he represents the kind of a writer I have never seen before . . . who knows instinctively or through long experience exactly where and when a scene will play, and where it won't—how much is enough for the camera and how much is too much. It is really a pleasure to see him go at the job, workmanlike and brisk, and knowing he knows.

If I were a satirist, Lord knows I could find plenty of vulnerable spots. This is an industry which now is all hot and bothered by Hitler and fascism. Yet this is the industry which, by its setup, is run pretty much on a Hitler basis. The head man is God and lesser men connive to get his ear and there are palace politics all over the place. This is the place where a smooth line of talk and a few clever words and an aggressive front will take a man a long way—far beyond his talents. This is the place where the left had frequently knoweth not what the right had doeth. This is the place of show-offs and phoneys.

But I am not a satirist and what I see is a tremendous business heaving and stirring and moving in strange, complex, slow-motion, indirect, half-blind and half-unsure fashion towards one objective, which is entertainment. Sometimes logic hits it, sometimes it rushes down an imitative alley, sometimes it responds to nothing better than a hunch. Nothing succeeds here like success. One man turns in a good part and every studio in

> town rushes for him, and he works himself to death doing drunken doctors over and over. One western succeeds and now we've got a cycle of them, and the cycle is wearing out. The new cycle, when it comes, will probably be more Nazi spy stories, since *Confessions of a Nazi Spy* went over so well.
>
> My job is done. I did a treatment of a thing to be called *Seventh Cavalry*. A treatment, as I have said, is God's own whimsy, being a present-tense synopsis full of adverbs and bad writing. If you saw it, you would not be proud of me, but it was liked. Now, either I go home or I do another picture for Cooper, cowboy theme. I do not know yet. All I know is that about six more weeks is my outside limit. I do not transplant well.

When the contract assignment was near completion, the studio would suggest a lengthy add-on involving a trip to Tahiti or some other island paradise where Erny could soak up atmosphere and produce original South Sea Island drama for actor Jon Hall, who was popular in native-boy roles (*The Hurricane* is best remembered). Precedent to this, it was necessary for the writer to see all of Hall's film work. Over several evenings, private screenings were arranged for this purpose, with cartoons added for the kids. Jim and Mary Ann knew their father was a celebrity of sorts, but probably not a very important one. They had never seen anybody ask him for his autograph. However, free movies night after night were something else. Maybe, they speculated in whispered tones as Mr. Hall tussled with the giant squid, maybe their father was a great man.

After minimal consideration, the South Seas project was politely refused. Erny knew before he got there that Hollywood wasn't his town; and even in mid-1939, the far reaches of the Pacific Ocean had lost much of their romance. Jim Marshall, who had metal fragments removed from four locations in his body and was partially paralyzed for a time, testified to that. Equally, construction of the new home in Portland could hardly be supervised from some beach several thousand miles removed. He spent the last of his studio time doing a film treatment of his story "Stage Station", which ran in *Collier's* while he was there; and then, in early June, the vacation ended. ◆

Ken Littauer visited Erny in Portland in early 1939 and they discussed, among many other things, the magazine's continuing interest in the writer's modern fiction. He had done a few contemporary shorts for *Collier's* and two of the serials were modern things—*Rough Air* in 1934, in which the leading man was a pilot, and *The Silver Desert* in 1935, with its stereotypical Hollywood characters hanging around the corral. More to the point, the writer was presently working on a serial novel about an Oregon girl who won a beauty contest and went to Hollywood, and this horseless drama for which the Hollywood trip had been a secondary justification had the magazine—and for that matter the writer himself—both curious and apprehensive. Shortly after Littauer returned to New York, he received the following communique from Portland:

> Now this is 1939 and all I see ahead is a terrific accumulation of words chopped off in little sections and appropriately labeled "A Rainy Afternoon" or "Pride and Sacrifice" or "The Lady Called Lily." I suppose I'll be throwing a number of such at you, some of which you may like.
>
> I read Hemingway's last one recently and find I have been looking up to a master who is at times something less than half a master. The poor devil is all sweat and sex; now and then he opens the door part way to something beyond but presently the wind blows it shut. It is a demonstration of his power, of course, that he's able to open the door at all. Something is missing in modern writers; perhaps because something is missing in modern life. Without wishing to be mystical I think it must be faith and positive belief . . . even if nothing better than faith in man's regeneration through a buttermilk diet.

No doubt, Erny was a bit envious of that gentlemen with whom he shared ages, initials, and records of underage military service. But when asked what he thought of this giant of American letters, and he often was, he had but one unflattering observation. There wasn't any issue insofar as Hemingway's talent was concerned. What he didn't understand, Erny said, was how this immensely capable fellow could be satisfied with one book every two or three years. Ernest Hemingway, he said, was sadly wasteful of his marvelous gift.

Collier's had recently accepted a new Haycox modern short, "Illusion," but with some misgiving. Perhaps, on reflection, they weren't quite so willing to let their top westerner spend his energy elsewhere. Littauer would plead: "Could we, for a little while, call a truce upon these pensive laments and substitute for them some stories with movement as well as mood? I am thinking, at the moment, about 'A Day in Town' which while not physically an action story was full of menace and therefore rich in suspense." Part of the problem, Ken conceded, was that the magazine's inventory was overflowing with stories "of rather quiet appeal." As for "Illusion," which the magazine retitled "A Girl Must Wait:" "It has menace but the menace is subjective and subdued. It has conflict but the conflict is restrained. It has pace but so does a glacier. It's qualities are good but they are qualities that we must not display too often. So see if you can't give us a couple of hell-busters between now and Easter."

Erny finished the new modern novel in the summer of 1939 and fired *American Beauty* off. Probably not to his great surprise, *Collier's* rejected it. Littauer said it seemed experimental: "I can see you tilting the test tubes and watching reactions and shaking your head. I don't think the modern novel is beyond your range. It probably was the wrong choice of material. Or perhaps there was some confusion in your mind as to whether you were writing a novel or a serial. As it turned out, it was neither one nor the other." The writer concluded that he'd simply done a poor job of putting the thing together. "I tried to write a story without a conventional plot."

It was about this time that Bob Case became a candidate for public office, contesting a seat on the Portland School Board, and Erny agreed to manage the campaign. "Everything he put his hand to, he did thoroughly and meticulously," Case remembered. "The first step was to obtain the legally required number of voters' names on petitions to file. I think the required number was around 2,100. We compiled a list of mutual friends and acquaintances—86 in all—and Haycox interviewed them all, persuaded each to get names on the petition, with the result that around 7,000 names were obtained. Due to his management I was elected by the highest vote among the six candidates (for three positions). Once I was in office, he showed no further interest in school board affairs. It was purely a gesture of friendship."

Case evidently wasn't aware of his friend's political aspirations, for the exercise was priceless training for a man wobbling on the edge of his own candidacy. Erny weighed the idea of running for the state legislature a couple of times in the 1930s. If he won, he explained to Jill on one occasion, he would probably have to spend a few nights in Salem during the week; but the legislative sessions weren't long and he'd be home every weekend. "You can stay in Salem as long as you like," she told him. "But when you get back, I won't be here." ◆

Although he had been trying to attract Hollywood's attention for several years, Erny's blockbuster break into the motion picture market with *Stagecoach* in 1939 was happenstance. Agent Sanders was showing his client's material to studio representatives in New York from time to time and, for his part, as the 1930s unfolded, Erny was producing manuscripts in which film application was at least a serious afterthought. Passages in *Trouble Shooter* describing the unisoned mass of Irish laborers and the forward-leaping tracks of the Union Pacific Railroad, written in 1935, were clearly cinematic vistas in the writer's mind.

> The engine pushed a load of rails forward, dumping them in an avalanche of sound. Men lifted these rails to a small iron truck pulled by a single white horse. The horse, disciplined in this business all the way from Fremont, heaved forward and came on at a dead gallop to the exact end of track. What followed was smooth and fast. The steel gang trotted to the truck, four men to each rail—lifted two rails and ran them forward. A foreman yelled, "Down!" and the steel clanged on the waiting ties. The gauger knelt, and jumped aside; the spikers swung their sledges with a battering rhythm and withdrew; the bolters bent over and bent back, and the white horse lunged on to the new end of track. In this interval the Union Pacific moved toward Laramie as fast as a man might comfortably walk.

There is nothing to suggest, however, that Erny viewed "Stage of Lordsburg" as having unusual film potential, or that anybody else did either until director John Ford read it in *Collier's*. Some might have found this particular short story—as Ford said he did—underdeveloped, alluding both to characters and incidents that might have benefitted from elaboration. The business end of the transaction didn't reflect the expectation of a remarkable motion picture. Erny's short-story rate in *Collier's* at the time was $1,100. Mr. Ford was slightly more generous—$1,500.

The story's imperfections were, to be sure, magnified by magazine space limitations; and although it is not recalled that he ever said so, Erny may well have considered later that he should have let the thing run on, regardless. But even when compressed (to about six thousand words), it was a prize tale of high adventure on the frontier, relating the uncertain passage of a stagecoach with its driver and shotgun guard and seven passengers through a desert scourged by Geronimo's relentless warriors. It had a reasonably conventional Haycox hero (Malpais Bill, who became the film's Ringo Kid), who, though wild and bent on revenge, was an insightful and soft-spoken man. But in other respects, it seemed to defy the writer's conventions. The plot device of crowding a disparate cast into a small space wasn't his custom; and the heroine, Henriette (Dallas in the film), was the only prostitute he ever allowed a leading role. The differences probably reflected the genesis of the story. He seemed to be remembering Guy de Maupassant's "Boule de Suif," a masterpiece he would have read in college, which has its own crowded coach and woman of easy but equally admirable virtue.

The threat of Indian attack sporadically themed his western fiction as the 1930s progressed. "Stage to Lordsburg" had one version of the terrible result, which its travelers found in the smoking ruins of a ranch house along their route.

> The stage stopped and all the men were instantly out. An iron stove squatted on the earth, with one section of pipe stuck upright to it. Fire licked lazily along the collapsed fragments of what had been a trunk. Beyond the location of the house, at the foot of a corral, lay two nude figures, grotesquely bald, with deliberate knife slashes marking their bodies. Happy Stuart went over there and had his look; and came back.
>
> "Schriebers. Well—"

Malpais Bill said, "This morning about daylight." He looked at the gambler, at the cattleman, at the Englishman who showed no emotion. "Get back in the coach." He climbed to the coach's top, flattening himself full length there. Happy Stuart and Strang took their places again. The horses broke into a run.

The Border Trumpet, a 1939 serial novel of Indian warfare in the Southwest, contained some particularly grim and graphic passages which probably, and unfortunately, were reproductions of actual events. Here is Al Hazel, old Arizona hand and cavalry scout, who with Lieutenant Tom Benteen and the Indian tracker Nachee, is trailing Antone's renegade Apache band, and remembering earlier times.

Suddenly [Hazel] heaved himself erect with a quick outlet of violent profanity and began slapping his clothes. "Damnation. I been sittin' on an anthill."

He kicked around in the darkness, making considerable noise, and came back to Benteen, his tone somewhat shamed. "I'll spit in the eye of a diamondback any time and I have shook a lot of centipedes outa my blankets. But them damned ants give me the creepin' twitters, ever since Long Jack Bell's time."

"Never heard of him."

"My partner back in '65. This was pretty empty country then. We used to prospect clear up tords the Mokyones. Wasn't any troops around here and the Injuns had chased all the Mexicans into Tucson. It was a bad time, for fair. We was over in the Basin, Jack and me, knowin' better than to be there but havin' a hell of a good time, just trappin' and prospectin', when up comes a band of Tontos and jumps our camp. That's pretty rough country. I got away and hid in a hole in the rocks. But they caught Long Jack and had some fun of their own. I guess I was half a mile away but I sure heard him holler till he couldn't holler no more. You understand, Lieutenant? Jack wasn't a hollerin' man, but he did then. They beat the country for me and didn't find me—and pulled out. I crawled back to where the camp had been and saw whut was left of Jack. They'd cut off his eyelids and staked him over an anthill, facin' the sun. The ants sure took care of Jack."

Often as not, Erny's Indians were bloodthirsty brutes, although that characterization was dictated by his choice of material and the requirements of high drama. But there were also sympathetic portraits scattered throughout his work—of Native Americans and half-breeds and of those casual arrangements wherein a white man took an Indian woman because he had no other choice. Anticipating the Hollywood tendency to present the Indian as a bestial character or otherwise calumniously, Erny typed several pages of suggestions and instructions for the producer of *Seventh Cavalry*. Those Indians camped near the military post should reflect "the informal and cheerful side of Indian life," he said, with women talking and kids playing. "The stern and slovenly side has been overplayed. This story should give a little truer picture of what went on. The Indians should be shown not as savage types but as human beings."

— 10 —

Scenes from a Double Life

IN THE SUMMER OF 1931, ERNY AND EP HOYT HAD SPENT A LONG weekend together in a Signature Nash automobile, touring the vast and nearly empty spaces of southcentral Oregon. It was a promotional event designed principally to advertise the speed, comfort, and durability of the vehicle but, notwithstanding their second billing, Hoyt and Haycox had a marvelous time. Though fully employed by the *Oregonian*, Ep was also writing fiction on the side—westerns included—and this part of the world, including the sprawling ZX cattle ranch, was as atmospherically appropriate to that calling as either man could want. The partners cataloged the sights and cowboy personalities with some care and agreed that two such admirable and convivial gentlemen as they should do more of this kind of thing, perhaps should even allow women along.

Whether the Hoyts and Haycoxes ever did much traveling together is doubtful. They did make it to the Pendleton Round-Up once or twice and they discussed other expeditions, but things came up, as they often do for incessantly busy men, and Ep was climbing fast in his newspaper's hierarchy (to the top job, as publisher, in early 1939). They got as far as making reservations for a round-the-country tour in 1941 before the Hoyts encountered some intractable conflict. Reluctant to abandon the project, and with a raft of spare tickets and hotel reservations available, the Haycoxes pulled their kids out of school and hauled them along.

They were on the road for thirty-seven days in April and May and inspected virtually every museum, gallery, historic point of interest and first-rate tourist attraction in Chicago, New York, Boston, Richmond,

Miami, New Orleans, and Washington, D.C. They stayed at the Roosevelt Hotel in New York for a week and were Grill Room regulars, and after "The Strawberry Blonde" had been requested a couple of times, Guy Lombardo would interrupt his program with the song as soon as the family appeared, and Erny would quietly sing along. He was a respectable baritone. "In another life," he said, "I'd like to have been Crosby." The trip was amended in Miami to include a brief inspection of Cuba and the family was befriended on the return flight by three extremely blond and exceedingly polite German travelers who were, they concluded, disingenuously pleasant. Nazi spies, unquestionably, though the Haycoxes did not have sufficient evidence to report the infiltrators.

They did not make it to Cannon Beach in 1941, being diverted by a boat that Erny had recently purchased and moored at the Portland Yacht Club on the Columbia River. This was *Sunbeam*, a forty-two-foot cabin cruiser powered by a pair of 200-hp engines that at full throttle produced a sensation not unlike that of a laundry machine with an unbalanced load. The purchase was in some measure a professional expenditure, for no man could write with authority about early Oregon without knowledge of the great River of the West. It would be, however, a more open-ended commitment than he anticipated. Graceful *Sunbeam* had been some years in service and previous owners had not bothered much with maintenance. Within a year, both engines failed at least once, various pumps, gages, and lubricating mechanisms fell idle; and the steering cable parted. As a general precaution, *Sunbeam* did not undertake long cruises alone.

Her master was a decent navigator, miscalculating docking speeds or distances occasionally at the beginning but rather quickly settling in and, of course, learning far more of the mechanic's trade than he had ever intended. *Sunbeam* went downriver that fall to Astoria, where Jill landed four salmon one bountiful day, and there was a long haul upriver to Miller Island in 1942 to collect arrowheads and examine Indian petroglyphs. Mostly, though, the boat was a weekend escape to some sandy island or lesser river where companion boats lashed several abreast and their occupants shared drinks and meals and gossip and, in the early dark, the men sang old songs in approximate harmony. There were guests aboard *Sunbeam* on most of the excursions, typically old friends from Sacramento Street or new ones from the West Hills. In 1941, while it was still a novelty, a popular Sunday voyage was into the Willamette River and Portland Harbor to watch the launching of a Liberty ship from one of the Kaiser yards. Eventually, with a half-dozen shipbuilding facilities active, launchings became anticlimactic; from the yacht club one could see cargo ships and transports and small aircraft carriers splash off the ways at the Kaiser Vancouver Shipyard without ever casting off a line.

As soon as *Sunbeam* reached her weekend destination, Erny would lower the dinghy and Jim would paddle off on some exploratory mission. He pestered his father to buy an outboard motor for the rowboat, which was heavily constructed and slow-moving under oar, but father seemed to regard the idea as extravagant. As for Mary Ann and other young ladies aboard *Sunbeam* and its surrounding flotilla, the principal attractions were the young sailors of the wartime Coast Guard patrol who boarded occasionally to inspect papers. If the patrol boat seemed at first sighting to be uninterested, the girls would appear on deck in bathing suits and halter tops and these were unfailingly regarded as evidence of suspicious activity.

Gas rationing restricted *Sunbeam*'s use in 1942 and 1943 and, in any event, it became something of a nagging obligation; in the latter year, for these reasons, it was sold. The market for good-sized pleasure craft was surprisingly strong at the time, for a draft-eligible owner could volunteer himself and his boat for Coast Guard duty and look forward to a rather pleasant term of wartime service patrolling the Columbia or some other domestic waterway, inspecting bathing suits and halter tops. The *Sunbeam* returned its grateful owner's purchase price in that transaction and, if one were to value the experience overall, perhaps generated a small profit. Erny's 1946 novel, *Long Storm*, was a Columbia River steamboat story, authentically seasoned with vistas and practical navigational details assimilated by a recent voyager.

In its impact on family life, however, no event at the beginning of the new decade ranked with the move, in June 1940, into the spacious high-ceilinged rooms of the new house. Situated on seven remote acres along Humphrey Boulevard, a long, twisting passageway in Portland's West Hills, it was actually and spiritually far removed from cozy Sacramento Street. Some family friends opined that the Haycoxes had taken up residence in a hotel. The formal entry was a large, circular room, along which an elegant stairway curved up to the second-floor bedrooms. Directly beyond was a solarium that opened outside to a slate terrace supporting the stately columns of a three-story portico. Turning left in the "sun room," one entered a formal dining room, whose walls were painted with pastel scenes of wagon trains and Indians and, on its longest surface, the portrait of the riverine city of Portland in 1858. If you continued in this direction, it led into an elaborate pantry—the Spode-and-silver staging area for social events—and then into the kitchen and a smaller breakfast room, where the family took its meals.

If, on the other hand, you turned right on entering the house, you were first in a gaping living room furnished with Early American reproductions and then, separated by a passage, in the author's two-story study and library. Framed by bay windows at one end of this room was a substantial and carefully appointed desk that Jim Marshall said was "unworkmanlike" and unrepresentative of the casual man it served. The study's paneled walls were decorated with old maps and colored prints of military scenes. Western artifacts surrounding the tall room's fireplace included a Spencer repeater, a cavalry-model carbine introduced in the Civil War and carried on many frontier campaigns. Guests often assumed this to be the weapon that John Wayne had used so effectively from his perch on top of the stagecoach.* There were also eight small Albert Bierstadt oil paintings in the library—studies of native faces and elk and bighorn sheep—which Erny had purchased from an antiquarian dealer in the East. And on the upper level, reached by a winding metal staircase concealed in a wall, were all those books and documents. He was buying more than ever now, sometimes several hundred items annually.

* It wasn't. It may have been a gift from Hollywood, but the Ringo Kid carried a Winchester.

It was a room that could have been used for composition but its master seldom occupied it for anything beyond evening reading. The new books kept him busy; he also consumed some classic literature but western and American histories and biographies were his principal interest. He read contemporary fiction occasionally but, fearing he might be drawn unconsciously to another man's style, he was careful about this and avoided western fiction entirely. There was a typewriter by the desk but it was hardly necessary; his office, which he relocated to a building in downtown Portland in 1940, was his sole writing venue.

On weekends, he was almost always outside, often toiling in a monumental vegetable garden. Seven acres did not quite measure up to the farm he had always wanted, but he made do with long rows of vegetables and several varieties of berries. Unaided, he erected a row of outbuildings—the first one to house the pump and engine for the well he had drilled, the second devoted to tool storage and rough quarters for occasional hired help, and the third for hay and feed and three dozen chickens. There was a horse at one time, won in a raffle and requiring construction of several hundred feet of fencing. There was also an apple orchard to prune and harvest and a previous owner's fledgling nursery of holly trees to attend and an endless lawn to mow when Jim could not be induced to do this. In a basement workshop, which had a lathe as well as a table saw and a bulky power sander, he completed construction of the Star of the West, his model sailing ship. He dreamed of making furniture in the shop, allotting time for this endeavor that did not exist.

His weekend dress was casually tattered and often smudged with oil from the truck motor that was supposed to power the well pump or the ponderous, walk-behind Vaughn cultivator, which had a massive iron engine block and a mind all its own. His hat was a discolored fedora with part of the brim removed. At labor, he chewed more or less continuously on the stem of a corncob pipe or the stub of a cigar, and he was frequently taken by package deliverers and other unacquainted callers to be hired help.

Jill did her best to keep the mansion, into which the old place on Sacramento Street might have fit a half-dozen times over, in a clean and orderly state. That meant a great deal to her and it very nearly killed her. The house included quarters for two or more live-in domestics and Edith was one of them, often the only one. Finding other help during the war was difficult, for Portland's shipyards took most of the ambitious and able-bodied and paid a good deal better than housework wages. Those few women left in the labor pool expected rather grand treatment for their limited cooperation and usually told their employer before many days had passed that she was asking far too much of them. Beyond that, they would explain, the place was lonely; there was but one house within shouting distance and the only public transport to Portland, the Council Crest streetcar line, was more than a mile away along a lonely road. So the wife of the celebrated western author, the mistress of this grand estate, found herself occupied a good part of the time as simply one more family servant.

Her husband sympathized and urged her to relax her standards, but she was no more capable of that than he was. The children pitched in occasionally but not as much as they could have. Jill carried on in this demanding environment for several years and was often depressed by her circumstances. When her depression became unbearable, she drank. It was an unpredictable thing and, never knowing when Mother might blow up, Mary Ann was reluctant to invite friends over. Jim, lost in his own fog, knew his mother went to bed early on occasion but took his dad's word that she was "just very, very tired." That did not entirely misrepresent the situation.

Mary Ann was a high school freshman in the fall of 1942 and her parents fretted about her a good deal. She was small and quiet and, they feared, rather intimidated by the wide world. Erny worked with her on homework assignments many evenings and administrated exercises to correct a minor vision deficiency, and Jill socialized with other school mothers to encourage friendships in her daughter's behalf; they both pushed. Sister—"Sister" and "Brother" were the common appellations at home—said she endured this as best she could, not wishing to disappoint either parent but mostly trying to please her father. Between those two was by far the strongest bond in the family. They learned Spanish and algebra together and she would always remember an English composition that he was determined to improve. First, he asked her to rewrite it, eliminating all adjectives. Then she was told to redo it once again, putting back only those few adjectives that she liked best. When that had been done, he had other suggestions and she was at length forced to tell him that the document's deadline was well past and that, in some transitional form, it had already been turned in.

Jim was of less concern to his parents, being curious and vocal, reasonably social and sufficiently clever with schoolwork to create the impression of knowledge retained. His father assigned projects around the home that were fitfully accomplished, when remembered. Growing bored with mowing the lawn in straight lines, he devised a startling patchwork pattern. He piled wood oddly and, assigned to paint the flat roof of the portico, he included giant initials in red—so that passing airplanes would know who lived there, he explained. Erny found his son distressingly indolent, though willing to concede that there might be a physical explanation for the persistent lethargy, possibly associated with the boy's rapid growth. By high school, Jim was a head taller that his father, topping out at six feet, two inches. Erny was therefore patient, suggesting and prodding from time to time but never lecturing. Jim would remember only three instances when he was spoken to angrily by his father, in each case with irrefutable justification.

In the early 1940s, Erny often read aloud to the kids. Father-and-son favorites were W. L. White's *They Were Expendable* and *Queens Die Proudly*, both accounts of heroic failure in the early months of the Pacific war, and Richard Tregaskis' record of bloody renewal, *Guadalcanal Diary*. With paternal encouragement, Jim became something of a military expert, virtually memorizing the 1942 edition of *Jane's Fighting Ships*, which contained photographs or specifications of nearly every naval vessel in the world. The boy maneuvered his own fleet of miniature fighting vessels, which were sufficient in number for both Atlantic and Pacific squadrons. He also collected military shoulder patches and, to the degree that such information was available, knew where every one of his divisions and corps was engaged. In this he had been inspired by a young New York draftee who passed near the house one Sunday in 1942, was bitten by the St. Bernard, and adopted by the family until the 104th Infantry Division completed its training in the Willamette Valley and shipped out. The division's bold shoulder patch, the silver head of a timber wolf on a green background, held a place of honor in the boy's collection.

Jill never ceased doubting her husband's fidelity, focusing for a time on a young married woman who was Erny's secretary during part of the war and from whom he purchased a blue Pontiac convertible with red leather upholstery, Sister's sixteenth birthday present. The enlarging circle of his "big shot" friends and the continuing dependence of his father and stepmother were tales often recounted, though these disputes were generally private affairs. They kept up appearances for their children and, in truth, the relationship was not unrelentingly acrimonious. They got along for good stretches and were at their best, as thoughtful host and ebullient hostess, entertaining at the Big House, which is what the family called it. They had a routine: she would welcome the first guests at the front door and, as they entered, he would be at the piano in the living room, finishing the last few bars of some rather profound melody. He would then rise and join the greeting, having completed the only piano piece he ever mastered from one end to the other. In another life, of course, he would have been Paderewski too. ◆

In the year or so preceding America's entry into the war, Colonel Charles Lindbergh spoke repeatedly against his country's involvement in the growing European conflict, becoming in that short time America's most visible and vilified anti-interventionist. It was an isolationist view that Erny did not support, although he had little sympathy for his country's eventual allies. The rise of Adolph Hitler was in his view "the direct, inevitable result of the [post–World War I] diplomacy of England and France," and he wondered if defending democracy logically extended to supporting two powers that, in attempting appeasement in 1939 "to save their own skins, break faith and word with Czechoslovakia and feed it to the dogs." And he was genuinely angered by those in the

Roosevelt administration, including the president's wife, who sought to discredit Lindbergh by labeling him a closet fascist and Nazi sympathizer. Sometime during this loud debate, he addressed a letter to the *Oregonian*'s editorial page, denouncing Eleanor Roosevelt for an intemperate outburst. It wasn't dated and it isn't clear whether it was mailed.

> Undoubtedly Mrs. Roosevelt has furnished American history with one of its most remarkable feminine careers since the time of Dolly Madison. Extremely intelligent, as democratic as an old shoe, and blessed with the vitality of three ordinary people, she has demonstrated for us what it is to be a natural and unaffected person. Facing gossip and caricature and malice her answer has been to preach the steadfast gospel of tolerance.
>
> Yet when Colonel Lindbergh makes a radio talk in favor of the existing neutrality law, Mrs. Roosevelt steps completely out of character to label the colonel as pro-Nazi. Clearly understanding that the word Nazi is hated by the American people, Mrs. Roosevelt evidently intends to attach that label to Lindbergh. How strange it is that she, having suffered from so much harsh judgment, should herself judge harshly.
>
> What has been Colonel Lindbergh's crime? Exercising his right of free speech—as Mrs. Roosevelt has done a thousand times—he simply said that our country ought to have no part in the ancient quarrels of Europe, that our job was to protect our continent and to fight our battles on our own soil. Most Americans agree with him on that.
>
> Perhaps he waved the flag a bit, perhaps he was indiscreet. Nevertheless the colonel represents a sincere and widely held point of view and it comes as poor grace for anybody to use the tar-and-feather word Nazi on him because he has the courage to speak up. Name-calling answers no argument.

There was a second letter to the editor, possibly following the scolding of Mrs. Roosevelt, in which Erny said his country had its own reasons for going to war, and should. It appeared in late June 1940, shortly after the fall of France and at a time when, according to an *Oregonian* poll, sixty percent or so of its readers felt the U.S. had no business taking sides in Europe. But war was inevitable, Erny said; France had surrendered and England was tottering and, wanted or not, it was destined to be America's fight.

> If we wish to exist as a trading nation, if we wish to maintain our standards of wages and hours and living conditions, if we wish to keep our form of government, in fact if we wish to remain a first class power at all, we are going to be forced to go back to a philosophy that we used during our younger days as a nation but lately thought we were too safe to need . . . imperialism.
>
> We will need to arm to the teeth, to seize the strategic allied islands near our shores before Hitler seizes them, to follow our merchant flag with force in all waters, to concede nothing, to back up nowhere, and to be prepared to meet this man dead and square at every point he disputes our way.
>
> If we compromise we will be caught asleep and destroyed. There is no middle ground. Two systems so completely opposed cannot live side by side in the same world. One must survive, the other must die. Never should we let ourselves forget history's plainest lesson, which is that the conquerors of the earth have always marched upon whatever country was the great treasure chest of their time. Today Hitler is the conqueror and the United States is the great treasure house.

Intensely patriotic, Erny considered rejoining the army as the unavoidable conflict approached. He had remained close to some of his WWI companions and one of these, also a B Company private on the Mexican border in 1916, was Brigadier General Thomas E. Rilea, now commander of the Oregon National Guard and second-ranking in the next-higher echelon, the Forty-first Infantry Division. The idea must have been suggested by Gen. Rilea or someone nearby: the Forty-first needed a postmaster general, a major's commission, and it might be his if he asked. He brought up the subject one evening at the dinner table. Could the family manage? Did they not think that serving his country again was in some sense an obligation?

They, of course, did not. The children were terrified by the thought of their father marching off to a likely war and Jill, for whom the suggestion had wider implications, was adamant. "Certainly not," she said angrily. "You've had your war." Resisted in this, Erny looked for some other way to be useful and, in October 1940, shortly after passage of the Selective Service Act, he accepted appointment to Portland's Draft Board No. 1. He would be its chairman for the best part of six years, during which time he would hear enough accounts of personal hardship, suffering dependents, and disqualifying maladies to inspire a hundred stories.*

Board 1 administered one of the broadest cross sections of humanity in the country, its territory amalgamating wealthy neighborhoods on Portland Heights with waterfront tenements, much of the city's Chinese, Japanese, and Black population, and its industrial northwest and farmlands farther out on Sauvie Island. The district had its full share of responsible young men who accepted their fate gracefully, some eagerly, and of those who did not; and over its term the board inducted more than five thousand of them. This three-member tribunal tried to be even handed in its judgments, recognizing that no set of written regulations was equal to the task. There were fundamentally two classes of men, Erny said, "those who were able to state their case persuasively and effectively, and those who had no gift of speech; and I think we early learned that sometimes we had to evaluate the statement of the gifted pleader and that sometimes we had to help build up the case of the silent man who could not defend himself by words." Among the former, who were often the subject of angry evening monologues at the Big House, were enterprising city dwellers who suddenly acquired a parcel of land somewhere and planted something and claimed agricultural deferment. Parents, some well known to him, sought special consideration for their sons. These encounters were uncomfortable and a few were embarrassing, involving offers of one kind or another in return for his influence.

By the fall of 1942, Board 1 had exhausted its supply of unencumbered single men and was within weeks of taking the last of the single-with-dependents category. Childless married men were next, then those with

* However, he wrote but one, about a widowed mother who wangles just enough time for her son to marry and start a family before he is called up. ("Deferred for Life," *Coronet*, February 1944).

dependents, and he told an audience of Eugene Rotarians that every category would be stripped before long and they would begin drafting those with occupational deferments in defense industries. It was a grim analysis. There were still some who believed the war might by some miracle soon end but that, he said, was unlikely. America was fighting cautiously, as behooved the contestant with greater resources. It would take much time and cause much greater discomfort.

> If you, as a nondefense business, can manage to get along on skeleton crews, on men beyond the draft age, or men physically rejected by the service, that is your good luck. If you cannot survive under those conditions, you have only two options—either to translate your plant or business into defense work, or to go out of business.
>
> I speak with no official status on this matter. But I know, and every board member knows, that the longer this war goes on, the greater the need for armed men and defense workers. Personal services in this country are going out the window, one by one. Next year at this time, the shops along the streets of every town in this country will present different faces to the public. I say this with deliberate bluntness. War is a grisly business. The casualty lists are beginning to come in from abroad; you must expect your own casualty lists on Main Street. You cannot expect otherwise.

Board meetings and administrative duties occupied more than a full day a week and a chairman's duties were both great and small. Jim wandered into his father's office one afternoon and found it strewn with hundreds of draft identification cards on which the ink of his signature was slowly drying. Board members weren't paid but chief clerk Earl R. (Sarge) Goodwin, who was among other things a gravel-voiced announcer at boxing matches, found a modest means of compensating the "captain," which was how he addressed the chairman. Colorful war posters arrived at the office almost weekly and, as each completed its period of display, it was refolded and set aside and the captain thus acquired an almost complete run of the things.

Erny spoke often at events staged to promote the sale of war bonds and his modern short stories adopted propagandistic themes featuring selfless young women who bravely sent their men to war. Phil Akers in

"Paycheck" (*Collier's*, March 1943) was making great money at the shipyard and having a high time but found girlfriend Edie breaking dates to entertain lonely soldiers at the local USO. Phil got the message and enlisted. Erny became an air raid warden, although atypical: his territory was his house, which for some reason fell into no other district. He followed instructions, placing bags of sand and a thirty–gallon garbage can full of water in the attic (these to suppress fire caused by incendiary bombs), then forgetting about them until 1945, when the garbage can rusted through. His books went to war; he and Max Brand were neck-and-neck for the most titles issued as Armed Forces paperbacks with about a dozen each. Some people thought the program unnecessarily dismissive of classic literature, but adventure stories probably made better foxhole reading. The appleless apple pie made of soda crackers soaked and seasoned with cinnamon and lemon extract in *The Border Trumpet* was replicated on a Pacific island and was, its preparer wrote, very close to the real thing.

Erny watched the public mood swing from uncertainty and confusion to the belief that victory was certain, writing in late 1942:

> The only point of doubt is the length of time it will take. Authorities—who are certainly not infallible guides—talk of a German breakup by fall of 1943. As for Japan, they say it will be a far more prolonged affair if we must chop off the tentacles one by one.
>
> Rationing begins to bite. The publication of any news that an additional commodity is to be rationed brings an instant flood of buying. This week it is butter. At Fred Meyer's store, four girls are wrapping butter and ringing the cash register as fast as they can move. It will keep up until rationing comes, or butter runs out.

He observed somewhat disapprovingly, while standing in the butter queue, that public psychology ran true to form. ◆

He was by now one of the Oregon Republican Party's elite, a fixture and frequent speaker at banquets and Lincoln Day observations and Young Republican seminars. It was difficult, vaguely unpatriotic, to directly confront the federal government or the president during a war.

But fuzzy liberals and ambitious bureaucrats and Democrats generally were always fair game.

> It is slightly possible that there may be one or two New Dealers with us tonight. If so, they probably got here by reading the wrong number on the door . . . [and] I have observed that New Dealers have trouble reading numbers. I believe that comes from the fact that New Dealers do not use the same arithmetical system other people use. They use a system which is generally known as the Hopkins method.
>
> Under the Hopkins method, symbols are used for answers instead of numbers: thus, two shovels plus two shovels equals a project. Ten pigs minus five pigs is a subsidy. If you divide a man who has twelve dollars by a hundred men who have no dollars, you reach a result called social value. If you multiply national debt by more national debt—and this is the most fascinating part of the Hopkins method—you come out with a very interesting answer. The answer is that since we owe the money to ourselves, we really don't owe any money.
>
> I have observed that people who are interested in politics are invariably those who have a strong, human, folksy interest in other people . . . [and] I do not wish to imply that a love of mankind is the exclusive possession of the Republicans. Democrats also love their fellow men. But I seem to detect a slight difference between the two parties in respect to the quality of that affection—particularly with those Democrats who have been cashing in on the label since 1932. Those people love mankind too, but it seems to be an emotion they handle best by long-distance telephone, or Western Union. It is a sort of ethereal and platonic and intellectual fondness. They possess an undying reverence for the wisdom and beauty of old age—except on the Supreme Court.*

Dwight Griswold, who was then serving the first of three terms as governor of Nebraska, spoke at a Lincoln Day banquet in Portland in 1942. Erny, who was toastmaster, was greatly impressed by this sturdy,

* The Supreme Court allusion was to President Roosevelt's attempt in 1937 to increase the size of the court, which had angered him by overturning several pieces of New Deal legislation. His "packing" plan—to add a man (of more liberal disposition) for any sitting justice who wouldn't retire at seventy—created its own furor and got nowhere.

plain-spoken man whose concerns about federal encroachment and liberal solutions for the country's ills were very much his own; and he concluded that Governor Griswold was a comer, the kind of solid, sensible middle American who might with a bit of polished support play some role in the nation's future affairs. He would visit Griswold later in Nebraska and from this association came "The Nebraska Story," the governor's ghost-written assessment of New Deal failings, which appeared in the *Saturday Evening Post* in 1943. Nebraskans, the reader learned, were responsible and practical people who retained the independent spirit of their sodbusting ancestors, voted for men and ideas rather than labels, got along without income or sales taxes, and abhorred public debt.

> The story of our state capitol illustrates the point. Time came when we needed a new building, one which would truly reflect Nebraska. We decided to spend $10,000,000 on it and levied a property tax which would produce $1,000,000 a year. Each year we spend the million dollars we received in tax money, no more. We built on the old capitol's location, but we left the old building up as long as possible, transferring from the old to the new as time went on. At the end of ten years we had a capitol which is a truly beautiful and imposing thing. Thirty or fifty years from now we shall have to burn no bonds.

The article, probably the only post-college composition that writer Haycox produced under other colors, attracted five thousand letters and did indeed give the governor momentum, though not enough to swing the vice presidential nomination his way in 1944. California Governor Earl Warren was the odds-on choice and, when he refused, Ohio Governor John Bricker was anointed. Still, Dwight Griswold had his moment. Standing before convention delegates who faced the hopeless task of unseating a popular, wartime leader, he nominated New York Governor Tom Dewey as presidential candidate of the Republican Party. Erny proposed a further article under Griswold's name, on the Republican Party's urgent need to modernize, in 1945. The *Post's* editors declined, one of them suggesting the idea would have been more appealing had Mr. Haycox chosen to speak in his own name.

Therein lay the old temptation, the fascination with the political process and the recurring desire to get involved in some way. He was about as well known in the state as a man could be, and there did not seem be much question about his standing with the Republican rank-and-file. From high circles came the suggestion that he should offer his name for the top party position in Oregon, that of state chairman. Some urged him to run for governor, among them his friend Ep Hoyt, which insured the *Oregonian*'s powerful endorsement. Political office was, in short, a realistic possibility. Yet he could not convince himself that the voice inside came from anything more substantial than ego, tinged perhaps with a bit of authorial weariness.

> Maybe I have lost some faith in my writing ability, or maybe I am unconsciously trying to avoid the really brutal amount of labor which will be required in these next years; for the next years—if I am to be happy with my stories—are the ones of experimentation, great struggle, failure, and perhaps achievement. I have reached the end of one period; the western story, which I was so comfortably engaged in, is no longer enough and I have to go on.
>
> The temptations of self-expression are great, and the love of an audience is a powerful thing. I shall be lonely if I turn aside . . . and I shall regret it if I give up these political ambitions which I have been quietly nursing even as I told myself I was not anxious for them. But I've come upon this problem before and have tried to straddle it; and nothing comes from the straddle but a half-hearted writing day and much lost time in other things. As quickly and gracefully as practical, I must give up any participation in outside affairs. It is a hard retreat . . . I shall grow often sour from solitariness and often will regret that other men rise publicly when I might have done so. Yet this is the profession I took up; and it must therefore be the one I follow.

These semi-despondent words, from a September 1945 diary entry, seemed to anticipate a change in the content and method of his writing that would be both substantial and abrupt. But in fact, he had been fitfully moving toward new ground for several years. It was a slow trend, but clearly illustrated by a series of uncommon short stories written between 1940 and 1943 about the inhabitants of the new prairie settlement of Ingrid on freshly opened Indian land (Oklahoma Territory, no doubt, although he never said).* The stories maintained essentially the same cast throughout but constantly shifted focus and, read together, would remind some of the episodic, deterministic work of Frank Norris and Theodore Dreiser (although a bit more cheerful). Erny had first thought of this Land Rush series as a single, larger story, but wartime commitments and a couple of other things held him back. In any event, they weren't bad as is; Ken Littauer would suggest that some of them were better than *Collier's* deserved.

Haycox stories—short and long, conventional and experimental—were notable for their violent natural forces. Nobody's rain fell harder and few winter storms in all of literature were as cold and deadly. The good citizens of Ingrid were frequently tested by the elements, as in this desperate trial from "Deep Winter":

> The snow whipped against him, knifelike as it struck his exposed face skin; and sleet formed on his eyebrows. He stamped on the wagon bed to bring feeling back to his dead feet. There never was a moment when he didn't have to wrestle the horses back into the wind; they were taking a beating and they didn't like it. He got to thinking of how small a target Ingrid was—just a spot a hundred feet wide in a hundred-mile distance—and he felt the runners scrape across metal again.
>
> "Road fence!" said Charley Graves. "We're on the track!"
>
> He wasn't sure. The constant flicker of mealy snow threw his vision off; it gave him a feeling of unbalance, and the constant rush and roar of the wind disturbed his judgment. He had, he realized, lost his sense of direction completely. That was probably why so many men died when they got caught in a thing like this. He thought he saw the shadow of a

* *Collier's* published five of the stories, in this order: "Some Were Brave" (1940), retitled "Land Rush" in anthologies, "Dark Land Waiting (1940), "The Claim Jumpers" (1940), "Faithfully Judith" (1942), and "Deep Winter" (1943). A sixth, "Early Fall," was rejected in 1940 and the editorial reluctance was rather vaguely expressed. Erny must have wondered whether, at the bottom of it, the magazine wasn't quite ready for its hero, a Jewish merchant Jules Solomon.

> shanty on his left and he pulled over and found it only an illusion. He straightened again, but he felt the growing weakness of the horses. If they stalled on him there was only one thing left—tip over the wagon box and crawl beneath it with the blankets and hope to live out the storm. It wasn't much of a chance.
>
> The horses stopped and refused to go straight on, as much as he urged them. He hauled them half around, and got them started, but Charley Graves called, "Wait" and slipped from the sled, disappearing. When he came back he yelled, "That was the big survey post!" We've overshot Ingrid! Turn left! Half a mile to go! Feelin' a little cool?"
>
> "Sleepy!"
>
> Charley Graves hit him a heavy blow on the back. "Wrong place to sleep!"

As long as he wrote, there would be evil men in his stories. But as one work succeeded another, natural elements increasingly overrode them as protagonists. The West was a hard place, often too hot or too cold or too dry. It was a huge and sometimes trackless expanse, in which the spirit was isolated and might be entirely stripped of its certainty. The prairie nourished Ingrid's settlers and gave them hope. At the same time, in the summer grass, "a cold and immaculate deadliness waited, with no warning to precede it but a dry rattling that was usually too late." The sky could suddenly darken, and the wind could blow forever.

— 11 —

As Good as It Gets

WITH DRAFT BOARD WORK AND OTHER WARTIME DIStractions, Erny averaged one novel and half a dozen shorts a year between 1940 and 1945, about half the earlier pace. Fiction remained the first calling but speechwriting and other special projects were pleasant diversions; he reviewed books for the *New York Times*, continued to paddle his political canoe, reinforced his Hollywood standing with several motion picture sales, and savored his new occupation of small-scale gentleman farmer in the rolling hills west of Portland. His seven-acre kingdom paled beside the agricultural enterprise he had visualized as a young man; the house, on the other hand, was surely grander than any he could have imagined on that 1916 troop train.

And though the writing slacked a bit, it did not suffer from lack of effort. *Alder Gulch* (1941), *Bugles in the Afternoon* (1943), and *Canyon Passage* (1945) were solid serial novels with strong historic foundations and the Land Rush shorts included several of the best that he would ever write. There were, however, modest signs of discomfort with what he was doing; the routine was getting old. In an early 1941 letter to his publisher, he explained that newly minted *Trail Town* was "as much of a characterization of a trail town per se as an action story would permit; and to tell you the truth I would someday like to rewrite this same trail town idea in all its social and economic shades, via characters of course, as an extended book—which could not be serialized."

> I may never do it, but the urge remains constant. I look with a good deal of yearning at the solid historical. Nothing would please me better,

> for example, than to start a young man and woman at the Texas gulf, 1867, and follow them north and through the years of the cattle trail and the coming of fences and the changing of times. Coming up-trail in this manner, such a family would bump into every current moving from east to west—the covered wagon, railroad, the Indian campaigns, the sheepman, the settler, the bad men, the mining fevers. . . . In thirty-five years, from the end of the civil war to Teddy Roosevelt, the plains area bridged the gap from the autocratic patriarch and his flocks and his henchman to the corner drug store. The old and the new fought it out very violently and dramatically through Kansas, Nebraska, Montana and the Dakotas. A girl starting at twenty with her husband—the woman would be the continuing character—went through it all by the time she was fifty-five. She would have seen almost every western figure of any consequence; and heard of or seen almost every major fight.

Little, Brown editor Ray Everitt urged him to try, offering that "once we were convinced it could have real possibilities, we might extend ourselves financially." But for the author, the objections remained formidable. "If I embarked on it," he replied, "I'd require about a year of additional research and writing. . . ." He added that agent Sanders was not encouraging, "and he is the businessman of the partnership. . . [and] his attitude is based on pretty solid ground." And finally, Erny explained, creative questions remained. "I cannot write deliberate Social Significance, and do not want to. There must be dust and grunting in my stories, out of which the Social Significance finds its own sweet way, if any."

Financially, the early '40s were the best years. Shorts went for up to $2,500 apiece, serial prices were approaching $25,000, and movie deals could be that or more. He earned $60,000 in 1941, averaged about $35,000 for the next two, then $50,000 or so in 1944 and 1945. He was a steady borrower, loan balances occasionally running mid five-figures. Now, however, his wildly gyrating cash flow was offset in good measure by hard assets and the debt served other purposes, particularly stock and bond investments. He was no better or worse at the investing game than the average, hopeful speculator. There were respectable capital gains occasionally, but he wouldn't have made a living at it. His luck was better in bonds than stocks. He would if necessary sit on the former for a year or two, and patience often provided when his short-term market judgments, or his broker's, did not.

The long and fruitful "first offer" relationship with *Collier's* ended in early 1943 when the magazine rejected *Bugles in the Afternoon*, the Custer story. That was quite a surprise, for Erny knew the piece was as good as anything he'd done in the serial line. His friends at *Collier's* apologized, explaining that their editorial policy was evolving and that they now sought material which would appeal to the widest possible audience. They did not further explain but Erny assumed they were telling him that some of their female subscribers did not like the Wild West. The magazine's most productive contributor for a decade reacted coolly. He was grateful for "exceedingly fine treatment" over the years, he replied to editor Chenery. The turn-down had been disappointing "but not a shock. These things come with the profession and must be accepted as the normal variation on theme." Then he changed the subject, adding a long paragraph about wartime regulation.

The *Saturday Evening Post* associate editor, Erd Brant, had been quietly promoting a relationship for several years and when Sydney Sanders offered the novel in that direction, it found a home. That would lead to an uncommonly pleasant experience in the late summer of 1943 when *Collier's* launched its final Haycox serial, *The Wild Bunch*, and Post countered with *Bugles in the Afternoon*. For two months, Erny was about as visible as an American writer could possibly be. Syd ran into one of the *Collier's* people on a commuter train, reporting that the gentleman had congratulated him on the sale to a rival but was otherwise subdued. Erny brought the first *Post* issue home one August evening to show the family. Jim observed that this was probably a pretty good thing, being in the two biggest national weeklies at the same time. The father agreed and laughed. "About as good as it gets," he said.

He had now something over three million printed words to his credit and a growing international audience. All of the books had been published in England; Spanish-language editions were common, and a few years on, as Europe dug out from the long war, a half-dozen markets developed there. National weekly newspapers in the U.S. and Canada routinely acquired second serial rights and many of his short stories were picked up in English- and foreign-language anthologies. He was also becoming known in American literature and English language textbooks, the story of squaw man Frank Isabel's deteriorating union, "A Question of Blood" (1937), beginning a particularly long run in the scholastic press.

Reviewers were mostly complimentary. Mr. Cuppy had long since come around and those writing for the *New York Times* book review section and the dailies in other big cities, though not always overwhelmed by western adventure, gave him high marks for style and characterization and for the solid reality of his descriptions. Some went further, suggesting that the writer's talent was perhaps too good for his material. There were passages worthy of Conrad and Maugham in his novels, they said, and one headline writer, succumbing to alliterative temptation, christened him "Balzac of the Badlands." To be sure, some continued to find his heroes unworldly in their power and his women of mythical goodness, and they muttered about the infernal predictability of the western plot. That was the problem: they saw the western as a form of literature—subliterature, perhaps—that could not rise above its humble ancestry.

He was well aware of this view, of course, and suggested that his specialization was unfairly singled out. "The tradition of the powerful hero is firmly established in all adventure stories and goes back many generations," he countered. "The basis of it is, of course, that fact that the reader always identifies with the hero, and it offends the reader when the hero makes a fool of himself." He did not intend that his characters serve metaphysical or allegoric ends, and for that reason felt that no more elaborate defense of his work was required. As he'd said much earlier, you had to be of a certain mind to enjoy the robust/romantic kind of thing; that was all. He had larger goals, of course; what writer doesn't? In the 1930s, he talked about them in occasional correspondence with his friend and former instructor, Professor Thatcher. One of his earliest letters acknowledged the issue.

> With you, there can be no question as to the writer's real aim, and no excuse if a writer does not utilize such gifts as he may possess toward the very highest end. Brush economics aside, put comfort and friendship aside, and all the minor considerations that influence ordinary men—the writer must serve his function. He has got to make the gamble, someday, even if it ruins him. I realize that . . . [but] at the present moment the financial angle is the most important. It makes me less of a writer, but I can't overlook the obligations I have. I can't overlook the matter of security for the family.

Though still some distance from good work at this point, he knew generally the kind of thing he would eventually attempt. It would be "the meaty, detailed, inclusive, panoramic novel" and he had a model in mind, *Les Miserables.* That one was symphonic. "It has a thousand characters, all of some meaning and consequence—and the totality of the story strikes you like a ton of brick." But not yet. "Before that happens, I've got to write the adventure-romance-popular stuff out of my system. Because of the economic necessity; and—even more important—because I've got to completely finish that mental cycle, so that I won't ever want to go back to it. . . . When the shift comes—if it ever does—I shall be completely through the thing I do now."

Several years later, the question on his mind was the means of expression.

> With me, and I suppose with all of us, the surge and pound of feeling is so much greater than that which comes out as a finished product. That is precisely the writer's problem; to translate without too much loss of heat and color the vividness and the richness and the turmoil of his mind into images of black and white.
>
> I know what I want to do. I do not yet know how to do it. But I rather think that if I am to do it at all, it can only come by my breaking every existing pattern in my head and starting fresh. In other words I have built dikes in my head, between which the waters of imagination flow rather neatly and in orderly fashion. I think I am going to find it necessary to blow up those dikes and let the water smash hell out of the peaceful countryside.

The break would come but, as already noted, aside from the occasional off-tempo, experimental short story, its progress was evolutionary. In the 1930s, the heavy hand of breathless action was increasingly restrained and refined into a leaner style of expression and Erny's work—particularly the shorts—leaned more on allusion and implication. A single sentence could say a great deal. An example is the beginning of "Stage to Lordsburg": "It was one of those years in the Territory when Apache smoke signals spiraled up from the stony mountain summits and many a ranch cabin lay as a square of blackened ashes on the ground and the departure of the stage from Tonto was the beginning of an adventure that had no certain happy ending. . . ." It was observed that his leading men gradually had lost much of their reckless purity, becoming moody, imperfect, and therefore semihuman specimens. He had, said historian and critic Bernard De Voto, "added the Hamlet strain to the Sun God."

And in at least equal measure, the once decorous ranch maiden evolved into plausible womanhood. In his pulp magazine period, his heroines were dependably comely and courageous and were sometimes allowed to be wiser than their opposites. However, they were for the most part insubstantial characters and almost always victims—isolated and threatened by villainous males and, with some regularity, kidnapped. Helen Chavez in 1927 had been the first glint of change. In the thirties, the women in his stories became believable and, by the end of that decade, occasionally dominant, replacing men as lead players with some regularity. It was, he would later say, a transformation dictated as much by personal revelation as modification to please the palate of a more diversified and sophisticated audience. Over years of reading and pondering, he said, he had simply come to realize that the women of the West occupied a far greater role in its affairs than given credit for. Histories of that time and place were oddly silent as to the female contribution and the reason for this, he suggested, was that this literature was produced for the most part by men.

Western artist Tom Lea picked up on the male transformation, producing a modernistic painting of a melancholy cowboy sitting on a rock, which he titled *The Haycox Country*. Erny, who had no foreknowledge of the effort, first saw it as a Little, Brown bookstore promotion in 1940 (it also would appear on the jackets of the next two novels) and he loved it. "This, I think, is the precise note to hit," he wrote to LB's Ray Everitt, "action and out-of-doors, but a cut or two above the lurid and melodramatic which has so tarred and feathered the western. Bringing the western out of the kitchen into the parlor is a damned difficult feat . . . but if we are to get volume we've got to break over to other reader classifications . . . [and] this poster helps to spread the intangible essences of westerns to this larger audience."

Still, the sagebrush string was running out. *The Wild Bunch*, written in 1942, was the last of the horse-and-rider serials; he had not done much with the cowboy theme in short stories since 1939, now preferring frontier military episodes whose events and characters were only marginally fictional. In the conventional western plot, it was a rare thing now for the final accounting to occur in the dust of a suddenly evacuated street in Pistol Gap. As early as 1937, the locale for this kind of story was more likely a homestead freshly set in harm's way. He had consciously begun to give his leading men more intellectual substance, starting with *The Border Trumpet* in 1939, although it was subtle work, mostly apparent to him. Insofar as the novels were concerned, the visible break with magazine convention occurred in 1944. He reported the occasion in his off-again, on-again diary.

> The other day I began *The Strong and the Weak* [later, *Long Storm*]. It began as a serial and went along that way for thirty pages, at which point I let the hero take his own course in a certain scene. What he did was stop and look around him—to view his world and to have a reaction to it. I had done this before in other stories, but always holding the hero in checkreins. This time I let him view as long as he wished and to think as he wished. At that moment the story ceased to be a serial and became a man on the search for something. The rest of the story fell into a kind of rhythm and wrote itself very rapidly—7 weeks.

The plot was his favored mix of history and imagination, involving an independent steamboat man fighting the Oregon Navigation Company's freight monopoly on the Columbia River and, coincidentally, the secessionist Knights of the Golden Circle. Close moments and furious encounters were plentifully supplied; the reviewer who found the lack of gunplay refreshing failed to note that two men were clubbed to death and another blown to kingdom come. However, the novel's structure was in some respects undisciplined. Characters were introduced haphazardly, including a few colorful souls who were clearly unessential to the main plot—a luxury the serial formula had no time for. *Long Storm* also lacked the steady serial flow; at times the writer interrupted progress to meander over a scene that pleased him, and he permitted his leading character to muse in a stream-of-consciousness manner that, in earlier work, he had avoided. Looking down from the wheelhouse of the *Daisy McGovern*, Captain Adam Musick saw a deck packed with men bound for the mines of eastern Oregon and Idaho—and saw beyond that bright and hopeful river day:

> Maybe two or three would make a decent strike; the others would do no better than day wages and would spend it as they made it in order to live. By fall some of them would be dead, and some would drift back East empty-handed, their time lost and the world marched a year beyond them. The rest would never return; they would be the drifters of unknown whereabouts and their people would seldom again hear from them.
>
> He narrowed his eyes and he saw these men age before him and he saw their dreams die. It would go in such stealth, little quantities bled away by successive failures, by tragedies, by the lessening of that fire which made them men. A wonderful and merciful blindness now hid this from them; but one day the knowledge would come to them in their respective revelations. One man would repeat the old words of faith to himself and suddenly those words would be empty. To another it would be the impact of a stronger man's arm, making known to him his own vanished strength. A mirror would tell the story to some, or a slow and rising pain, or the realization that coffee and meat no longer had the old taste; and there would come the most cruel of all realizations—that the tomorrows were nearly done. And thus to each in his time the dream would end.

Until this moment, it had been an absolute article of his faith that lengthy "thinking" passages were poor excuses for good writing, evidence that the composer lacked the skill to convey his meaning with strong scenes and conventional descriptive tools. And there was a further danger in this method, that of excessive profundity; might not the writer appear "a romantic juvenile whose reflections and agitations look very silly strung out on paper?" In the end, however, there seemed no other way to achieve the depth and fullness of character that he sought.

He was uncomfortably certain that *Long Storm* failed as a magazine effort, although willing to let Sydney Sanders, who was predictably disturbed by his client's direction, give it a try. The *Post* and *Collier's* each declined, their editors expressing dismay at the number of subordinate personalities in the story and wondering where all these people were headed. Syd suggested that Erny could salvage the effort by redoing the first thirty pages but drew no takers. The novel was fine as far as Little, Brown was concerned. It became a book club selection, and reviewers were mostly supportive. But it was a financial disaster: book club sponsorship greatly increased sales but at the cost of heavily discounted royalties, which didn't come close to making up for the loss of a $25,000 magazine sale. And without the usual magazine exposure, Hollywood hardly noticed. Still, said the writer, though not the book he'd set out to write, it had been an instructive exercise—a step toward the next level. There was no turning back, he told Thatcher; he would somehow have to deal with all the rules he had learned over twenty years, many of which now seemed impediments.

> There is a man on *The New York Times*—I don't know who he is—who has read nearly all of my novels and has criticized them directly to the publishers. He has said two things which I value. One is that I am a spotty writer, somewhat unpredictable. I excite him with one piece of work and disappoint him with the next. The second observation is that he felt I wrote under too much restraint and that if I really let myself out I might amount to something. He came closer than he realized. Restraint is habitual with me. I boil inside but I am fairly placid outside. Nothing

excites me in the line of human behavior—I can accept the most unconventional and abnormal sort of behavior and thinking in other people. I can look into the dark spots and not be ashamed or repelled; yet I am myself pretty normal, pretty standard. I subscribe to Sinclair Lewis' conception of Babbit; yet I am a Rotarian, and enjoy those men even as I see the pewter in many of them.

I have had the thought for a long while that a writer needed a point of view—a firm and established philosophy—in order to write a good story; and I have tried to arrive at some philosophy these many years. I am now convinced this was a false idea . . . simply because I cannot formulate a philosophy which I'd [not be] dissatisfied with. . . . I'd immediately realize that neither life as a whole nor any sizeable chunk of life in particular could be reduced to a demonstrable rule. Life is far too capricious, arbitrary, changeable. . . .

I have come to the conclusion that I shall have to write somewhat like the referee who follows the players and uses his whistle as little as possible. Of course, my essential beliefs will condition my use of the whistle. Those beliefs, boiled down, seem to be that there is an immense amount of beauty and glory and wonder in the world—in people. We struggle and occasionally we come through. Otherwise we reach ends which are tragic or disillusioned; sometimes the tragedy is not of our making but usually it is. In the end we defeat ourselves. All of this, as a writer, I observe with a good deal of compassion . . . but when I look at the mass, instead of at the individual, it always occurs to me that the dead and the defeated make no difference in the general current of life. The stream keeps moving. ◆

In 1945, the writer-director James Algar met Erny in his office, which Algar found oddly spare, "as unembellished as a hard-used saddle." This is how Algar described him:

He was a smaller man than I had anticipated, having come by then to associate his name with the tall, rangy men of his stories. He was of slender build without fat, a dapper dresser. A naturally high forehead accentuated by baldness gave his face a domed, thoughtful appearance. His nose was large, long, and blunt-tipped; his eyes deep brown with grooved crow's feet beside them from much smiling. His mouth seemed meant to grin; it was a wide mouth with full, sensuous lips that found repose only when curled around his pipe or his cigar. He smoked both while we talked.

Bob Case remembered his friend as one writer might another, as a character of many facets, some of which reflected "a bitter and impoverished boyhood."

> He was hard to know—withdrawn, sensitive, suspicious alike of strangers, acquaintances and even those who classed themselves as friends. He had very few intimates. It was years before he decided that I was sufficiently trustworthy that he could "let his hair down" and talk to me in uninhibited fashion.
>
> Little of this appeared on the surface. He was easy to meet, polite, well-mannered, using impeccable English when he chose to do so (though with me, in private and ofttimes humorous conversation, he would deliberately use "ain't" [and] "guardeen" for guardian and "sireen". . . .)
>
> . . . he was almost Puritanical in matters of morals and ethics. He was rigidly honest; never drank to excess; was intolerant of off-color stories; was faithful to and considerate of Jill in spite of their obvious incompatibility.
>
> He was not a handsome man—somewhat under medium size but would have been very muscular except for his wartime injuries which left him with constant stomach trouble . . . ; bald in his 30's; with an enormous beak of a nose (of which he was secretly a little sensitive though he took the jokes of his friends with good grace and occasionally joked about it himself).
>
> His distinguishing characteristic were his eyes: deep-set and apparently gloomy at first glance, but when you met his gaze fully you were at once aware of the keen and kindly intelligence lurking in those somewhat cavernous depths. When he scowled, which was seldom, he looked like a *very* mean horse.

There were, for the record, no war wounds beyond that overactive thyroid. The stomach trouble was real enough, discomforting, producing frequent bouts of indigestion, rather than serious. It was later traced to a slight stomach deformation—an odd pocket that tended to save bits of food overlong. A glass of milk in the evening sometimes settled the problem. Case did not say whether he thought that his friend was Jewish, but was greatly amused by an banquet incident involving a waiter's assumption of that progeny. The main course included a large ham slice, Case said, and the server solicitously inquired: "'Is ham all right for you?' Whereupon Haycox grabbed his [own] nose firmly and said to the waiter, '*Vy not?*'" Case and other friends were certain Erny's delight with large cars and oversized dogs and the mansion were rebuttals of his early poverty and small physical stature. A degree of arrogance would have been consistent with this analysis, and some seemed disappointed not to find it. Bob's wife, Evelyn, who had this expectation, found him unfailingly considerate and particularly fond of children. Erny often struck up conversations with youngsters, she said, particularly singling out newsboys.

He was gentle with editors, normally accepting their suggestions without protest. Those toiling for national magazines were, after all, better than fair judges of contemporary literature; and if they had a problem with something he wrote, it probably *was* a problem—and it could usually be fixed right by changing a few sentences. He would occasionally express irritation at the *Collier's* penchant for changing titles, although his weren't always perfect—the editor who thought *Wings and Slippers* odd, and *Rough Air* better, probably deserved a medal. The situation at Little, Brown was a bit different, for, although its editors were working with the same manuscript that *Collier's* or the *Post* had accepted, it was often larger in final form, including material that the magazine had condensed out. For whatever reasons, Little, Brown had its idiosyncrasies—as to punctuation, for example, which the writer viewed as simply an artistic tool and was inclined to avoid in a sweeping descriptive sentence (the first sentence of "Stage to Lordsburg," for example). LB's copyreaders had difficulty with this, and he had difficulty with them. "I will yield on the matter of grammar any time," he would on one occasion explain to them, "since my own grammar is strictly functional and any resemblance to rules, living or dead, is purely coincidental. But on the matter of commas—no. I spend most of my time clipping commas and semicolons from this tortured style of mine, so that each strophe of beautiful English will not resemble Aunt Maggie's ball of yarn after having been dropped on the floor. Let us be penurious with commas."*

Although he could easily do without backslapping and boisterous behavior, Erny didn't impose his own reserved manner on his judgment of high-spirited or unorthodox acquaintances. He admired writer Richard Wetjen, whom he had known early but never well, though Wetjen was a somewhat bizarre fellow to his mind—really not much better than a bum, he said on one occasion, but "much more iconoclastic than I am, much more impatient, more usually in a state of ferment—and therefore possibly a greater hand." His tolerance extended to race. Through friendship with University of Oregon football coach Jim Aiken, he arranged to have halfback Bobby Reynolds, who was black, attend a Lincoln High School football dinner in 1946. He brought Reynolds by the house early that evening to meet the family and have a drink, and he tried to pull strings later when Reynolds graduated and found that a well-known and impeccably mannered black man with a diploma was of no particular interest to Portland's business community. Reynold's cold reception was inexplicable to him.

Still, it would be difficult to claim that he was much above his generation's standards. In his talks at high schools, he sometimes offered Lancaster Jones as an illustration of the need to expend effort toward any worthwhile goal. Lancaster, a southern black boy, was found by one of his friends leaning wearily against a tobacco shed. Asked why he did not lie down, Lancaster responded that he did not have the strength to do so, prompting his friend to observe: "Boy, if you want to rest, you got to work at it." This, in the 1940's, passed for inoffensive humor.

Given something of a hard edge by his draft board experience, he did not object to the wholesale relocation of Japanese-Americans at the beginning of the war.

* This particular copyreader would vigorously deny guilt. "I find he has objected to exactly two of my commas, all the other changes he has made being revisions of his own punctuation. In fact, he's turned most of his own dashes into—of all things!—*commas*." (An undated note which Little, Brown probably didn't send on to EH.)

> When we moved them away from the coast a considerable outcry rose from perfectly good citizens who thought this was a brutal and undemocratic way to treat people. Maybe it was and maybe it wasn't. But the point is that war is brutal and undemocratic—and if we draft millions of Americans and thus break up millions of homes—and if at this moment thirty-five thousand of those Americans are dead in action—if this is true, why are we shedding sentimental tears over the far lesser hardships of our Japanese-Americans? Sometimes we don't get the picture quite straight.

Whether they were true or not, he believed the stories about wartime sabotage at West Coast ports and clandestine radio transmissions to Jap submarines. Some Japanese-Americans had "proved their disloyalty beyond any doubt" by refusing to sign a draft-board loyalty oath, he noted. His opinion also had been influenced by an event at the next-door neighbors on Humphrey Boulevard, an older couple named Gangware. When their Japanese houseboy was hauled off to internment camp, they assured the young man his job would be waiting for him. His answer rather appalled them. "No," he said, "when I come back, you'll be working for me."

On the stump as the war ebbed, his message to Republicans was one of exasperation with a party that had now lost four successive presidential elections. To the Democrats' credit, they had ideas and were willing to try them. It almost didn't matter that their programs often failed, often wasted great sums of money; the voters rewarded them for the effort. Republican leadership, on the other hand, was tiresome and sterile—quick to complain but unable to offer better. To a Republican gathering in January 1945 he would thunder: "The one shining contrary example in recent weeks was the Vandenberg speech . . . and yet Republican leaders are criticizing him for going along with the president. Just how many times do these old guard Republican leaders have to be licked before they know they're licked—before they realize that Americans do not want doubt and despair and negation and penny-ante tactics—and will not follow men who preach that gospel?"

In late 1944, Republican Senator Arthur Vandenberg of Michigan, once an isolationist, had spoken in favor of a strong U.S. hand in peace-making efforts. It was a view Erny expressed frequently between 1944 and 1947 in his public addresses. The country's withdrawal from international councils after World War I had been a dreadful mistake; it dared not retreat to splendid isolation again. In a June 1945 address to fellow Rotarians, he likened the issue to a debt obligation—in this case, that which a present generation of Americans owed to selfless predecessors.

> Now it is our time and our turn. The first of our problems, this war, we have met—and history shall never be able to say that we did less than was expected of us. But now we must make the rest of our contribution, which is to take this power which is America, and these principles which are America, and to apply them to the struggle for peace.
>
> This is the problem which a previous generation failed to accept. It is our problem now and one which we must meet with that same driving energy, with the same imaginative daring, with the same cold purpose which we gave to the prosecution of the war.
>
> This is what we must do. If we fail to do it there will come a day when future generations, looking back upon us, will say: "Those were small, blind people who threw away the destiny of a country." ◆

There were two movie sales in 1944, *Trail Town* and *Bugles in the Afternoon*, and another in 1945 involving the last of the magazine serials, *Canyon Passage*. It was filmed in Oregon in the summer of 1945 and the Haycoxes were on one of the sets, at Diamond Lake in the southern Oregon Cascades. Jill would remember the two leads, Dana Andrews and Susan Hayward, as standoffish while lesser actors—Andy Devine, Ward Bond, Hoagy Carmichael, and Lloyd Bridges—were as common and friendly as Baker City cousins. Some said Andrews was preoccupied by an approaching scene in which he would fight the much larger Bond, perhaps suspecting the giant, who carried a bottle about the Diamond Lake lodge as one might a book or a small dog and was insistently generous with its contents, planned more fun than the script allowed.

The family did a good deal of traveling that year, having returned from a cruise to Alaska shortly before Diamond Lake and spending Christmas in Los Angeles, where *Canyon Passage* was being edited into final form. The Alaska party included Dr. A. A. Knowlton, a physicist of international standing who for many years instructed at Reed College. They had played a good deal of shuffleboard on the *Princess Nora,* there being few other diversions on this small steamer that still carried 20-mm. guns and was only beginning to reacquaint itself with tourists. A shuffleboard court was reproduced in the basement of the Big House that fall and Dr. Knowlton built the canes and round wooden counters with which the contest is played. Some of the parts came straight from the college's physics lab and, all together, they may have comprised the most precisely engineered and balanced set of tools for a simple game that the world has ever known.

Canyon Passage came to Portland in July 1946 for its world premiere. Actors Andrews and Hayward were unavailable but producer Walter Wanger found popular replacements, principally voluptuous Yvonne De Carlo and comedian Lou Costello, who was the event's unrestrained presence. It hardly required a mistress of ceremonies but nonetheless had one, Elsa Maxwell. Carmichael, a singer of dreamy ballads, was the teenage draw, and Mr. Wagner's stately wife, Joan Bennett, was an enthralling presence for Portland's adults. Attractions included a Yakima Indian village in the city's Park Blocks, a mounted manhunt, a reception at the Big House, and a parade overflowing with movie stars, pioneer associations, and almost every horse-propelled club and sheriff's auxiliary in Oregon. Erny endured a testimonial dinner and an honorary degree and editorial-page tributes and the parade, in which he was joined by Sister, ever the good soldier. Jill would not touch that event, saying with some justification that she had enough to do feeding three hundred people. Jim, now fifteen and profoundly embarrassed by his father's fame, skulked on the far fringes but did consent to see the picture with his family.

The summer of 1946 overflowed with activity. Erny explored the western Oregon countryside, absorbing scenery and atmosphere for the next novel. Jill and Sister spent a week in New York on a pre-college shopping expedition. Father and son packed into the Wallowa Mountains and the family spend the last of August at a resort in central

Oregon. They did not think that this would be the final family vacation, but it was assumed Sister would sooner or later meet her young man in college and Jim was about ready to test the summer-job market.

Jill and Erny continued to worry that the world would somehow overwhelm their shy and mild daughter. They suffered far more than she during sorority "rush" week at the University of Oregon that fall, fearing Sister might not be accepted by her first choice; and when she was, their concern shifted to her studies and her social life. Letters of advice and encouragement flowed from Portland; he produced at least one a week, which, though cheerful, throbbed with parental angst. He and Jill found frequent opportunities to visit Eugene in the fall of 1946, for he was at that moment in the first of two terms as president of the university's alumni association. Getting football tickets wasn't a problem.

There were two Hollywood assignments in 1946. Warner Brothers commissioned him to write a western for Errol Flynn, which it was hoped would invigorate the actor's flagging career; and producer/director, Albert Rogell, lured him into a profit-sharing arrangement to adapt an implausible yarn about the good deeds of a misplaced angel (Robert Cummings) in a western setting. These tasks were, respectively, *Montana* and *Heaven Only Knows*, and the latter provided all the information Erny would ever require about profit-sharing deals in Hollywood. In 1946, for the first time in twenty-four years, he wrote no short fiction. Almost the only brief discourse was an essay for a Portland writers' conference in which he sought to answer the question, "Is There a Northwest?" He thought not, disagreeing with some (including fellow speakers Case and Holbrook) who saw uniqueness and found it hard to understand how Erny of all people, who knew the place so well and had described it so often, did not.

Aware that he was letting a good deal of air out of the Northwest writers' conference balloon, which was intended in part to elevate awareness of the region's many qualities, Erny did his best to soften his impiety. He did this by lacing his opinion—that the Pacific Northwest really wasn't a unique place—with humor. The reverence of regionalism, he would suggest, was universally practiced to excess.

> We are, we feel, a region set apart; west of the Rockies and indefinitely north from the California line lies a world with its own particular past, its own distinct traditions and values, its own future. We have not forgotten the geographer's remark that here in the northwest was every element needed for the man and the civilization of the future. This is our land, like unto no other.
>
> So we do believe. Yet love of one's own acre is so universal a love that there is no patch of earth which does not have its proud devotees faithfully weaving around its songs and legends and that whole body of beautifully colored literature which becomes a minor patriotism. We send east our gift boxes of holly and choice fruits to express our spirit of regional richness; immediately back from the east, in like spirit, come boxes of maple cream, smoked turkey, Virginia ham and Iowa sausage. We believe our apples to be the world's choicest. Your upper New York state farmer prefers his own apple which gets its juices unassisted by an irrigation ditch. We admit no potato to equality with our Netted Gem. The man of Maine simply smiles. All this is good and accustomed rivalry; it symbolizes our ability—which God gave us to subdue our natural discontent—to associate ourselves with a place and to see that place as incomparably fair. The cooking may be unbearable, the fleas darken the earth, the corn turns black under the heat—but the air, the air my friends, is the finest air a man can breathe.

As this issue was resolving in his mind, he was also settling down to *The Adventurers*. This was the project by which he intended to leap the chasm between the serial format and the honest-to-God, sprawling, smoldering, historic-romantic novel that *Long Storm* had not quite managed to be.

Erny Haycox and agent Syd Sanders. Sanders served as Erny's agent for seven years, beginning in 1930, before Haycox met him in person.

A scene from the movie, *Stagecoach*, the film created from a Haycox short story that launched John Wayne into stardom in 1939.

Erny Haycox with Sam Goldwyn in Hollywood, 1939.

The *Sunbeam*, a boat Erny purchased in 1941, used for weekend escapes, and sold in 1943.

Jill, Jim, and Mary Ann in 1941 during the family's round-the-country tour, which included Cuba, where this photograph was taken.

The Haycoxes began construction in 1939 of what they called the Big House, located on seven acres in Portland's West Hills, and moved into it in 1940.

The two-story library and study at the Big House, which Ernest Haycox used more for evening reading than writing. He did the latter in an office in downtown Portland.

Erny Haycox, with ever-present cigar, at the library desk that friend Jim Marshall regarded as fancy and formal and thus unrepresentative of Haycox.

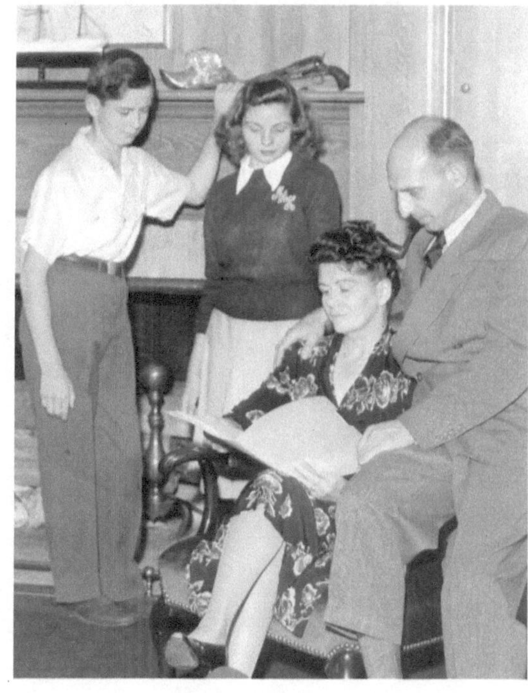

The Haycox family at home, 1943.

Fedora and pipe in place, Haycox pauses for a publicity photo in 1941.

Erny Haycox with an aging Duchess in 1941.

Ernest Haycox with Chief Clerk Earl Goodwin (standing) of Multnomah County Draft Board No. 1, which Haycox would chair for almost six years during World War II.

Mary Ann and Jill at the launching of the *Patrol Craft* 572 at the Albine Engine and Machine Works yard in Portland in 1942.

Erny and Ward Bond admire a six-shooter in fall 1945.

Erny (center) joined (from left) Lloyd Bridges, Dana Andrews, Patricia Roc, and Andy Devine on the set of *Canyon Passage* at Diamond Lake, Oregon, 1945.

Erny and Mary Ann ride in an open car during a parade marking the Portland premiere of *Canyon Passage* in 1946.

Dwight Griswold, three-term Nebraska governor, vice presidential candidate, and postwar foreign aid administrator, invited Erny to Greece in 1947.

A relaxed Erny Haycox in the Wallowa Mountains at Minam Meadows in 1946.

OPPOSITE: A head-table grouping at a *Canyon Passage* dinner event in 1946 included (left to right): front row—Haycox, Joan Bennett, and her husband Walter Wanger (the film's producer); back row—Hoagy Carmichael, Yvonne De Carlo, an unidentified woman, and Oregon Governor Earl Snell.

Erny and Jill on the beach in Hawaii, 1947.

Erny takes a break in Hawaii during a year he termed his "second adolescence."

Father and son on the Rogue River in southern Oregon in 1948. The hard-used hat was his weekend and casual-wear companion for many years.

Father and daughter in 1950, following Erny's operation for cancer.

Tools of the trade.
Erny Haycox's typewriter
and homemade typing stand,
in the Haycox Memorial Library
room, University of Oregon, Eugene.

—12—

The Accidental Profession

OF ALL HIS WRITING YEARS, 1947 MAY HAVE BEEN THE MOST dispiriting. He struggled with *The Adventurers* into summer, could not make it right, and finally set it aside. He then began research for a new serial novel, *Head of the Mountain*, though he had earlier sworn off that brand of fiction. He had reconsidered for economic reasons but admitted later that his heart wasn't in it. Fortunately, though he hadn't written a short story since December 1945, he hadn't forgotten how. Between April and October, eight shorts rolled off the line and *Collier's* and the *Post* both seemed pleased to have him back.

He had sworn to limit distracting activities but agreed to lead a fund-raising drive to help finance a student center at the University of Oregon, and that involved a good deal of time and travel. It would also lead to an incandescent moment when the university president, H. K. Newburn, and several associates appeared unannounced at the Big House one evening. Erny ushered them into the library, from which could shortly be heard loud voices, his above all. They accused him of misdirecting campaign funds to his own account and it did not dawn on him that they were kidding, that this was simply part of an honorary-society induction ceremony. He seethed for days.

Unexpected visitors in 1947 also included actors Thomas Mitchell and Ward Bond. The pair were returning to Hollywood from a shooting location on a summer Sunday and found themselves in Portland with several hours between planes. Unable to buy or beg a drink anywhere else—

Oregon being dry on the sabbath—they came to see their "dear friend." The modest Haycox liquor supply was quickly exhausted and Jim was sent abroad on his bicycle to obtain augmentation from neighbors. Mitchell was charmed by the Big House, which may have reminded him a bit of his grand residence in *Gone With the Wind*, and retained its architect to do one for him in California.

In addition to fund-raising jaunts, travel this year included a January holiday in Hawaii with Jill and three other couples. The Hawaiian vacation put Jill in a good mood. "Daddy is a swell guy," she wrote to Sister. "Don't think I don't know it." He also spent time in Hollywood, where producer Wanger was proposing a long-term deal, and went on several local expeditions for story material. The best of these in Erny's mind were a couple of summer days with former Oregon Governor Oswald West (1911–15), who helped him locate some of the first roads and land claims in the Willamette Valley. He greatly admired West (many still do) and, had there been time, West would have provided background and probably a character for a novel flavored with the smoke and spice of early Oregon politics. Late in the year, Erny took two months off and went to Greece, where good friend Dwight Griswold had been appointed by President Truman to head an American aid mission. He was classified and paid as a government consultant but the objective was to publicize and rally support for America's postwar involvement in Europe. Back home in late December, he summed the year in a note to Ray Palmer Tracy, a teller of tales like himself and therefore a proper confessor: "As with any other writer, my soul (sic) has had its wandering spell, and we, my soul and I, have asked the old, old questions concerning the future, concerning art, concerning immortality, concerning personal happiness—concerning every goddam thing but that of the next story. It has been, perhaps, the second adolescence that comes to every writing man. I hope it is ended; but of that one never knows." ◆

In the first half of 1947, *The Adventurers* was that subject most on his mind. The first draft was four days from completion when he wrote to agent Sanders in March:

It comes close to 400 pages, twice my normal story. You can see the immense amounts of nonsense to be cut out, the tightening needed, the adding, subtracting and modifying of characters, the changes and pointing up of values. The best character is the bad girl. She never changes on me, beginning to end. Number Two girl—who marries hero—is thoroughly consistent but possibly suffers by being out of too many scenes. The hero needs work done on him. As with many of my leading men, he searches for the light never seen on land or sea and as a result he has his formless, footless moments. The story has a tendency to ravel out, to straggle to an end rather than to come to explosion. My serial training spots this at once; novelistically it may be all right, but I believe I'll need to strong-arm the ending to some extent. I won't modify my earlier appraisal of this story. As of now it is—in the light of what I wanted to do—a stinker.

Nevertheless, my story ideas have been further clarified. In the ancient romantic-realistic classification system (which is an unreal concept at best) I have been on the romantic side. All my stories take the up note and all my characters are touched by a natural optimism, and by a certain gilding. My precise difficulty has been to inject realism into my people and to remove the Oliver Optic touch, the thought that God's got his eye on us and we're all right. So then I've been at war with myself. I don't want soapy romance but I cannot abide the modern concept of realism which I think is nothing better than a dreary accent on unimportant facts.

The best I can say of *Long Storm* and the present novel is that they've taught me to reject the whole romantic-realistic idea. The thing I want to do is clearer than it was—though the method of doing it is still not wholly clear. A valid story for me must drive straight down to the most elemental urges and confusions in people. Actually that's about all I'm interest[ed] in. There is a certain austerity, or simplicity or actual grandeur in people involved in their own fundamental conflicts which the moderns don't catch at all in writing. I suppose that's the way I'm trying to drive.

I think, too, that I have a chore to do in the matter of actual prose. I can, at times, in the clutch, deliver a certain amount of sweep and feeling. Otherwise, when it's a dull morning, my style gets somewhat crabbed and

> unenlightened. Some of this lack rises out of deliberate restraint on my part, a fear of slopping over. It is self-conscious in that I don't want to move over to the corny side, which is very easily done, and which I sometimes do, I fear.

Three months and two revisions later, the story still wasn't right but he let Sanders take a look. Excerpts from three letters in June and early July reflected his own displeasure, and his agent's as well. On June 17, he wrote:

> It's down from 395 pages to 270. It will require another revision, for the cutting has left it lumpy. More than that there will need to be a revaluing of scenes. And—this is the important thing—I shall have to make up my mind about the need of a greater conflict (business conflict) for the hero. It's not the novel I set out to do, I'm sorry to say.

> We return to the thing which probably causes most of the characters to turn out as they do [he wrote on June 26]. The idea that nothing matters—that there is no pattern and no logic to any life. Clara and Revelwood end up that way. Sheridan, believing in pattern, gets kicked around but keeps going. As long as his energy holds out he'll keep going. That's about all the justification his life has—or any life, according to the philosophy of this story. Since that's the idea, it follows that none of the characters can be carving out their destinies.

> You comment on the two brothers of Katherine going over the falls [he noted on July 3]. Your reaction was, "Why does she deserve this?" That is the point of the story. She doesn't, but it happens to her. It happens, one way or another, to all of us. Nature—including that part of nature which is our own waywardness—is the villain of the piece. My trouble is that I didn't get it across.
>
> My failure in this year goes back to something we've discussed many years. I do intrude too much thought into a story, via the character's reflections. That is a symptom of what is probably my major weakness as a writer, a lack of inventiveness in scenes. For want of an effective scene I sometimes strong-arm the thing across by means of thought. Still, I doubt

a straight scene would entirely please me, since it would pretty much destroy the undertones which come out of a character engaged in his internal struggle. A scene has two dimensions. The gestures and reactions of the characters supply something of a third dimension; but that is still not entirely enough. It is the soliloquy of a Hamlet without the benefit of quotation marks which supplies the fourth dimension.

Meanwhile, Walter Wanger, who had produced *Stagecoach* as well as *Canyon Passage*, was suggesting a long-term movie deal. It sounded great, Erny told Syd, although the benefits and details weren't entirely clear to him.

Two or three things probably motivate Wanger in suggesting such a set-up. First, he makes no outright payments, but has the deal on the cuff till the money comes through the box office. That is his protection, and my wait. This of course is offset by a possible advantage to me in the shape of larger income. Second, this is nebulous but might be in his mind—with [the] American Authors' Authority being discussed in Hollywood, and so strongly favored by the Screen Writers' Guild—that he could protect himself against this kind of a closed shop by having a prior contract with a writer which subsequent closed-shop conditions couldn't legally touch. As a third motive, he might think I can supply him with stories at a certain standard level. He's had luck with two of them.

My program seems to look this way: *The Adventurers* will be done in three weeks. Then I turn to research on the next serial which I want to be a *Post* or *Collier's* serial on the *Canyon Passage* order. I'd like to get in a short or two during that research time—or do the Hollywood job if it develops. Then the writing of the serial. If there's anything left of the year it will be shorts. I want to get back on those.

On the Wanger deal: We started this thing with the idea of tax savings, via a long-term capital gain set-up. It turns out there's nothing like that now involved. What we've got is in effect the sale of one story a year for a certain number of years at a fixed price, plus a bonus of 20% of the profits. On the plus side it gives us an assured market for a considerable time. I like that.

> On the negative side, it pins us to a sale price not to exceed $50,000 per story. Assuming the possibility of one of my stories coming in as a best seller, our agreement would cut out any possibility of a sale to Hollywood at a really handsome price. The 20% stock interest is, of course, supposed to offset this—and might do so if dividends were yearly declared, and if no unreasonable costs were added to the operating budget.
>
> I trust Wanger's basic honesty. Yet I realize he's an excellent businessman, and one who will probably be the number one producer in town before he's through. I'm perfectly willing to go along, provided we've got our own interests fully protected.

Mary Baker of the Sam Jaffe Agency, Erny's direct representative in Hollywood, was involved in the Wanger discussions, and to her Erny confessed:

> I've never gotten this gross and net business unraveled. In a normal deal—Rogell's deal or the proposed Wanger deal—what percentage does the producer stand to receive? In either of these deals I scarcely know whether I'm talking about money or marbles.
>
> As for the picture we saw [*Heaven Only Knows*], it looks like it might have possibilities. The first half of the story had weaknesses here and there. Against that was a fine job by [Robert] Cummings, by Jorja [Curtright]—and an adequate performance by [Brian] Donlevy. The little boy, I suppose, is all right. Since I break out in a 100 per cent rash at the sight of any child star, I'm not competent to judge him. The dialogue was put out with nice restraint, and the ending is quite strong. What's your hard-boiled opinion?
>
> I note Hedda Hopper says "it is rumored" that it is a sneaker. That's the beginning of the build-up, I presume.

As *The Adventurers* wound down, he looked ahead to the next project—the serial novel—and gave Syd Sanders a quick tour of the scene.

> The first story (1864) is the opening of Eastern Oregon. The emigrants passed over it earlier but never stopped. A gold discovery brought people back to it. Auburn, the first town, was nothing but brush on the side of a hill; six months later it had 500 houses and five thousand people. Four

years later it was back to about 100 people. Today there's nothing at all, not a stick or stone. Canyon City, another gold rush town, came up from nothing and became the kind of place Bret Harte romanticized. Joaquin Miller began there. People didn't think much of him. I still don't.

These two towns, plus a few other strictly stag camps, were a long way off. Supplies came up from Portland, via the Columbia, to The Dalles. That was the depot town. From The Dalles pack outfits struck into an empty country, high desert, deep stone rivers, heavy pine forests, badland formations—every known variety of scenery. It was around a two-hundred mile run from The Dalles into these mining settlements, with an occasional isolated ranch or so-called "hotel" here and there (meals in a cabin, bed in the brush). The Dalles was the jumping off place. Anybody wanting to disappear just took the boat to The Dalles, bought a horse and grub, and vanished.

It was Indian time. There were no major battles, no decisive campaigns. It was a case of perpetual threat from roving bands who now and then caught somebody off first base and butchered the outfit, or knocked over a single family. The trails were guarded by small detachments of regulars and volunteers who rode themselves ragged. The regulars were too few and did very well; the volunteers sometimes did well and sometimes were strictly on the comic opera side. Some of them got killed.

There were highwaymen on the trails and stories of "white savages." Many murders and much crude violence. In Canyon City the cemetery was on a ridge several hundred feet above town, with a switchback road leading up to it. They tried a man, convicted him and sentenced him. (There were no minor penalties. You went free or you got hung.) They put the fellow in a wagon and started him up the hill to hang him conveniently near the cemetery. People swarmed up the hillside, running past the condemned. He called out: "What the hell's your hurry? Nothing's going to happen till I get there."

As was his custom, Erny would flavor the new story with eyewitness accounts of that era and Oregon's 1860s gold fever. One whose boyhood memories came close to both period and place was Phil Metschan, a Portland hotel operator and a friend. Erny asked him:

> Can you close your eyes and recall these descriptive bits: 1. The appearance of the stage you rode on, the driver, the passengers, the fare. 2. The appearance of the stage stations, inside and out. Yard, dining room, bedroom, facilities. Meals. Type of house construction. How settled or unsettled were the various stretches of country? Can you recall if people were still wearing much hardware? Was the Dayville-Mitchell area sheep country at that time?
>
> ---
>
> Harney has turned into nothing but a scatter of ranch houses. Do you recall what it looked like in the '80s? About what year was the appendix operation performed on Pleas Hankins by Fell and Ashford? Was chloroform used? Can you remember when the waltz came into vogue to supplement the square dances? Can you recall when you first saw the two-step?

Metschan received several such detailed requests for information and composed a half-dozen long letters in reply.

Aspiring writers asked for help and, although sufficiently burdened with his own tasks, Erny tried to accommodate, particularly if the petitioner was a war veteran. To a young man who was writing of his experiences in a Japanese POW camp, he offered a lengthy critique:

> It is not dramatic to say that you set out on a certain day, traded six bars of soap for a shirt and six pesos, transferred the pesos into canned goods and came out with a profit. The dramatic way is [to] set a scene. You start in the morning. You meet a man with the shirt. You sit down in the sun and start haggling. It's a hot sun and you sweat. He sweats. You see slyness in him as he dickers. You try to outguess him as he's trying to outguess you. Ideas flash through your mind. Some incident happens nearby—this brought into the scene to give it reality and breadth. You conclude your dicker. You rise and go on. This is a scene. It is story. The other way—a straight recitation of a given number of facts—is not.
>
> Men under strain talk of a lot of things. There is tragedy, humor, lust and brutality in this conversation. Men betray themselves in talking. A married man in this camp will think about his wife. Is she faithful? That will torture some men. Others may be past the point of caring. You've seen men break. In terms of scene, what's it like? I throw all of this in rather

indiscriminately to highlight the point that you need to review those days and to bring back specific instances which you can set down. You began this way. Later the story flattens and runs along too much on a level.

To another beginning writer, he recommended verbal compression:

> You are trying to make this man into a very tough character. You seek to do it by laying on the adjectives. This, I think, points to another writing rule. You create the effects you are after not by laying on the words but rather by putting a character through a scene and permitting him to demonstrate himself. Naturally, you must use adjectives when you write the scene, but it is not necessary to load them on until the sentence breaks down. Visualize your scene carefully and draw an exact picture. Use your words sparingly and you'll find your scene or your incident coming out as sharp and definite as you wish.

An offer of payment for this personal consultation was declined. The advice, Erny explained, "isn't that good." He had no use for collective authorship, explaining to one fellow that he wouldn't consider a joint venture and, to another, that the claimed benefits of American Authors' Authority, in addition to being spurious, were inappropriate. The AAA proposed to increase the bargaining power of writers through cooperative effort, but this sounded very much like a labor union to Mr. Haycox.

> I guess the answer now is the same as it was ten or more years ago. I don't read other men's manuscripts, and thus I may pick my story backgrounds and situations without the charge than I have improperly borrowed from anybody. Over and above that is another reason: I could not work with another man—for then the idea would be neither his nor mine, and if I am to do a convincing job of story telling, the idea's got to be mine.

> The proponents of AAA have pointed out that it will bring to writers the same advantages now secured by musicians under [James Caesar] Petrillo. I can think of nothing I would rather not have than a czar of the Petrillo type controlling my business.

> There can always be improvements . . . [but] writing is and can only be a matter of the survival of the fittest. No power, no form of guaranteed security, no type of socialization, can guarantee a mediocre writer an audience. The man has but one obligation, which is to tell that story . . . in such a way that people will read it. If he can't do that he is not entitled to any kind of protection.

It was in some ways difficult to understand his profession, he said, or to fully explain some of its current, tortured trends.

> It is a strange thing that writing—the most common of the arts—is perhaps the hardest to teach and has less of a formal approach than any of the arts. Music, painting, sculpturing, acting—these all have accepted routines through which the beginner must pass. They all have organized classwork, study methods, studio hours, finger exercises. Writing never has been thus set up as an art. Universally, writers straggle into writing by the back door, the side door, or through the cellar. There isn't any front door. Stevenson possibly came as close to being a conscious learner as we have to show; yet he had to organize his own procedures. I've often wonder[ed] at this and have come to feel that perhaps the lack of teaching routes in writing is the result of the way in which writers are recruited. Seldom do we begin this business as young people dedicated to the idea. The common story is that of a man turning to writing after he has failed at something else, or has given up some other profession. More or less, writers are accidents.

> Everybody wants to read good adventure, yet our times are not in tune with simplicity. The taste, or the mode, is to overlay everything with an extra layer of meaning. We have become quite conscious of schisms, social implications, propagandas and artistic definitions—to the point that nothing apparently is what it seems. If indeed a story is what it seems—according to our intellectuals—it is a poor thing devoid of stature in their eyes. Most American writers, by consequence, suffer a bit of a complex. They try to measure up to the standards of significance and almost always they press their stroke and overwrite.

His frustrations in 1947 weren't limited to novel work. One of his modern shorts stirred up a small tempest at *Collier's* and another, he told Sanders, had somehow gotten away from him.

> I had no intention of advocating free love in the story [which was "Affair's End," published in *Collier's* in August 1947]. My thought was to take a couple of people through the turbulence of first meeting and first adjustment. The ending was meant to indicate that they were on their way to the usual . . . ending. If it seems otherwise in the fade-out, I suppose it is obscure writing—which can be clarified in about three sentences. Tell Ken I'm not yet moving out into the wild blue yonder of unregulated sex.

> I write so painfully, and rewrite so much these days that when I'm through with a job I've lost contact with the essential story result. Next week I'll send you one in which this is particularly true ["Dead Man Trail," which would appear in *Saturday Evening Post*, September 1948). It is nothing but one man chased two hundred miles by four men. I had a hell of a good story in the beginning. Eight pages of rewrite later I don't think I've got a story. So it goes.

He was depressed but undeterred and, to a disgruntled Jim Marshall he expressed the faith of renewal and diversity.

> It's been a long, hard year for me and I understand that jaded feeling. I've had it. My prescription is nothing more than sleep and rest; it makes all the difference with me. I've done nothing but experiment the last two years in stories and have little to do with the markets—except Hollywood. Now I'm breaking out of the cycle and will begin to appear in print again. But it's been a tricky time. One of those times a man invents for himself in order to prove something or other. A man can look at one set of walls too long. Go somewhere and pick up seashells for a couple weeks. Or build a big basement and go in for model railroading. Wouldn't mind doing that myself.
>
> I'm in the middle of a campaign to raise $600,000 for my university to build a Student Union. After that's done I've got notions for a much larger

deal, over a period of ten years. to raise five or ten million for endowed chairs for professors who are big enough to teach youngsters what ought to be taught—in the way it ought to be taught.

Somewhat withdrawn from politics, Erny kept in touch, advising Senator Harry P. Cain (R-Washington) of the mood in Hawaii and Senator Guy Cordon (R-Oregon) on tax policy.

> I have been over in the islands for a month and find those folks hotter than mustard for statehood. The big owners are not too happy about it, feeling they can operate to better advantage under the existing situation. Looking at the strict politics of such an arrangement it appears that statehood would add two Republican senators. Economically, I can't see much ahead for the islands. There appears to be no way of breaking up the existing three-crop system—sugar, pineapple and tourists.

> Almost every businessman in Portland today sooner or later faces the question of expansion. Should he put six more stools in his restaurant and hire another waiter? Should he add a couple more machines and take on three new mechanics? His answer—among the many men I've talked with at least—is to deliberately stop growing at the precise point the added responsibility and risk seems unjustified by diminishing returns. In contrast, every large corporation is divorced from this personal management strain and risk; it therefore expands to get a greater and greater dollar volume from which to slice its pennies of profit.
>
> What you have then is a tax law driving personal management one direction and corporation management another. The penalty is on the little man and the incentive is held out to the big one. It is a nice thought to first cut the lower bracket tax rates and to leave the existing load in the middle bracket; but if that is the present policy, another policy automatically flows out of it—which is the encouragement of big business. We will not have in this country, under such a philosophy, the annual crop of new ventures springing up.

And to a Portland business friend, he put his foot down—not too hard—on gubernatorial aspirations.

I can think of a good many ways of being miserable for four years, one of which is to be governor of Oregon. I am by nature somewhat of a political animal, and I have fooled around the shady fences of politics for several years, never permitting myself to become too serious. Two things are required of any man who runs for office, (1) a good deal of vanity, in which I fully qualify, and (2) a decent bank account, which the government, through its internal revenue department, has fixed up just dandy. There is probably a third qualification—some desire to do a bit of good. I have that desire but think it would be probably a very smart thing if I stuck to my writing a bit longer.

Congresswoman Helen Gahagan Douglas (D-California), best remembered as Richard Nixon's liberal opponent in a 1950 senatorial contest, asked Erny to lend his good name to the creation of a Roosevelt national forest. She shouldn't have bothered.

I do strongly wish to see such a national forest, and I am flattered that you wish me to be a national sponsor. If it were only the redwoods involved I'd be happy to be considered one of your group. Unfortunately—from my point of view—you have added an extraneous and unnecessary thing in making it a memorial to Franklin Roosevelt. I can't join you.

The late president had many strong and great qualities. With these he also had some petty qualities, one of which was to permit Secretary Ickes to wash out Hoover's name on a dam and substitute Boulder. I have always regarded that tacit approval to be something less than plain charity of spirit. Possibly I expect too much consistency in greatness, and perhaps I ought to overlook the heavy streaks of plain yellow fat which interlard the lean and good streaks of famous men. I ought to but I find I can't, for I recall that Franklin Roosevelt, seeking an everlasting record for himself in history, could not beat the competition of other strong men and destroyed them politically wherever he could, and had very little kindness and magnanimity toward them.

He will have his record, and many things shall be named for him. As for the redwoods, other men worked faithfully to preserve these trees long before Roosevelt gave them attention, and if there is to be a memorial it should go to one of them.

He wrote regularly to Mary Ann, seeking to buoy her spirits—she wasn't all that keen about college—and polish her social skills. Some of his observations were decent character analysis, but Sister must have found him a bit of a nag at times. He followed up on a visit to Eugene in this well-intended but pestering manner:

> When we pulled out that afternoon, I noticed that you walked right by a fellow waiting on the Kappa steps for his girl. He looked at you—but I don't think you looked at him. What have I been telling you about slowing down and turning on the charm? He wasn't your customer, but that's not the point. The point is, you ought to have a smile and a word for people you pass. As for boys, they're not as aggressive as they like to think. They need a break—and that's what a girl does by her smile and her pleasant, natural manner.
>
> One other thing. Don't go overboard too fast when a man gets interested in you. If you show your seriousness too fast, you may scare the fellow. Just see to it that your charm is working on him—by being wholly natural, and pleasant. Have a line of talk, and make him feel you're having a nice time with him. It's up to a girl to create the warm atmosphere around a man—if she likes him; but she mustn't let him see that she's pitching.
>
> You've got all the qualities; you've got everything. It's just a matter of technique—and self-confidence. Just lift your head and step out. That advice, my little cucumber, comes from your old man who was, in his youth, far more reserved and shy and introverted than you'll ever be. You get some of your reserve from me—but you haven't got nearly as many kinks and doubts and fears in you [as] I had.

> I've been watching folks in the lobby [he was now in Washington, D.C., on his way to Greece]. . . . The southern women are not as pretty as tradition makes them out to be. . . . Only in one respect do these gals—the young ones—seem to live up to their supposed glamor. I observe that when a girl sits with a man, or walks through the lobby with him, she seems to give him plenty of attention. She pays him the courtesy of making him believe she's quite interested in him. She talks, she laughs,

she listens to what he has to say as though it were important. Some of these men don't look so hot to me, but still the girl goes to work and does her stuff.

Erny received a good deal of fan mail—almost all of which he answered—and many communiques from those who professed admiration but, more to the point, needed a favor. Would he mind sending a copy of a song written by a certain lady to Roy Rogers, on the assumption that the cowboy singer would more likely open his envelope than hers? Would he please examine this or that piece of the correspondent's writing and, if merited, recommend it to one of his publishing contacts? Would he lend his good name to a good cause, one of which was a mail-order fish business, and to which he replied:

I did some commercial fishing in Alaska after the first war, and as a result of the experience, I have no earthly use for the salmon—either to eat them, to look at them, or to praise them. Standing hip deep in those things in the hold of a boat, with gurry all over me, and smelling the end product of fish piled together two days too long, I have a well developed antipathy for the brutes.

Here and there, he offered mild rebukes. His Rotary Club's dismissal policy was unfair.

I noticed in *Spokes* the dropping of Curly Llewellyn for nonattendance. That struck me as not being quite cricket. I hope a final warning is given errant members which will permit them either to adjust their affairs for better attendance or, if they can't do that, resign without embarrassment.

The Boy Scout organization, while commendable, was overdone.

With cubbing we now start too young and on the other end of the trail we hold youngsters too long. At one stage scouting is all very real to a boy—but presently he reaches a point where the thing is self-conscious play acting. To the outsider, too, it is sometimes a jarring note to see a six-foot lad all trapped out in uniform, badges, medals, whistle cord, etc.

The state highway department was missing a bet.

> We have little breathing spaces along the Coast Highway, and an occasional one scattered elsewhere. But along the 300 miles plus of 99E and W, I cannot at this moment recall a single acre, half acre or lot which the highway commission has set up as a pull-off spot to give the motorist a breathing spell beside a drinking fountain and underneath a shade tree. A piece 200 feet long and 200 feet deep would be ample for most places. A dozen or two of these would not be terribly expensive, and Lord knows they'd be appreciated on a warm day.

And he observed to a newspaper friend that the city's Protestants, with whom he was nominally affiliated, were not well served.

> Were I a minister it's possible I might feel rather bitter toward the hypocrisies of my congregation. Still, I must say that the Protestant ministry of Portland is scarcely a challenging or particularly spiritual body. The Jews and Catholics have certain ancient disciplines and rituals to support them. The Protestants must go it entirely by spiritual depth and spiritual flaming out. But where are the ministers with that quality which make them the shape of fiercy swords illumined against the dark skies? Their leadership is comfortable, prosy and agreeable.

These were small, private thoughts. He did not wish them broadly cast and when it was suggested that his ministerial appraisal might contribute to a useful public discussion, he insisted that it not be published. "Of all subjects that's the worst to publicly argue," he replied; and besides, he'd had plenty of exposure, more than enough for a while. To another writer, he responded.

> I do appreciate your feeling that a Sunday piece on me would be justified. My feeling is that we ought to wait until another day. Four or five years ago somebody did an article on me for the *Sunday Oregonian* and meanwhile, I have been interested in activities—such as the university alumni work—which have given me a certain amount of publicity. Frankly, I don't think I justify any more mention at the present time.

Early in the year, Dwight Griswold, now part of the American occupation government in Europe, suggested that Erny come over and have a look around. He was interested but didn't finally commit to the trip until September, by which time Griswold had one of the toughest jobs in Europe—head of the American aid mission to Greece, where a full-scale civil war was in progress. Erny would be employed as a government consultant with no particular duties spelled out, but the clear task was to justify to an ambivalent public this early U.S. effort to thwart Communism in southern Europe. "The trip will have some prestige value," he explained to Syd Sanders, "and perhaps in addition I can sell a piece or maybe two on it." As his friend Griswold harboured senatorial ambitions, there were incidental benefits to be gained from publicizing the aid program, of which the writer was possibly aware.

—13—

"They are also terrifically democratic"

IN 1947, GREECE WAS IN TATTERS, RAVAGED BY A LONG AND BRUTAL German occupation during which hundreds of thousands died by starvation or execution. Inflation had destroyed economic activity and personal wealth. And now there was a civil war, Communist-backed guerrillas attempting to dislodge the country's fractious democratic regime. The United States had come to the rescue with $340 million of economic aid but this was a new game for a traditionally wary and isolationist nation and Erny, in a letter to a friend, wondered how it would play out.

> The test of our policy is not in Washington. It's in Greece and in Turkey—in terms of using this money effectively to fill bellies, restore industry—to keep it out of the wrong pockets and make every dollar work well. If we're smart enough to do that, I believe the money's well spent. But if we're not, then we've wasted our money, and presently the public will say, "To hell with it—let those birds go their own way." In that event we've lost Europe and we'll fight the next war in a very lonely fashion. So it seems to me that Greece is a testing ground for us in the way of applied savvy. It's the thing England did so well for so long—her administrators and public servants in far off places. It's the thing we know so little about—and have got to learn so very damned fast.

Erny spent about a week in the East before going overseas. He was briefed, medically and psychologically evaluated and inoculated in Washington D.C., and then hung out at the Algonquin Hotel in New York for a couple of days, waiting transportation. He dined twice with Jack Chord, who, after a spell with a couple of big midwestern merchandisers, was now display director for Montgomery Ward in Chicago. A frequent business traveler, Jack had managed several Portland visits in the '40s. He always remembered birthdays with inventive tokens and produced entertaining, rhythmic letters. He was a widower now; his wife had died in 1946, an event he mentioned in a letter to Mary Ann with odd detachment. It had simply been a terrible week, he explained: a car accident and a traffic ticket, a slip on the ice, the loss of some clothes in a small apartment fire and—oh yes—Dorothy died after an operation. ◆

Erny crossed to Europe in one of the earliest commercial transatlantic flights, an adventure in itself. The airborne passage on a four-motor Lockheed Constellation took thirty-six hours, with stops in Newfoundland, Ireland, Paris, Geneva, and Rome. It was, by modern standards, rather basic transportation; on the Atlantic leg, security was a pair of large, inflatable life rafts for the ten crewmembers and thirty passengers. Breakfast was a tired Spam sandwich which, he was certain, had preceded him on at least one flight.

> There's no radio or directional beam as there is on land (writing this while 15,000 feet over the Atlantic). We fly strictly by navigation. Every so often the navigator takes his sextant and shoots the sun, the moon or the stars through a glass bubble on top of the cabin, does a little arithmetic and comes up with his guess. Well, Ireland's a big country—and how can he miss?
>
> The captain of this packet, I discover, has never made the Atlantic hop before; neither have the co-pilots. They come from the transcontinental run. But the navigator has. May the Lord bless this little man.

In Greece, Erny spent a fair amount of time visiting and travelling with Griswold and his aides and much more in his own pursuits. But he was never alone, requiring an interpreter and, almost anywhere outside Athens, an armed escort—for he was, after all, in the middle of a civil war. He interviewed officers of the American and British military missions, a number of aid-program specialists, several members of the Greek government, journalists, and many civilians. The latter were a treat—an indomitable, autarchic, querulous, and cheerful caste that no writer of fiction could possibly have improved, let alone imagined.

The article he wrote was respectful of Griswold ("an excellent governor of Nebraska, he was perfectly equipped for this kind of work") but brutally frank about early, disappointing results of the aid program. Erny wasn't anybody's press agent, observing that the Greek army appeared reluctant to engage and the government, a coalition, seemed incapable of action. Griswold and his state department bosses would have to be more forceful and that, in turn, required the American public's support, which wasn't entirely evident. "Any gap between public opinion and administrative policy," his article would conclude, "is a weakness the Russians will at once capitalize; for they believe we will not remain firm."

Jill did not accompany Erny to Greece. He asked her to come along, but she refused and then fumed when friends assumed she hadn't been invited. In Athens, he received his first letter from home—a bitter, accusing thing.

> You must be having a fine time amongst all the big shots; anyway they are the kind of people you enjoy, and they speak your language as the saying goes. It seems funny to me that you have had no social life of any kind, except for the little trip out to Sanders. I suppose it would be so unimportant to you that it would scarcely be worth mentioning. I have changed quite considerably, I think. Just as soon as I get through with the things that I'm doing, I plan to look for help in a big way. Figure I have been a servant too long. If we have money to give away, I might as well spend it. Hope you are enjoying yourself and dropping ashes everywhere. ◆

His letters home often described living conditions in Greece. They were bad, food being scarce and, like everything else, prohibitively expensive. But things had been worse.

> There's one smell in this country that I caught the moment I got here and couldn't identify—and you know I'm very good at detecting smells.

At first I thought it was DDT, which has been sprayed in and on almost every house in Greece. But it wasn't that. During the latter part of the week I began to detect it on myself. It's in the buildings, in clothes, everywhere, not a really offensive smell but still fairly easy to catch. I talked to other people about it—and finally found the answer. It's olive oil. All cooking is done in olive oil and everybody eats olives. That's the only fat the Greeks get into their bodies. There are no other fats available.

The Germans made no attempt to feed the Greeks. They stripped the country of all food and animals and sent [everything] back to Germany. Melas [a Greek attached to the American mission who was Griswold's interpreter] said that people—many of them his friends—would fall on the streets from hunger and he'd help them home. Then the time came when he had to turn his eyes away from people who fell. There were too many of them. The Germans had a policy of shooting fifty Greeks for every German who got ambushed in Athens. They'd walk into an office, or a store, take the first fifty they found and lug them off to jail. Nobody would hear any more about these people. Maybe two weeks later there'd be a list of people in the paper . . . "accidentally dead."

He would get a sense of the country's economic collapse from Leno Melas, who took him home for dinner one evening, and from encounters and observations on the street.

He's one of those fellows [this is Melas] who comes from an old and rather prominent first family who's come on hard days and now works at whatever he can get. On the way to his house we crossed one of the main boulevards and he pointed to a huge stone house which was three stories high and occupied half the block, exactly like one of the old millionaire mansions on 5th Avenue NY. "I was born in that corner room," he said. Now it is used by the Greek supreme court. So then we went up a very narrow street, turned into an alley and stepped into a dark hallway of a rather ratty looking place, walked up a flight of stairs and stepped into a room—his living room. Coming out of rather gloomy and drab surroundings, this room took me by surprise. One end was solid, from floor to ceiling, in book cases made of black carved wood out of Greek temples, many hundreds of years old. The cases were solidly filled with all the Greek and European classics. Some of the books were printed as far back as 1592. He had a glassed table with bits of ancient jewelry, hammered gold bracelets. He had a whole string of clay figurines across another wall — stuff dug up from before the time of Christ. On still another wall he had a panel with the silver crusted pistols and swords which had belonged to his family when they fought in the Greek war for independence, in 1820. Apparently he had once had a much larger collection, but during the occupation the Germans had appropriated many things, and since then he has sold off pieces bit by bit to live on. He told me the story of a beach house which had been in his family a long while. Around 1944 he decided to sell it. Then inflation set in and he said that in two weeks' time he used up all the money he'd gotten for the house, just for living expenses. ◆

Just three years ago, the government, by decree, wiped out its debt, and all bank accounts and life insurance policies and all securities by declaring the old drachma valueless and then setting up a new drachma. So the average Greek's got no faith in paper money. As soon as he gets a few drachmas he converts . . . into gold sovereigns. There are about ten million of these coins floating around Greece—English money which the English government long ago ceased to circulate. When I came here two weeks ago it took 180,000 drachmas to buy a sovereign; now the price is 192,000 drachmas. . . . Almost every morning the first thing a merchant does is find out what the day's value of the sovereign is—and then he reprices all of his merchandise. Some merchants are reluctant to sell anything. The goods they have on their shelves are at least a solid thing.

Much of his family reportage described personal encounters. One of these involved General Nicholas Plastiras, who would have comfortably occupied a regimental command in one of the writer's cavalry episodes. The retired officer and politician, a national figure, was "a striking guy—six feet tall, white mustache tilted upward at the points, sharp brown eyes, a tanned, smooth face, a good sense of humor, and straight as a pole."

In the war with the Turks in Asia Minor in 1922, Plastiras was one of the officers who got the Greek army back from Asia without being

> completely destroyed. On the long march his troops became exhausted and lay down one night at the foot of a hill to sleep—the Turks chasing them. Plastiras didn't put out guards, knowing that the guards were so tired they'd fall asleep too. So that night his regiment had a rest and he went up to the top of the hill to stand guard. In 1922 he lead a revolt of the army and kicked the Greek king out of the country. Later he was prime minister and ordered the execution of certain army and government people he thought were traitors. After the war, the British brought him back again to be prime minister. That lasted for a while. . . . He's regarded by all people as honest and patriotic—but lacking in political judgment.

Erny's first expedition outside Athens was—of all things—a bird-hunting expedition involving Griswold and a few Greek notables, including the minister of security. Erny tagged along to see the countryside; he had no interest in the sport and, other than the .45 he had kept in 1919 and perhaps never fired after that year, owned no serviceable weapons. The expedition was accompanied by two truckloads of soldiers. The Greeks were understandably concerned with their Nebraska friend's safety, he observed: "If the guerillas captured Dwight, there'd just be hell to pay—and no $340 million for Greece." That night the Griswold party stayed at a large ranch "that occupies the entire valley. Mountains are on all sides of it, and guerillas are in the mountains. Occasionally they come down, raid the town, rip up a bit of railroad track . . . and go back to the hills. Sometimes they burn a house, kill somebody, and sometimes they capture a few village boys and take them back into the hills to forcibly serve as guerillas."

On the following day, Erny and Dwight Griswold tagged along with the hunters for a time but, tiring of this, returned to their vehicle and began talking to passers-by, people trickling down a mountain road to find work in the valley. One of these was "a pretty wild looking cooky, tattered pants, shoes about ready to fall off, blue shepherd's coat, black wild hair and whiskers, and a free and independent manner." He carried a shepherd's crook that Griswold erred in admiring, for the fellow insisted he accept it as a gift. The governor declined, momentarily.

> But the interpreter warned him to accept the gift, or [he would] offend the man. So Dwight did. Then the man invited us over to his village. He said: "I'll get a lamb and cook it, and we'll have a talk." I would have enjoyed it, but the interpreter said: "That means we'll spend half the afternoon getting to the village, then the fellow will take a couple hours finding his lamb. By the time he gets it slaughtered and cooked it will be late night, and of course, he'll insist we stay overnight." So we didn't. We gave him a drink . . . and asked him what his politics were. He looked around at the soldiers and got cagey. All he would say was, "We're all right," meaning he wasn't a communist.

The trip back to Athens would provide two more striking impressions of the people.

> As we left a lot of the men came up to say goodbye—and you'd have thought we were old friends sailing off the America, and one young man went over to a patch of a garden, picked some flowers, and handed them to Dwight. They are a sentimental, emotional people with wonderful manners, a fine sense of humor, and extremely intelligent. They are also terrifically democratic. Coming home, [Constantine] Rentis, who is a cabinet minister in the government, got in a argument with the driver (just a guy hired by the mission to drive cars at maybe $100 a month). The driver sailed right into Rentis and Rentis sailed right back at him. Neither the driver nor Rentis had the faintest notion that there was any difference of age or position between them. I've seen this everywhere I've been. Everybody in this country genuinely feels that he's as good as anybody else.

He attended a Rotary dinner in Athens and another at the local post of the American Legion, its membership consisting of Greeks who had earned U.S. citizenship through World War I army service. The head of this group was lucky to be breathing, he said, having enduring both German occupation and an equally unpleasant time when communists briefly controlled Athens and he had been jailed. "One by one men were taken upstairs to be tried by the commies. He heard some of his friends being beaten and killed. Before his turn, some communist who knew him and was friendly, got him out of the place and turned him loose. This sort of violence and narrow escape is a very common story here."

He gathered information during a string of lunches and interviews with Greek ministers and business executives. Mission sources were useful too, although, he thought, worth confirming. "My policy in this thing has been to go to the division chiefs in AMAG (American Mission for Aid to Greece) and hear what they're doing, and then go out in the field and actually see if they're doing it, or if it's just hot air . . ." On one day, this led him to the docks of Piraeus to observe the progress of incoming relief supplies. His driver insisted they visit the city's cemetery, where its director pressed him to examine its records for two years. One was 1942, under German occupation, during which almost 11,500 graves had been dug. Then there was 1946, the first year of American aid. Burials had declined to 1,800.

On the afternoon of this day, Erny boarded a sizable private yacht in the city's harbor for an overnight cruise with the Griswolds and several other couples to some nearby island. The vessel's owner was the local beer baron whose brewing ancestors, he was informed, had moved from Germany a century earlier when the Greek king of the moment was a thirsty Teuton.

> This morning, we went ashore on the island, saw a village and talked with a couple of ancient sisters living on a little patch of land—some cabbage, some olive trees, two goats. They pack water from the village, half a mile away. "I walk fast and make it in ten minutes," one of the sisters said. Her dress had been patched in every possible place, and the patches had been patched. No stockings. Old sandals, a scarf around her head. With people around her, it wasn't the place to ask a lot of sharp questions, so I didn't—but Griswold did. He asked her what she needed. She grinned and pointed around the place. "Everything," she said. She had been on the piece of land all her life—and her people had had the same chunk of land for perhaps 500 years. It looked pretty worn out, very thin and rocky. Most of Greece is nothing but rocks.

He spent his last days in Athens writing his article and Christmas shopping and arrived back in Portland on December 21. He had been gone seven weeks, which was for him a very long separation from his primary profession. Before resuming it, however, he would spend a couple of days on a letter incorporating his observations on Greece and suggestions for the aid program to Oregon Senator Wayne Morse.

The greatest roadblock to AMAG's operation is a complete lack of unity among the people. There is no sense of emergency, crisis or desperation in them. There's no feeling whatever of a national will slowly working its way toward decisive action. In Athens, you'd not know there was shooting going on in the north. Greeks have been individualists always, and their recent trials have made them more so. All they want, as individuals, is to be let alone, to make a living, and to take care of their own affairs.

It took us twenty-five years to subdue the Apache and the Sioux, who used precisely the same methods the guerillas now use. It is also a border warfare, neighbor against neighbor—the most demoralizing kind of a war. The guerillas pick their time and place; they have the initiative. The army is actually on the defensive. Every American and British military man believes it could do much more than it is doing, yet it is a puzzling thing to know just where the indecision and lack of enthusiasm originates. It may be among the rank and file who have no stomach for fighting, or who see no great urgency in it; it may be among the officer ranks who are afraid to take the responsibility for decisions; or it may be at the very top—among the civil or military leaders.

Griswold has great power. He has, actually, more power than he can use at this moment. Of necessity he must look over his shoulder at American public opinion. This the Greeks know. They have also come to the conclusion that the United States is committed past the power to withdraw. That makes them somewhat more independent in their bargaining.

As a flyspeck item, I think we ought to have a corps of investigators in Greece who will watch the flow of our goods from the time these goods land at Piraeus to the time they reach the hands of the ultimate users. And

> purely as personal opinion, I don’t think the important thing now is to have a liberal government in Greece for the sake of window-dressing. The important thing is to have any kind of government which will function.

It had been a long respite and he was probably refreshed by it. He would need that renewal, for the new serial novel wasn’t to be any six-week wonder.

—14—

"I said I'd not write one of those again . . ."

HIS MAGAZINE ARTICLE ON THE AID PROGRAM, "THE GREEKS Have Many Words for It," was passed on by his usual buyers as duplicative of other recent efforts. The *Reader's Digest*, which had run a Haycox piece in May 1947, found it short on the human-interest angle, which was their preference. Substantially condensed, it would find a home in the April 1948 issue of the *Atlantic Monthly* as the lead editorial report, unattributed. He supplemented this with more than a dozen foreign policy speeches in the Pacific Northwest, and he was the master of ceremonies at a January dinner in Portland at which British trade representative Sir Frederick Puckle addressed a national radio audience on the importance of U.S. participation in Europe's economic recovery. Sir Frederick was introduced by Senator Wayne Morse and the senator was introduced by Mr. Haycox. That was a task, for, as he explained to a Seattle friend, he had become disenchanted with this recently elected Republican lawmaker. "I voted for the guy [in 1944] on the assumption we needed ferment in our party," he grumbled. "I don't low-rate egotism. All our public performers have got it—and need it. But with him it appears to be an obsession. Ambition drives him too desperately. I get the impression of an indecent, impetuous greed for fame in the man. He's not a liberal. He's nothing but an opportunist who's not got finesse enough to put a decent cover on it."

As to writing, 1948 was no improvement on 1947. He had a terrible time settling down to the serial piece, *Head of the Mountain*, and it wasn't finished until December. He hoped it would do as well as *Canyon Passage*, which earned better than $60,000 in magazine, book, and movie rights. But he found that, having gone beyond the serial format, he couldn't return to it with any enthusiasm. The new novel didn't impress Erd Brant or Ken Littauer, the latter explaining somewhat weakly that *Collier's* had a huge backlog and really wasn't buying anything. *Esquire* took a much-shortened version in early 1949, paying all of $2,500 for it. The short stories were, again, his best efforts of the year, particularly three about an Oregon settlement family, the Mercys, and their first, hard year. These were "finger exercises" for the future panoramic novel, which was the thing he thought about most.

There was also a modern short, "Beach Fire," which both the *Post* and *Collier's* found disturbingly unreserved. Within the editorial ranks of *Woman's Home Companion*, it caused something of a squabble over the magazine's direction. "I don't think we could use the more or less frank treatment of sex here, and to delete it would damage the story," one reader opined. Another disagreed: "A very intelligent story, one in which the characters says things . . . that most authors don't let their characters say, preferring to gloss over them coyly or to ignore them. Cut a bit here and there, it would contribute to building a reputation that we are printing *adult* fiction."

He had contracted with Little, Brown to produce a massive anthology in which the principal events and trends of the American West would be illustrated through its fiction, but had to beg off. It would take five years to read everything that deserved consideration, he said. Sydney Sanders died of cancer in May 1948 and, although Erny would remain with the New York agency under Syd's wife, Marde, it was on a reduced basis. Unhappy with West Coast results, and made more so by the aggressive representations of a Hollywood agent who badly wanted the account, he pulled motion picture rights from Sanders. On the publishing front, Doubleday & Company tried to pry him away from Little, Brown, offering a $20,000 advance against a three-book deal. The proposal was momentarily brushed aside.

He and Jill spent three weeks in Mexico in March. Mary Ann worked in her father's downtown office that summer, and he wangled Jim a summer job in the US Forest Service. Father and son rode a drift-boat down the Rogue River—stopping by Zane Grey's empty fishing cabin at Winkle Bar—in September. He spent many weekends repainting the Big House, which was for sale but not attracting much attention. The market for terraced Georgian Colonials in 1948 wasn't buoyant; nor for that matter was the stock market, in which investor Haycox lost about $12,000. It couldn't have come at a worse time. His writing income had dropped by half since 1946 to about $25,000, the lowest point in a dozen years. ◆

He continued to believe that domestic confusion represented a far greater threat to Greek aid and the Marshall Plan than all of Stalin's divisions. In a letter to *Saturday Evening Post* editor Ben Hibbs, one clearly designed to suggest editorial content, he deplored the hesitancy of American public opinion.

> Having professed ourselves adherents to democratic principles and Christian ideals, we now find ourselves in a rough-and-tumble fight and yet cannot bring ourselves to use a club to defend those ideals against plain footpads. We understand there comes a time when, as private citizens, we can not longer permit ourselves to be pushed around and must sock the pusher; and all other private citizens applaud that vigor. But as a nation we go into the same thing with a shamefaced, mumbling apology. We sidle into it. We're not sure of ourselves. We look over our shoulder to see who is watching us. It's a moral conflict; or else it's a feeling that, having stood so long in the pulpit, we'll look very silly to the world when we descent from the pulpit. If we stay in this world business very long we'll learn better—but it palsies our hands now.
>
> In one direction we have made a great advance—the idea of setting foreign politics above . . . party wrangling. Someday, I'd lay a bet, [Senator Arthur] Vandenberg will get his paragraph in history for strengthening the beginnings of that tradition.* But the rest of it lies with the citizenry.

* It was a good guess. Senator Vandenberg is perhaps best remembered for his advocacy of bipartisanism in U.S. foreign policy.

We've got to wrestle out this problem of when morals are painless and when they must be applied with force.

Responding to a note from Dwight Griswold, who would shortly resign his foreign post and return to Nebraska, Erny offered somewhat reserved praise of President Truman.

Truman, frankly, seems so frequently to do the right thing the wrong way. I'm all for his tough policy. I think it the only way to play poker. Yet it rather appalls me when he permits one of his officials to publicly state that our bombers can now reach any part of Russia. That's fine meat for Stalin's boys. They'll spread it out to all their poor damned people and build up the American menace. We ought to have the bombers . . . [but] our job is still to search for peace, not to create incidents out of pure carelessness.

Shortly before Syd Sanders died in 1948, a Los Angeles–based agent, William Herndon, pitched the Haycox account, suggesting he could do much better than its present representatives—which for motion pictures were an uneasy combination of the Sanders group in New York and Mary Baker at the Sam Jaffe Agency in Hollywood. Herndon lit a fire, although his bold manner made Erny uncomfortable. Discussions ran on for a couple of months and, although Herndon's campaign ultimately failed, it wasn't by much.

Confidentially [Erny asked Walter Wanger], do you know anything about William Herndon? I'm collecting background on him, as an agent. He's made offers to me and . . . I'm temporarily intrigued. By letter he's quite brash with his words; face to face he makes a somewhat better impression. If he's as good as he says he is, he's very good—and maybe he is. My view is that I do not wish to deal with dynamiters.

Reports from Wanger and several writer friends being favorable, he decided to give Herndon a try. He addressed him:

To be fair with Syd and Mary, as well as with you, I'd better make this as explicit as possible. You've got my permission to handle anything I've so far published, though not on an exclusive basis, for pictures. Mary Baker also represents me, and that arrangement must continue, as a decent matter, until you have shown what you can do. When that happens, we'll take another look.

I've had a letter from Sanders which, while not 100 percent enthusiastic, indicates his cooperation. As for publishers, that's another story. I'm not ready for any change in that field until I have a much better grasp on the full novel which follows the present serial.

You'll note in the carbon I said Wanger was very interested in seeing the next serial. For your private information, his story gal is one of those who's put out with you—but don't tell her I said so. In case we do business . . . you may have a bit of a smooching job to do with her.

However, a few weeks later, having heard the other side of the story, Erny pulled the plug on his new representative.

Syd, I find, first tried to market the stories with the picture editors in New York and then, as a second bet, let Mary Baker handle them. It has not been a good arrangement; it's taken the bloom off the peach. That, as it now appears—plus the fact that Syd did not give anybody in Hollywood exclusive rights but instead invited offers from all comers—was the root of our problem.

I propose to cure the trouble by giving one agent in Hollywood exclusive rights at the full commission, withdrawing all such picture rights from the New York agent. The hard thing for me to say is that I must give —and am doing so—the first try at this exclusive deal to Mary Baker. She, it appears, has been laboring under the difficulty of receiving material after Sanders had tried it out . . . [and] it is only fair that she have the opportunity to demonstrate what she can do in the new situation. I'm sure that were you in her place you would probably feel the logic of that.

So, he said to Mary Baker, it's your job, but know where I'm coming from.

I think the root of the trouble has been, as you state, the divided authority. This is why I'm making the complete break and giving you the full job. I hope it solves the problem. To be utterly honest with you, if it seems not to solve the problem, I shall try another guy. I don't mind telling you that I had been leaning toward Herndon and had so indicated to Herndon and had agreed to let him have a nonexclusive try on all the material hitherto published. That I shall of course withdraw now.

William Herndon did Erny one immense favor, introducing him to Howard Cady, a skillful appraiser of the written word then representing the Doubleday publishing house on the West Coast. Erny mentioned his problematic novel, *The Adventurers*; Cady asked to read it, and the author considered his critique first-rate.

Your criticism is a better job, I think, than you realize. In changing from one vehicle to another, serial to novel, I had to abandon certain shorthand methods of characterization and hunt for fuller devices. Any man changing methods finds his touch shaken by the shift. In the experimental novel I went for the full-out statement and this, as you have pointed out, becomes too explicit, too tiresome. I think that's the best point you make. From such explicitness flows another fault which you didn't mention: a repetition of the obvious, plus an empurpling of prose. This weakness doesn't often crop out in my shorts or serials since the economy of space imposed by those two forms has kept my nose pretty clean. The experimental was designed however to throw everything onto the page and to see how she looked. She don't look good.

The correction is (so far as plain technique goes) obvious, and in line with decent writing practices: restrict the story to objective descriptions which set the scene, give each scene its mood, and let dialogue carry the exposition. This will remove much of the trouble, but not all; for it will still be necessary to occasionally put the character in a stance and have him deliver his silent monologue. A certain amount of introspection can't be avoided, nor should it be. A story needs this fourth dimension; to try to create depth by strictly objective writing is to place too much load on your objective devices, the result being often a brittle story without shadings. You can see this in many of Hemingway's shorts; he meant for his explicit descriptions and his dialogue—particularly his dialogue—

to break through the surface narrative. Sometimes it did; sometimes it didn't.

The theme's perfectly sound. The characters are not entirely right. I believe it was Thackeray who brooded over an idea and couldn't get anywhere with it until one day he thought of Becky Sharp. Then he had it; the whole pattern rolled out before him. I'm in somewhat the same position with this story. We need a character.

The short-story work in 1948—he produced eight stories—involved occasional communication with Ken Littauer at *Collier's*. These varied messages included an apology of sorts and a couple of general lamentations related to weather and will power.

You'll recall that at our last lunch together I discussed a possible series of shorts which would tie a hundred years of Oregon history together in terms of one family on one piece of land—Mercy's mill. I wrote the first story. Meanwhile you had just turned back one of mine on the thought that you had a backlog of Haycox. . . . Miss [Jo] Stewart [at the Sanders agency] assumed it would therefore be bad marketing to ship you another of mine so soon, and sent the Mercy story to *Post*, where it landed.

I lay no blame whatever on Miss Stewart. She exercised her judgment in the matter, and you can't shoot people for that. It was a decent story and you might have liked it, though it was of that type that *Post* has often liked—the Walter Edmonds sort of thing. But I do want to stress the fact that it was intended you should have the first sight, since we'd talked about it. There was no funny business involved, but it embarrasses me slightly.

Never was a spring like this in Oregon before. Rain every day for 30 days. It's the kind of a spring the earliest settlers used to describe in such forlorn terms and which we in later years more or less discounted as the exaggerated reaction of transplanted and homesick people. No such thing. We've had it in all its sticky-wet, variable, clammy, steaming, chilling, foggy fullness. The effects of Hiroshima at last reaching here, I suppose. Everybody else is using that excuse for everything else, so we might as well.

> I'm finishing a serial of the usual content and find myself very bitter, for I said I'd not write one of those again—and afterwards changed my notion. I should have stuck with the original decision. I do have two or three long projects which, if the Lord does not scorn me too much, may show something. I lay me down to sleep with that pious hope and think that if I am a good boy, I may be rewarded. Writers do like to kid themselves.

In August, *Collier's* purchased "Cry Deep, Cry Still," the third Mercy short. It appeared in November 1948 and, in addition to the $2,500 purchase price, won the magazine's best-story award for that issue, a $1,000 bonus. At the magazine's request, for a weekly column about its current contributors and their stories, Erny explained what had inspired him to write it.

> In Oregon, in the early days, no man could break 640 acres of land and at the same time handle the thousand-and-one chores that were so large a part of a handicraft society. There were no corner stores, seldom doctors, very few neighbors and not much surplus to live on. The rule was that if you grew it you could eat it but if you did not grow it or make it you went without. From daylight until long after dark it was the women who had to keep so many of these chores going. Often a man might have a breathing spell . . . [but] by and large, these early women had no time at all and were never caught up with their work. This never-ending drudgery plus the isolation and hardship broke many a woman in the West and those that survived were spiritually very strong. That is why I wrote *Cry Deep, Cry Still.*
>
> A man is normally a very poor observer. Many women can give him cards in spades in the business of seeing the small details which, after all, constitute the true picture of daily life. To give you an idea of the difference . . . here is the way one man reported it: "Made 14 miles today, camped by the river in the rain, shot a deer, very tired." A woman in the same wagon train reported the same day as follows: "We pitched camp in the driving rain. The fire wouldn't burn and the smoke was so strong in my eyes that I cried. I couldn't make the beans boil and all the time I heard Mrs. Jackson's dying baby crying in the next wagon. Out on the river the

> waves were four feet high and I didn't know how we could ever survive going down that terrible place."

He turned down the usual number of story-consultation and joint-venture proposals, but did spend time answering the questions of one inquirer who asked about magazine standards and the tendencies and practices of writing professionals.

> In the matter of taboos, I think you could classify them all under the heading of good taste. What would offend average people—in reference to religion, politics, morals or human decencies—would offend *Post*. I suppose those things that you and I might think twice about before mentioning in company would be the same things *Post* would think twice about before printing, though here I might add what one *Post* editor is supposed to have said concerning the morals of a certain heroine: "She cannot commit that act on our pages but, of course, we can't be responsible for her actions between installments."
>
> To return to the formula question. Every writer has a certain field in which he does his best work, and it usually happens that he restricts himself to this field. He has certain themes he likes best, and repeats them. There are certain kinds of people he understands better than others, and these will recur in his stories. He has certain preferred methods of telling a story, and he often leans on certain tricks, consciously or unconsciously. Beyond this we must add one last and important qualification: a writer has limitations and though he may dream of the perfect story, he can only do what he can do. He has lush periods, dry spells; he has days when it's impossible to get a character in and out of a room without violating all the rules of grammar and economy, and he has other days when things run along nicely. There is no such thing as a uniform day in a writer's life—and no such thing as a uniform product.

The campaign for an all-powerful organization to represent the interests of American writers evidently had calmed down but Erny caught a strong whiff of authoritarian sentiment when the Author's League instructed its members to withhold radio material, and he resigned from it. Assuming his objection was financial (dues having been bumped up substantially), mystery writer and league president Rex Stout ask him to reconsider. Money wasn't the issue, he replied.

> I understand very well that the I-can-get-it-for-less boys we sometimes deal with in the markets will have their advantage if we remain professionally weak; yet if the alternative is to be a League strong enough to penalize its members for noncooperation in bargaining matters, I'd unhesitatingly drop. Possibly I misread the smoke signs, yet I can in no other way interpret the recent letter of the League requesting its members to send no radio material to the market pending settlement of a dispute.
>
> [The League] needs to be strong and, in the hands of temperate men, the strength would be justified. But should the zealots, of which we have our share, have their way, nothing should suit them until the League's bargaining power was absolute through its power of compulsion upon its members. This far from New York, I can't know how much influence, existing or possible, other and more militant Guilds may have with us, nor do I know how much influence the zealots have in the Guild. I'd wish to do nothing which would help them wrap up their package.

Erny backed youthful Harold Stassen's bid for the Republican presidential nomination in 1948, but Tom Dewey upset the Minnesotan in Oregon's primary election.

> It's conceded that Stassen had this state 3–2 before Dewey showed up. The latter's personal appearance made the difference. Frankly he's turned into one of the most potent campaigners I've ever seen.
>
> He gave the impression that he had thought about a lot of things and had jelled his own thinking; that he had accumulated great masses of information and experience—and that he drew from this mass a pretty seasoned viewpoint. Before he arrived, I think people rather accepted the notion . . . that the sum total of Stassen's experience exceeded that of any other candidate. After Dewey got through I don't think the verdict stuck. He just didn't create the air of seasoning that Dewey did or the sharp competence. (Mind you, I was a Stassen man.)
>
> I ran a poll at a Rotary meeting. 93 Dewey, 51 Stassen. Then I asked: How many of you were for Stassen before Dewey came to town? About 20

had switched over. That switch-over was pretty spectacular all over Oregon.

Erny didn't support Portland mayor Earl Riley's bid for re-election—the mayor would lose to a prim and proper reformer Dorothy McCullough Lee—but he refused to join a chorus of his business friends condemning Riley for links to corruption.

> At this point the evidence convinces me that the operators lay protection money on the line and that Earl must know of it or be pretty thick. I don't know, however, how far up the line the money reaches. I don't defend him and I do have growing doubts about him, but I cannot take the final step of adding my name to the public charge that he himself is a receiver of such money unless I [have] more evidence. Almost every mayor of Portland within my memory has been suspected of corruption; it is a public pattern to suspect mayors, and in this case does seem more damaging to Earl. Still . . . I'll have to stand aside.

His dislike of Senator Wayne Morse—which his January introduction in Portland poorly concealed—also may have signaled the slightest drift from mainstream Republicanism, although, as events would establish, the senator was drifting too.*

> The senator with us tonight [Morse] is not the ordinary type of political figure. He is rather the uncommon sort that once in a while rises up from the plain to explode into sudden brilliance. He has brilliance—and he has some unorthodoxy in his system. He has a well filled and disciplined mind—and an extremely quick mind. You may remember that recently another senator, not from this region, held a hearing and cross-examined a rather prominent witness, the witness making somewhat of a spectacle of the senator. A newspaper commentator described that scene by this brief phrase: "The senator entered the duel of wits completely unarmed." That would never be said of Wayne Morse.

* The outspoken legislator decamped the Republican Party in 1952 and, after a brief period as an independent, joined the Democrats.

> At this point, Wayne, I must explain something to you. Usually, constituents don't explain to their senators; usually it's the other way round—so we have a man-bites-dog situation here. But on one or two occasions I have been so emotionally disturbed by the decisions you made on those occasions, plus your reasons for making them, that I could have wrenched up the Burnside Bridge and thrown it in the general direction of Washington D. C. And on those occasions I fear I have used some violent language upon you. I am not apologizing, you understand. I'm only explaining. I know you'll understand—for you have sometimes felt the same way, and have used much the same language upon other figures in public life.

The University of Oregon fund-raising campaign he managed had succeeded, although someone evidently questioned Erny's personal generosity. He explained his position to school President H. K. Newburn:

> We both know as between things done and things that could have been done there was a considerable gap during my tenure as alumni head. We'll just put down on the bronze plaque (figure of speech, Harry) the wistful inscription: "He meant well."
>
> I think you are entitled to one candid explanation. At the beginning of the [student union] campaign [Walter] Darling came to me and suggested that I set an example by making my own contribution early. At the time I told him that to a writer money and time were completely interchangeable items. I do not know of any profession in which this is so literally true. I told Walter I proposed to give time. I shan't tell you what my cash book tells me in respect to diminished income this year, but there has been a pronounced drop—perhaps $10,000 of which can be directly attributed to my part in this Student Union campaign. It is unfortunate of course that this figure doesn't show on the records—unfortunate only in the sense that people will wonder where the hell I was when the plate was passed.

A bit later, Erny delivered to President Newburn a blistering analysis of a cooking course that both sister and he found unnecessarily encompassing.

> The thing [course] is loaded with theory . . . [and] all this takes time and effort away from the only reason a girl at the university would want to take the stuff—which is to learn to cook. There doesn't seem much reason for a cooking course at Oregon to go into the histology and pathology of the coffee bean—and though this is a slight exaggeration, it's a fair index of some of the padding in the course. I suppose it's the old academic routine again. Give a professor a three-month subject and he'll round it out and stuff it . . . until he's got something that looks like a chunk out of the Britannica.

The family was fine, he reported to his mother, and WJ was momentarily employed.

> Haven't seen dad for a couple of months. I got him a state job, over in the license division. He writes out auto license applications for about $160 a month. That's ample to keep him going, and nice light work. I've told him to save his dough, for this will be the last job he'll be able to hold. I gave him a hell of a lecture . . . told him to get along with his boss and not get dissatisfied, which he has a great habit of doing . . . and for X's sake to keep out of [office politics] and mind his business. He also figures he's written a book on Columbia River steamboats that ought to make a lot of money, and was considerably put out when I told him it wouldn't make a dime. He figures that if I can do it, he can—maybe better. I must say, he's never lacked confidence in his ability, but the sad thing is he's never stuck to anything long enough to demonstrate whether or not he could succeed.

And the following were a few of his discrepant thoughts in 1948—to an admirer, an editor, a name-borrower, one of his experts on ancient weaponry, and Marde Sanders, respectively.

> There has been as you have noticed a spell of writing laziness. I think you will see more stories this year. I hope you enjoy them. Meanwhile I shall send you my favorite book, as you have requested. Actually it is not my favorite book—that's like asking which one of my children I like best—but it is still a good book, according to my likes.

No, I don't believe that age necessarily brings wisdom. I once thought so; then the Townsend Plan came along and I wasn't so certain. Age brings insecurity; insecurity brings the soft and uncertain voice—and the soft voice often passes for wisdom.

I have your letter suggesting I add my name to your national committee which will welcome Mr. [Menachem] Begin to this country. I must regretfully decline. My sympathies were originally and entirely with the Jews in Israel but of late months I have been disappointed by the acts of terrorism which seem entirely beyond patriotic resistance and also by their lack of cooperation with the United Nations. Surely the Jews of all people must know . . . the eventual consequences of terror.

After much messing around I find that I have my dates and my guns balled up. It's 1868. I have a .44 revolver, which implies a muzzle load and caps. Ducked in water, that's the end of that. I have additionally some rifles. I assume these would use fixed ammunition. But do we need caps on the nipples for these? I can't see any reason for caps but for some funny reason I had an image in my mind of a fixed-ammunition rifle with a nipple on it. Now where would I get that?

Last night I found "The Sheriff of Crooked Rib" and read it. It's a nice sagebrush story such as I used to do 20 years ago but I can't see it as representing me in a collection of short stories. If the publishers still want a story of mine I shall recommend something more recent.

Erny's search for reality and its means of expression inevitably led to the conclusion that sexual activity could not be ignored. Hemingway and some of the others, clumsy and repetitive as they sometimes were in this territory, were at least honest about it—and at their best, damned good. In *The Adventurers*, the hero and second-lead female spent a night together but, fresh from a shipwreck and chilled to the bone, they did so out of virtual necessity. It was in the modern shorts that he did most of his experimenting with the issue, as in the never-published "Beach Fire." Sex there is by no means explicit, but the meaningful glance and the brushed lip, which had been the approximate limits of the old Haycox, were on their way out.

"Beach Fire" described the meeting of two people—weekend vacationers—in a remote coastal hamlet. Chance encounter in a market leads to a conversation, then a hike and a picnic, and later a dinner prepared in a house lent to him by a friend. They puzzle over pencil marks grooved into a sill. Was one of the former occupants, the wife, marking the years of her imprisonment, or does this record of time have another meaning? They share the final evening by a roaring fire near the ocean.

> She fell silent, lying full length on the blanket, face to the sky. Her hand —the one nearest him—rose and dropped, long-fingered and supple and cupped as though waiting to be filled. Her whole body had the same expectancy. It was like one of those wartime mines washed ashore, waiting with the terrifying patience of every inevitable thing for the touch that would bring it on to its purpose. He dropped to an elbow, looking directly into her face; he shielded the firelight from her face and saw nothing in her eyes. He let himself quietly down, finding her mouth and was gentle with her because now he was afraid he'd lose her. Her hands came around his back and held him until he drew away.
>
> She said: "Is anything to come of this, or was that goodbye?"
>
> "I want something to come of it."
>
> "A night on the beach?"
>
> "No, the whole forty-seven years."
>
> "If I'd not been in the store, if you'd come there half an hour later, a thousand ifs, I'd never met you."
>
> "I don't know why it works this way." But what he felt was that he had no more control over anything. He had stepped inside the field of her attraction and the rest of it was as certain as the force which held these grains of sand together on the beach; maybe it was the same force.
>
> "Now you can ask me why I'm thirty and not married."
>
> "All right."
>
> "We've all got to put in our time the same as Mrs. Ralston. But we do try to begin it right, or the years would be much too long. Like this—first night and first year, one black heavy mark."

He said: "I'm eight years older than you are."

Her lips made the shape of laughter. "That's about the right difference, Frank." He was drawn down by the light pressure of her hands at his back. "In the morning, first thing, you answer that phone call. It worries me."

The ocean's roar was a great drum roll flung into the enormous night, signaling this occurrence here. Stars and sky were gone, everything was blotted out so that the fire of their collision—two lone fragments on the far shores of a far planet—would shine more intensely against the black; and this warm brightness was a cell in which they were safely enclosed.

"Beach Fire," which he wrote in the summer of 1948 and toned down a bit at year-end, was his last attempt at modern fiction. There had been several dozen such stories over the years, evolving from frothy yarns involving society girls and rodeo hands in the thirties to somber tales of young women waiting for and, shortly following, young men struggling to reacquaint themselves with a postwar world. The present grinding and groaning in magazine editorial offices may have suggested to him that, insofar as the new reality in his fiction was concerned, there wouldn't be a comparable market, if any at all. No doubt, that suspicion added to the allure of big-book adventure fiction, where, to a considerable degree, a good man could make his own rules.

—15—

Hard Rules in the Golden Land

IN EARLY 1949, ERNY PUSHED EVERYTHING ASIDE TO CONCENTRATE on the large and many-layered novel that would be *The Earthbreakers*. Ahead were several months of searching pioneer records and recollections and of elaborating plot and scene and character. This required a new piece of office equipment, a tilt-top stand next to his desk with a large artist's sketch pad on which—in addition to the customary typewritten notes—the various story lines and incidents were visually recorded. He calculated that, following these preliminaries, there would be an uninterrupted half-year required for composition and then further time devoted to revision. It added up to a lengthy period during which there would be little money coming in, for he would be too busy to break away for short-story work and the late, lamented serial novel was going nowhere. Thus, he told Doubleday's Howard Cady, he would be amenable to their earlier offer—of a $20,000 advance against a three-book deal—if the advance could be structured in the form of monthly $1,500 installments as 1949 progressed.

He didn't tell Little, Brown of his decision until a late hour, not wishing to appear manipulative; after all, Doubleday was committing to a degree that Little, Brown never had and, so far as he knew, never would. So much for assumptions, as will be seen.

The Big House sold and he and Jill were gone from it at mid-year, renting a much smaller one a couple of miles distant. He thought he was going to miss the old place badly but, he told his mother, "we both look back on it as a hell of a lot of work and wouldn't care to go through it again." He did go back, but only to retrieve the dog; Honey, another St. Bernard, did miss it. Sister met her young man at the university. They announced their engagement in February and she skipped spring term, coming home to figure out the cooking business; they were married in August. Brother, who had an imposing job title that summer (he was the lookout on Bull of the Woods Mountain in the Oregon Cascades) came out of the hills for the event and was a freshman at Oregon that fall and had become, Father observed, a rather serious and stubborn cuss. Erny thought his son's girlfriend of the moment rather more reasonable and a good deal more cheerful than the boy.

In Portland Rotary's occupation-classified membership, Erny was the sole literary representative—indeed, literary Rotarians were rarae aves nationwide—but his election to the club's presidency that July had nothing to do with celebrity. He was simply one of the hardest-working members they ever had—and had been for seventeen years. To be sure, he was unable to walk down many streets or enter many rooms in Portland as a stranger. When a group of Portland pilots decided to fly across the country on a promotional air tour in May 1949, they pressured him into coming along as the home-country spokesman and luminary. A Portland Chamber of Commerce booklet soliciting conventions made him a leading local attraction, described in those terms that Oregonians normally reserved for the Douglas fir and Tillamook cheese. He had slimmed down his commitments to the extent of resigning from the Oregon State Library Board and declining a few speaking dates but, turning around, was elected a director of the Oregon Historical Society and put to work writing copy for markers and roadside monuments; and the university had found another use for him, this time as president of the Oregon Dads' Club. On and on it went.

As for *The Earthbreakers*, its writing produced days of soaring spirit and days when everything seemed doubtful, but he was wise enough to discount both extremes of mood. On balance, it seemed to go well, although he would observe to a friend, "Writing is not a simple business and the thing we want to do is not always the thing we do. It's a good deal like a pole pushed into a creek; above the water the pole is straight—

which is the writer's conception of the story he wants to do; but beneath the water the image of the pole takes a slant, and that's the way a good many stories turn out." ◆

While Doubleday was in the picture, Erny gave Cady a lengthy account of his struggle to break the bonds of his serial-novel background.

> There were two ways to go, it seemed: 1) the thematic, clinical, case-history novel or 2) the big circus wagon story with everything thrown in but the kitchen sink, every element weighed for its box-office value, battle pieces, bosoms, bedrooms, stock figures, assorted trumpet flourishes and some flag waving. I never seriously considered the Number Two method; for this is usually five hundred pages of heavily plotted, mechanical story creaking at every joint.
>
> I did do much experimenting on the thematic novel. The net of it was that I realized it wasn't for me, and thus I returned to the conviction I had when I began writing twenty-three years ago: A story is the result of characters in action. The serial form, actually, is a closer approximation of ideal storytelling than the thematic business, for at least a serial requires pace, a knitted plot, and people who march. Its limitations are of course obvious: there are taboos, mechanical contrivances inherent in it, and a space economy which makes full characterization and round development almost impossible.
>
> Perhaps the clearest definition of the kind of story I want to do lies in a review of [R. C.] Hutchinson's latest book in SRL: "It must be exasperating to all the little thesis writers—the existentialists, the Marxists, the psychoanalytic writers, and the rest—to come upon a full-blooded, magnificently alive work such as this. . . . All their philosophical trapeze work seems suddenly puny in the presence of a natural artist who can create people instead of literary skeletons, who can depict solid, opaque, glandularly active life instead of a transparent, carefully designed existence to fit some esthetic pattern." Nobody could say it better [than the reviewer, William Soskin].

> American novels have suffered from clinical treatment: in rebound they have also suffered from the attempt to do something "sweeping and epic." It appears that writers have difficulty escaping a theme; but in pounding on a theme they starve character, or discipline it into poor channels; and they forget often that characters are often willful, and often have no point except the point of their own lives played out for better or for worse.

The people in his future works would be common as clay and they would be in vigorous motion. "I wish to tell the story on a buoyant, driving level," he declared. "I have written action too many years to fall into the analytic, melancholy, motive-below-motive pit now; and I have dealt with fairly folksy people too long to specialize in the bizarre and neurotic."

What he had in mind, he continued, ran well past the first project, which was the Oregon settlement piece. Beyond it, there were at least a half-dozen other episodes marching through time, one of which, at turn-of-century, was to be partially autobiographical. "I've had it in mind for years."

> And on the tail end there's a modern story. Each story is an independent thing. . . . Each period in this state had to fight its own particular battles; each generation had its own survival problem, and so did each family. We are not exempt from that battle today: the security we seek as a society does not exist. I rather think that's the core of the modern story.

He had great expectations and if things went well, he told a colleague, the next decade of his life would be fully occupied.

> The first will be the story of settlement in Oregon around 1845—taking up the story where Emerson Hough left off in *The Covered Wagon*. I have got it pretty well projected . . . and will spend the rest of the year writing it. We shall have first-class promotion and we are shooting at a book club and a movie deal. If this works out satisfactorily I have got five of the beasts in my system . . . all of which will take me about ten years to do. I shan't be doing any serials this year and if the novel goes over I shan't be doing any serials ever. Probably no short stories either.

> It's sad to hear of Ken leaving *Collier's*. My grapevine tells me the situation there has been getting worse and worse and I understand he is glad to go. The magazine has been getting increasingly unpredictable and it has fallen off.

Two shorts sold in January 1949 were his last—although it is hard to believe that on occasion he wouldn't have come back to a form to which he had been so comfortably attached for so long. "I would like to do some more moderns . . . in the same vein as 'Beach Fire,'" he had recently told Marde Sanders. "That of course removes both *Post* and *Collier's* as a market. I can't write cream-puff modern so the question is—who's printing and decently paying for moderns which are not cream-puff?"

> As you say it is sad to throw away so large an audience and so successful a story form [the serial novel] after all these years of building. But the surest way to die is to play anything safe and small and in my case the serial form has gotten too stereotyped and too thin. Were I a hamburger merchant I could of course go on for years turning out the uniform product.
>
> Syd and I discussed this many times and he was always reluctant to see me throw aside a very fat yearly income for the sake of something different. Deep in his mind, I think he doubted my ability to make the switch. For that matter, I had the same doubt until quite recently. I think now I see the way to do this little trick.
>
> I don't wish to convey the impression that I am turning literary and artistic, for I have no earthly use for the consciously sought art. I shall always have to operate right down in the mud and dust where all of us do our business and live our lives.

In February, he advised his principal contact at Little, Brown, editor-in-chief Angus Cameron, that he would affiliate with a new publisher. He emphasized the issue of financial security, although he didn't describe Doubleday's offer or suggest that Little, Brown might counter with one of its own. It was, he thought, a done deal. He addressed Cameron:

> As you know my last magazine serial to appear in book was *Canyon Passage*, four years ago, and my last book, not serialized, which you put out was *Long Storm* . . . and during the intervening time I have been very prayerfully squatted over the crystal ball in search of stories for a full novel treatment and for a way of telling those stories. The result is that I shall be embarking upon the first full novel this year . . . [and] to take as much risk from the gamble as possible I felt I needed the strongest possible guarantees in advance from a publisher; and since my name has so long been associated with sagebrush westerns I have also thought it necessary to make as clean a break as possible so that the new Haycox—if he turns out to be new—might have whatever promotional benefits accrue from a fresh start in a fresh wrapping. I do regret to tell you this, and possibly it may offend you that I should make this decision without prior discussion with you, but my decision is to change publishers. Had I discussed it with you, it would only have meant a haggling and a horse-trading between publishers which I do not think you would have cared for.

He had kept the Sanders agency out of the loop, too. "For many years I gave no thought to the business end of things but was very happy to let Syd carry the load and do all the bargaining," he explained to Marde. "The change in your shop naturally made me review [matters] in light of my own future—and therefore these conversations came about." He elaborated:

> . . . My thinking in the matter [now] has come to a point and I have outlined in very tentative form several full novels that I wish to do—and propose to do. This represents a complete break with twenty-five years of writing practice; it's a gamble with no sure answer; but it's something I must do because I can't do anything else.
>
> As soon as I got this clear in my head I made certain propositions to Doubleday and these have been accepted. Obviously I have gone over the head of my agent in this matter which is ordinarily not at all a good thing. But I think you will understand that change in offices which naturally led me to take all things into consideration and to act as I thought best for my

> own interests. What I must tell you is quite painful. I propose to close the deal with Doubleday which will involve a direct relationship with them in the matter of all book rights. Since they are fully equipped to do this and since in the future we are dealing with a simplified program of not more than one novel a year with no magazine dickering involved, I can't feel I need an agent for this particular business.
>
> Other things remain with you for the future . . . existing contracts, plus whatever short stories I may write, or other casual pieces. Do you . . . wish to go on under such an arrangement?

Little, Brown was outraged, calling Doubleday many unBostonian names and mildly reproaching the author for his lack of faith in their wisdom and generosity. Within a few days, Doubleday stepped back, suggesting a moratorium and appearing to Erny somewhat spineless. And for those few days, having resigned one house only to find its replacement backing off, Erny was in that curious and somewhat tenuous position of having no publisher at all.

> It was to avoid the suspicion of such jockeying [Erny wrote to worried Doubleday editor-in-chief Ken McCormick] that I carried our negotiations to the contract stage before notifying Little, Brown. Frankly, this does not stem from my system of ethics; as a writer I look to my own advantage. I was rather trying to play this game according to the publishers' ground rules. I owed Little, Brown the courtesy of informing them of my step, before I signed, and did so. In a way it's a pleasant surprise to know that I could kick up such a hell of a fuss. It's now clear to me that had I signed your contract before notifying Little, Brown, we should have had the same amount of strained emotions, Little Brown feeling they had been left in the dark, and you feeling you had bought a dubious product. There's only one way to unwind this. I am enclosing your contract, unsigned. We are now both perfectly free.

Cameron was quickly on the plane to Portland for talks, and Erny decided to stay on with Little, Brown, which matched Doubleday's terms. He seemed disturbed by only one element—that Howard Cady, for whom he'd developed a considerable appreciation, wouldn't be involved. He told Cady:

> I shall say again that I regret not being able to work with you on the books. Strictly between us it might have come about had not our friend [McCormick] gotten so terribly nervous about the ethics of the proposition. His last letter to me—not explicitly but between the lines—indicated a quite virtuous viewpoint and, also by inferences, suggested I should have made up my mind much sooner. I might have suggested to him that the making up of minds works both ways, but such mutual reproach, even by indirection, buys nobody anything. . . .

Later, as *The Earthbreakers* took shape, Erny would give Little, Brown occasional progress reports, although he never offered samples. He had, of course, described the opus to Cameron in person and in a long letter in which fifteen or so characters were introduced and various story lines revealed. Further disclosures to the publisher were general, sometimes the rambling of a writer who seemed to be talking to himself.

> It must be the novelist's first preoccupation to build his sheer storytelling frame; the rest, assuming he's a good writer, will find its way into the cracks and fissures of background and character, and so make roundness and/or significance. But the writer concentrating on significance becomes so often a propagandist or a tractarian, whereupon he ceases to be a novelist. Wells did that. Or he becomes so damned obscure that nobody reads him and his values are quite lost. I'd put Joyce and *Ulysses* in that bracket.
>
> ———
>
> They brought the seeds of every sin with them; and the expectation of a golden land couldn't possibly materialize. The thrifty, the shrewd, the energetic and the lucky got along; the rest either died or sank to the level they had been on in their other place. Disillusionment came to all . . . and the first year was an ordeal. In fact it was sometimes so much of an ordeal that many of them paid out too much of their strength during the first year and were never quite the same people again. All of this leads to the major point I wish to rub over the story—like a clove of garlic . . . over a

piece of bread: There is no escape, no golden land, no security; it is a timeless illusion. We must sweat and cry. This will be in every future novel I write.

In writing a short story I am always conscious of the space limits . . . and therefore I dig right in. It is a precision job requiring short, intense strokes. By contrast the novel [has] plenty of room and the tendency is to sprawl and not to achieve the clean-cut definition of people. The novel—the serial, that is—has always been to me a run-along thing with the emphasis on action and suspense. The plot frequently overpowers the people . . . [and] it frequently happened that my leading people were standard dimension pieces straight out of the lumber yard. . . . It points [to] the problem in the novel I am writing. I have got to be highly inventive in these scenes. Should I find myself repeating one set of tricks and mannerisms scene after scene I shall know that I am only building stock figures. Each succeeding scene must convey some new quality of the character or carry the old quality to deeper places.

In his final progress report, he was 400 pages along with 100 to 150 more to do. "I begin now to see what I must do in the way of revise," he said, and there followed a long list of commands to himself that included the following: "Cut some of the introspection, make it a bit less authorial and a bit more colloquial. Evaluate the space given to some of the characters. I don't yet know who's hogging this story beyond just merits." There were nine large tasks in all: "That's about it," he concluded, "and that's damned well enough."

The new arrangement with Little, Brown included plans to republish a number of Erny's short stories in three anthologies, the first of which took shape in 1949. The writer was uncomfortable with one of the selections.

I am returning the galley proofs on *Rough Justice* today to your editorial department. I have used the pencil most sparingly . . . but one story troubles me much—"Wild Jack Rhett." That's a good story, but it was written 15 years ago at a time when I hadn't learned that one adjective is better than two, and no adverbs better than any adverb. It was also at a

> time when I was experimenting with words, and it mortifies me now to read some of the strange results. I'd like to . . . take some of the purple pulpiness out of the story. Can the budget stand this . . . ?

Meanwhile, the Haycox household had been slightly enlarged, Mary Ann finding reason to leave college midway through her junior year. Erny had on several occasions encouraged Sister to stay the course. However, when she decided shortly after becoming engaged that enough was enough, he was sympathetic and, in a letter to Professor Thatcher, somewhat retrograde in his view of higher education's impact on young womanhood. For an adoring father, of course, this backtracking may have been the logic of necessity.

> Yes, Mary quit at the end of the term to come home and learn to cook. Anyhow she had enough education for her purposes. When the desire for marriage comes, and the chance to fulfill the desire comes, education can be a dimming of the lamp, for a woman. I must truthfully say that in recent years I've seen young women out of the University, unmarried at 25 or 30, who seem to me to have been badly balled up by education. That's contrary to what it's supposed to do; but rationalism and enlightenment [have] got some of these gals so at war with themselves it's pathetic.
>
> We've sold, or are about to consummate a deal on the house. We'll not move to California. I think we play out the rest of the piece right here. We'll probably go into a small apartment for a year or two, then possibly build a little modern place, when prices come down.
>
> I've spent six weeks doing nothing but plot and build[ing] characters. I want a consistent story that runs along with vitality, doesn't drag, and comes to its climax like a play. I have a Number 2 love affair between two fairly educated people who don't belong in this mud and dust at all; it goes hard on them—to show that the original breed out here had to be coarse-grained and a little bit insensitive to take the beating. But these two start a love affair (woman's married) with self-consciousness, rational enough to look on themselves partially as spectators. That's my fling at education; it gums up something wholly honest, until biology settles that nonsense.

Perhaps Erny's long study of frontier life had influenced him to the degree that he could not possibly have been an altogether modern man. There is nothing on record to suggest that he was overtaken by this concentration, but his immense admiration of settlement society was undeniable and his work—now more than ever—reflected this in its fusion of fact and fiction. The Mercy family was real enough; he had initially misnamed the wife.

> The original Mercys left several children who in turn left several children who in turn left several children. The descendants of Mrs. Mercy fall into two groups—the line of the Mercys and the collateral branch of the Tubbses. When I wrote the first story I consulted the surviving Mercys. They said her name was Nancy . When I wrote the second story I had meanwhile contacted the Tubbs branch, and they said her name was Martha. You can readily see that I was presented with a problem, but inasmuch as there are more Tubbses than Mercys nowadays, I followed the usual rule of evidence and gave heed to the preponderant testimony of the Tubbses. So Mrs. Mercy's name is Martha. I hope this satisfies the reader as an explanation.

Over the years, some readers found characters in Haycox's work so familiar by name or deed that they wondered, and asked, whether he had intentionally borrowed their family's tree. No, he would reply, he wasn't aware of this ancestor or that; it was just a name or an incident he'd run across somewhere that had a strong western scent. But all of his characters, stock figures and minor actors included, were, as he told one inquirer, "as representative of the period . . . as I could make them."

So were his plots. *Saturday Evening Post* columnist Ralph Knight asked him how he had come to write "Outlaw's Reckoning," which appeared in the magazine in early 1949. Well, he said, with a chuckle:

> The readers of your page are sufficiently indoctrinated by now in the ways of writers to know how these things go. We had our setting, which was the [Deschutes River] canyon, and we had also the inevitable stage station at the bridge. The station keeper came up as the leading character

> by virtue of squatters' rights. The wild young man moved in, which meant trouble for the station keeper. But such straight-away complication seemed insufficient and so our genteel sheriff moved in to give the additional depth to what would otherwise be a fairly surface story. We needed a bit of the eternal urge, which brought in the three women in the various stages of experience. Add to that a broken-down hired hand—of which the West was full—and a stage driver whose purpose in the story was to see and understand everything the hero saw and thus perhaps add a touch of suspense. Mix well, let stand overnight, and shake before using.

In twenty-five years, he'd gotten his facts mixed up a few times, on one occasion using a type of lantern before its general introduction and on another harvesting strawberries rather earlier than they are known to ripen. But by this time, he had more knowledge of the early West than most, as one punctilious and entirely errant critic would learn.

> I presume from the tone of the letter than you figure the author to have been a white collar man living in Newark, New Jersey. Some authors do, but I live out here where the story came from, and since you believe in the frank approach I shall be equally frank. Some trappers were wonderful men and some were just plain bums who had only the ability to stand punishment. You bet they got drunk. Also some of them, when they settled in this country, made their own liquor. The most celebrated mountain man who came to Oregon, Joe Meek, was a tremendous figure but he was also the greatest deliberate liar on earth and took a lot of fun in his lying. He had a choice land claim but starved half the time because he neither knew how to farm nor wanted to farm.
>
> You mention the impossibility of growing wheat on the wet meadowlands of Oregon. However diary after diary mentions that the first labor of these people was to turn the ground and get in their wheat. They were not of course suckers enough to plant in the swampy part of their claim. You mention the impossibility of cutting down a cedar tree with an axe. Again the records show that they cut down trees all winter long with whatever implements they had at hand.

You are wrong in your statement that the first wagons got to Oregon in 1848. The first large wagon train . . . was in the late fall of 1843, comprising about 1,000 people. Most of the wagons were left at the Whitman Mission but some came to The Dalles, were put on rafts, were portaged at the Cascades and rafted down the river to the Willamette. I shall give you half a point on the cow. Maybe Mercy should have known it would have strayed. On the other hand this cow had walked twenty miles that day and she was a damned tired cow.

I enjoyed your letter my friend, and come again, but your final statement—that I don't know this environment—intrigues me. I was born here a long time ago and, continuing our amiable frankness, I shall have to insist that I know a hell of a lot more about it than you do. Even if you objected to this one story, keep right on buying *Post*. You will find a good story in it every once in a while.

Most of the reader mail was friendly and was answered in like tone. If he had a favorite among 1949's many incoming dispatches, it was probably this one from Governor West.

I took the *Sat. Eve. Post* to bed with me last night and read your well written story "The Land That Women Hate," and then laid awake most of the night thinking of the many angles to such a life. I got to thinking of the summer trips taken through Montana, The Dakotas, Kansas and Nebraska . . . and the God damn dust the farmer families had to face year after year. And I thought of friends and acquaintances that lived it in Eastern Oregon and Eastern Washington. Dust in their clothes, dust on their hides, dust on everything in the house and in the food. I had often declared to myself that I wouldn't spend my life under such conditions were I given a deed to whole damn Palouse country as a bonus. I had to get up and take a shower before I could get to sleep.

If the story made you bathe, Erny replied, "then I suppose I have thereby done my full share in contributing to your cleanliness which, as you remember . . . " He continued:

Somewhere along the line . . . I want to do the story of a young man with political ambitions coming from some small Oregon town in the '80s. I want to show him going through the jumps as he moves upward toward the governorship. I want to lay down the fundamental battle between conservatism and liberalism . . . [and] to portray the Victorian morals of that era . . . [and] to paint a nice, realistic, warm story of our situation during the so-called chinwhisker era. That's why I wanted to get together with you, for you are close enough to that time to know the people and your own personal life is not so far removed. . . .

To be sure, the daily mail and the telephone and streetcorner conversations produced inquiries and appeals that were wholly unrelated to literature. In particular, Erny's well-known association with the University of Oregon led some to present their concerns about that institution to him rather than to appropriate authorities in Eugene. On one occasion, he tried to help; on another, he was no help at all.

> A father has come to me today [he advised President Newburn] with a problem concerning his son Wilberforce. It seems that Wilberforce, who is no student, put up at the Vets' Dorm while making his grades for rushing. The son is doing poorly. He reports to his father that conditions in the Vets' Dorm are completely out of hand. There is no discipline, no supervision, no study hours, the radios are going full blast after 7:00, men are horsing in and out of the place at all hours and furthermore Wilberforce reports to his father that he has seen all phases of life in the Vets' Dorm.

> [Drinking] is as much an alumnae as an undergraduate problem . . . [and] frankly I know of no way to handle this [he confessed to a woman who had written]. I am not myself a reformer and when the spirit moves me I like to drink. I try to be moderate about it and I wish we could all follow moderation . . . [but] drinking is such a personal matter. This I suppose takes us back to . . . the kinds of lives we lead as individuals . . . and those moments in which the world either goes completely haywire for us or suddenly becomes for an instant so good that we have to do something about it. I am completely at sea insofar as offering practical suggestions. . . .

Strong as he was for the improvement of higher education, he argued against the establishment of a new state junior college in Portland. It would simply bleed money away from the university and Oregon State, he explained, and both were seriously underfunded; and a modest JC in Portland would not—he accurately forecast—remain a small institution with minimal funding needs for long.

> I'm afraid the idea of the state building a junior college in Portland reminds me of a man buying a Cadillac on an income of $20 a week. Oregon has a champagne appetite but refuses to pay the price. When [Harvard President James Bryant] Conant suggested bringing education to the centers of population, he meant a first-class education, not the bargain basement kind.
>
> Do you see what the establishment of another state school will do to us? It will only spread the money thinner and make the quality poorer. There is no use talking about greater services until this state is willing to face the problem of taxation.

As the year came to a close, another writer asked him if he thought Portland's new mayor, whose gender and reformist manner had begun to attract attention elsewhere, might be worth a national magazine spread. Though no particular fan of the woman who had put tainted Mayor Earl Riley out to pasture, she was, Erny thought, fully deserving of the attention.

> [Dorothy McCullough] Lee is a cool, careful, determined lady, not bad looking, wears precise hats which add ten years to her age, and has ambitions politically. She has practically no sense of humor, is sensitive to criticism, and has a certain charm but very little warmth. As to sensitiveness. At a banquet, in her presence, I made a crack about slot machines and punchboards, which furnish her with a very good ammunition. Remark was intended to draw a laugh, which it did from everybody but Mrs. Lee. Half an hour after I got back to my office she was on the phone, deadly serious, wondering if I had any information about punchboards she didn't have, and if I had would I give it to her. She has a husband who would have to be a very easygoing and obtuse character to stand the usual ribbing of a husband in such a situation. He is.

As to her success: The proper elements of this town, church, serious-minded, upright, etc., are probably all for her because of her intention to make the city pure. Naturally she draws resentment from the little businesses which get their rent money from punchboards. Innocuous punchboards—question and answer type—are now licensed by the city, but it's well known that a Texas Charley is still a Texas Charley and if you've been playing the Texas Charley at your favorite counter, you still play it there and sink your dough, never mind the questions and answers. It is one of these pyrrhic things, Dotty pointing with pride, cigar counters still doing business in a discreet way. Somebody launched a recall movement against her. It got nowhere. Mrs. C. S. Jackson, who controls the [*Oregon*] *Journal* here, calls her Mrs. Airwick.

I'd say she's still in the ring and could win again. You can't point to much solid achievement as major. How can you ever do that in such a thing as a modern American city? Against her can be no rumor of personal corruption such as [is] laid against every mayor in every town. If she goes on politically it will be because of the quiet citizen who approves her, the women's club—that route—not because of great personal appeal; and if she goes on, it will be against the record of mayors generally. Very few get beyond the job. They're too close to neighbors, automobile fines, dog controversies, petty stuff. But she's stubborn and she plugs. And I think she'd be well worth a story. Expect no cheesecake. She dresses well and makes a nice appearance, but the total effect is not glamorous.

— 16 —

Beyond the Obvious Functions

T*HE EARTHBREAKERS*, WHICH AT ABOUT 200,000 WORDS WAS double the size of any previous novel, was completed as the year turned but still needed work. Erny spent the first two months of 1950 on revisions and, after Little, Brown's Angus Cameron and others in that shop had their first look at it in March, undertook further adjustments. There were a good many suggestions from Boston and he agreed that some characters might benefit from a bit of polishing and that some of the conflicts could be more sharply drawn. Still, he was disinclined to stray far from the original inspiration. In this view, he was supported by Howard Cady, who read the manuscript at his request and told him to hang tough.

It was during these last turns at the project that he sickened. The first symptom was jaundice and its persistence required hospitalization. On May 17, a day-long operation revealed cancer at the upper end of the small intestine. A good deal of tissue was removed, including one duct that his surgeons replaced with plastic tubing. He came home two weeks later, weak and badly underweight but spiritually undiminished. He managed a half-hour at the office eleven days later, then half-days, and on July 5 celebrated his first more-or-less full stint.

That may have been the day that Jim picked him up in the afternoon and waited in the car while he visited the doctor's office. It was a financial consultation and a nurse explained that the charge of such elaborate service as he had been provided generally ranged from $5,000 to $15,000. "Fine," he said, "why don't we split the difference?" He wrote a check for

$7,500. A few minutes later in the car, it dawned on him that his math had been none too good and that she had been too polite to correct him. He chuckled all the way home.

Some months earlier, Jill had read about a locally sponsored student tour of Europe open to all ages and decided that she and Jim should go. The idea was pretty much abandoned in May but with the apparent recovery and Erny's continued encouragement of the project, Jill and Jim left for Europe on July 15. They weren't notified that Erny was hospitalized again in early August and that a second operation found his condition hopeless.

Had he survived, the marriage probably would not have. They had remained together for their children and, that obligation having been satisfied, the union was now explained only by convenience and routine. Sometime earlier, he had informed Jill of his interest in another woman whom he did not identify, saying only to his wife that "it is someone you know socially." Details of a possible separation had been discussed; she was thinking about moving east to be with brother Jack, then living in St. Louis. Whatever the arrangements—and perhaps nothing was firm—the illness interrupted them and she would later say that she thought they might have reconciled their grievances.

As it was, he lay in bed at home, uncomfortable and increasingly sedated. He told his wife he did not want to see Bertha, desiring to avoid that predictable commotion. He had quietly given WJ $5,000, explaining to the old man—although it was hardly necessary—that if something happened, Jill would be unlikely to continue the subsidies of now twenty years' standing. He was baptized, perhaps at his wife's urging, although it may have been his thought or Sister's; his daughter came home for the last weeks. Extended conversations weren't possible, but he did on at least one occasion express a wish. It was a writer's supplication. "I hope I'm remembered," he said.

Quite by chance, Ernest Hemingway was at this moment tipping his cap. *Across the River and into the Trees* had recently appeared and a writer for the *New York Herald Tribune*'s book review section queried him about his Cuban lifestyle and reading preferences. Responding to the latter, the author rattled off a list of foreign and domestic periodicals that he read with fair regularity and which, he said, extended to the "*Sat. Eve. Post* whenever it has a serial by Ernest Haycox." *The Earthbreakers* would remind some of Hemingway's earthy manner; Erny's vision of the frontier in this last iteration of it left some long-time readers and reviewers rather stunned. It was indeed a new Haycox. ◆

The 1950 correspondence file isn't large. Novel revisions commanded his attention and, after illness interfered, he never would reestablish a normal office routine in which occasional afternoons could be devoted to the salutation of distant friends and the expression of ideas on writing and mankind's lesser affairs. Fortunately, the book was well along by summer. He had further revisions in mind at this late date, but of minor scope.

The Earthbreakers recounts the arrival of an early (1845 or so) wagon train and its occupants' first year in the timber-fringed wilderness of the Willamette Valley. Cabins rise and split-rail fences stretch out and precious seedlings from remembered farms go into the moist dark earth. Rice Burnett, once a trapper and still a restless man, has come to establish a gristmill and will in time cleave to Katherine Gay, a wise and patient young woman. Before this happens, however, he is enticed by the bold advances of another of this new settlement's daughters, Edna Lattimore. Cal Lockyear, more mountain man than pioneer, has tagged along but is increasingly troublesome, becoming finally the lawless outcast whom Burnett must confront. George Millard is restrained while Dr. Ralph Whitcomb cuts off his leg. Whit Rinearson finds bad company and sheriff Joe Meek kills him. Squaw man Bob Hawn's wife sees regret in his eyes and goes away. Recently widowed Mr. Irish watches her frail son attempt a man's labor. Lucy Collingwood dallies with Dr. Whitcomb while her politically ambitious husband George travels the countryside (and goes too far, being swept over Willamette Falls). Noisy fundamentalist Lot White rails against sin, of which there is much, and shriveled Gram Gay sees grim portents in strange places. Thirty or so characters were introduced into the story and a smaller, wiser number survived its telling.

In early January, with a first draft completed, Erny gave Angus Cameron his final presubmission report.

> Katherine got pushed away from center stage by Edna too frequently; that was my fault, not Katherine's. I was preoccupied with Edna. It is curious, too, that I avoided bringing [the hero] into conflict with our cosmic villain, Lockyear, very much. That comes about from my fear of making this another serial thing in which hero and bad man are always slugging it out.
>
> After this revision, I'll send it on. Then there must be another revision —for style's sake and economy's sake. I throw a lot of punches in this thing and some of them don't land. I'm at the point where I don't know which ones do and which ones don't. That's where you come in.
>
> Modern writing—Hemingway—tends to convey a sense of discovery and search and confusion within people but to keep these things unexpressed—to let the reader's imagination do the rest. But writing is something more than music and painting; it must not only evoke, it must state. I grow leery of some of these pieces of modern fiction which require a bird dog, a compass, a map and a set of critical reviews to become plausible. *In Sicily*, for example, is a delightful story [by Elio Vittorini], a downright pleasure to read. But when the critics get through with it, it has more layers of meaning than the Empire State Building has floors.

In a pair of notes to his mother in January and February, he gloomed about the inevitable dissolution of a family that, although discordant in some respects, was the only functional one he had known. And his son, the unlikely scholar, mildly ruffled him. He seemed not to notice his slight imprint on the boy.

> The kids [Sister and her husband and Brother] came up from Eugene and put in ten days with us, which made things seem much more like old times. It might possibly be the last Christmas we shall spend together as a family, for if Jim Wallace should get a job on a magazine, it probably wouldn't be anywhere around this part of the country.

Jim H. is working like a truck horse at his studies, trying to keep his grades up to last term's level, which is a mighty hard thing to do since he got so close to the top. The work's getting harder, of course. He surprised us with his determination and his girl, Susan, complains he's taking it too seriously and not having enough fun. But you can't tell Jim H. anything. He's got a square head and he must learn things the tough way.*

After receiving and digesting Little, Brown's comments on the manuscript in late March, he turned again to Howard Cady, whose analysis of *The Adventurers* had so impressed him. He conceded some of his publisher's criticisms while others seemed niggling nonsense. The story needed some work; but how much?

Therefore, between editor and writer there's a no man's land in which the editor seeks to imply and suggest without offense and . . . the author tries to evaluate the things meant in the things said. Almost always the writer looks for brusquer meaning behind the gentle editorial statement. So between editor and writer there's a sort of process in which they extend their antenna and seek to identify vibrations rather than words.

That's my position now. I have had answer from the east. In the beginning are the gentle words. "This is a big, important, satisfying novel—surely a book club choice." This is from a reader, who continues by saying that some of the scenes are repetitious and ought to be cut. Angus . . . says the repetitiousness rises from values not yet fully developed in the story. His reaction is that the characters walk out of the scenes pretty much the same people they were when they walked in; and from this he concludes that the basic need is to develop the hero, Rice Burnett, into a more dynamic figure.

Since writing the story I've let it simmer. From the simmering I've concluded to beef up Katherine. She needs to be somewhat more aggressive in the community, which is no great writing chore. She needs to

*Father and son had a bit of a blowup when Jim declined an invitation to join Delta Tau Delta, Erny's fraternity at the University of Oregon. There hadn't been any prior discussion of the subject between them and, for a time, Jim didn't realize why he was berated "for not following through on anything." The incident helps explain Erny's dour assessment of his boy at this point.

consider herself in relation to the big guy she had intended to marry . . . [and the hero] needs to emote a little more. I kept him pretty well under control; and in the scenes he has with both girls, a greater pull and haul wouldn't hurt. To that extent I subscribe to Angus' reaction. The difficult part of the evaluation begins beyond that . . . [and] the question seems to be: do we have a story which is actually weak in terms of story, conflict and drama, or do we have a decent story which, with sharpening, could be a more sure-fire thing? I avoided certain head-on conflicts, not wishing to make this a contrived story on the serial pattern. It's somewhat a problem in my mind whether I avoided such complication too much.

A writer . . . has to discount his own views, up to a point; he has to recognize the validity of other judgments, up to a point. Where is the point? . . . I'd say that a writer's version of a story, no matter how sprawling it might be, is better then a critic's version, no matter how tailored it might be; for a writer's version—if he felt the thing—at least has a pulse beat, whereas tailoring sometimes removes heart, lungs and liver. A bit of snipping here and there won't hurt—never does. In the end the corpus will, I hope, remain intact and improved.

I look forward to [the next novel] with a certain amount of eagerness, for I think we'll have a robust adventure story mixed in with Oregon background, circa 1855—eight years after this present novel. The little Oregon towns were coming on and life in these parts had acquired another flavor. It was a nice time. Then came the Indian wars in Southern Oregon.

There followed a long dispatch to Little, Brown in which he examined all of the scenes involving the principal players, to suggest to Cameron where modifications did or didn't make sense. The villain, Cal Lockyear, would be made a less brutal character at the outset so that his evolution into a murderous outcast packed more wallop; and the dithering lovers, Lucy Collingwood and Dr. Ralph Whitcomb, were indeed redundantly hesitant in spots. There would be several hundred nips and tucks, although the title, which neither he nor Little, Brown much cared for and Cady said had dull, agrarian connotations, never was changed.

There were other, later messages from Erny to Angus, one written eighteen days before his operation:

> I got about 100 pages of novel revised when I came down with a case of jaundice; so now I'm in bed, and will remain in bed for another week, and that will delay the completion of the revise by damned near a month. Don't get this particular ailment if you can choose any other. It's not at all painful but everything tastes very bad, and smells very bad . . . and reading in bed is a very much overrated pastime.

And a further message written nineteen days after Erny's operation, focused on the philosophic essence of several characters.

> The clue to this conflict lies in Burnett's growing awareness of the essential evil of Lockyear's philosophy . . . which is essentially anarchy, negation, nothing-comes-to-nothing; Lockyear hurts everything he touches, so that Burnett sees there is no such thing as live and let live . . . or indifference to any cry of misery; we are all obligated.
>
> In the story, the doctor sees the concept as clearly as Burnett . . . [but] doesn't take a position, for education has infected him with as much skepticism as it has conviction of perfectibility. But Burnett is another animal . . . a better instrument than the doctor because it is in his makeup to discharge his usefulness as an instrument. The doctor would say: "What's the use of all this?" Burnett would say: "I was put here to do something, and I'll not waste my time figuring out why."
>
> But I won't be at work for two or three weeks. It was a rough routine and I have got to get back 20 pounds and some energy.

In Europe, Jill and Jim were enthusiastic travelers despite Spartan accommodations and student-tour services that fell far short of economy class. The boy, now nineteen, considered himself beyond need of maternal oversight and this created occasional friction. But unaware of the bad news back home, they had a fine time, as these reports (first from Jill, who quickly forgot shipboard limitations, then Jim) attest.

> I am in a cabin or dormitory [aboard the *Volendam*] with about 20 other people (two babies) . . . [and] I have the lower bunk. Now I can

realize how it must be in the army. Everyone perspired all night. . . . Dinner and breakfast, we were sort of herded into a place where we sat at long tables. They use a lot of something I've never tasted before; it sort of turns your stomach.

You would get so much out of the people on this boat; it's a shame you aren't here instead of me. Of course, it's very democratic. Jim plays canasta a lot with a married woman . . . going to Germany to join her husband. She is probably 30. A little on the smart side. Thinks she is an authority on canasta. Well, I licked the socks off her.

There is also a section of the boat that one of our members was told to stay away from as she wasn't that kind of person. Apparently a lot goes on that I don't know about. My friend Minerva [someone she'd met, Jill explained, once married "to the ambassador of someplace"] started telling me how one time in San Antonio she was attacked by a man. He had a gun but she seemed to hold her own. Well, she went on and on, waving her hands and getting all worked up . . . [and finally disclosing that] the man is on board. She had gone to the Catholic priest about it and then to the captain. I am beginning to discount quite a bit she has said. If she is so darned important, why is she on this ship?

We have worked out a system where everyone gets on the train and bags come on or off through the windows [Jim wrote]. The sad part is that the two heaviest bags in the whole group are (first) hers and (second) mine. God! And does Ma ever worry about them.

As for the two of us, all has gone very smooth. There was only one small flare-up the time I forgot our two small bags at the hotel and (she says) carried some dame's stuff to the train. Now there wasn't a speck of truth to it. . . .

Late in July, before the second operation, Erny wrote to his mother:

I have returned to work but I'm not very forceful about it yet. In the middle of the morning I break off for a glass of milk or a banana. After lunch I lie on the office couch for half an hour, or so long as it pleases me. Middle of the afternoon I have another light snack. And I go home fairly early and get to bed fairly early. My strength picks up little by little. I'm

138, still 12 pounds short; but these hot days I don't have appetite enough to lay on weight. This week I've been battling with a bit of stomach flu which is going the rounds, and that has slowed things down somewhat. Otherwise, everything's swell.

Erny had recently moved his office to another downtown building, and Bob Case, with whom he would briefly share secretarial services, was next door. He wrote the following messages to Jill after his second operation in August. About the end of that month, he gave up trying to go downtown. It had become more than he could manage.

Bob Case moved into the two offices adjoining mine but . . . I don't see much of him, which I suppose is due to the fact that when we last talked over the subject I impressed him with my liking for privacy. We got Ann Case's [marriage] announcement yesterday. Bob says that they are putting their house up for sale and will live in an apartment, so there's the dissolution of one more Great American Family. They've certainly had bad luck with their youngsters after marriage. Oldest girl somewhere in the south, Bobby Jr. at Oak Ridge, Tennessee, and Ann will live in Connecticut.

Perhaps I had better brief you on one thing that's happened here during your absence. I had to go back to the hospital for a second operation.

You were just a day from Rotterdam when I went to the hospital and you were in Munich when I was operated on. It would have been a sad thing to have told you, spoiling your trip completely and maybe ending it. Nothing would have been gained; as it is, things turned out okay. Naturally, I wish you were here—it's been a kind of tedious business, but I could not bring myself to ruin something you had looked forward to for so long.

Erny died in the early hours of October 13, 1950, twelve days beyond his fifty-first birthday. Jill called Bertha later that morning and his mother said she already knew that her son had passed away. She said he had come into the kitchen of her small house in Paradise, California, on the previous evening and had asked for a glass of milk. He drank it, Bertha said, and then quietly departed. ◆

Early in *The Earthbreakers*, as the wagon train suffers a howling storm in the Columbia Gorge, Rice Burnett, alone on a trail, comes across Alpheus Stricklin in a collapsed tent. The man is deathly sick with fever and diarrhea and Burnett, suspecting Stricklin won't survive the night alone, stays with him. It was one of those scenes enlightened by introspection, which Erny mistrusted for most of his writing life but without which he could not convey the picture in his mind in later works or in this particular passage:

> Night moved in full of sound; the little river roared over its stones, the racing clouds broke above the camp and the rain rattled like buckshot and blackness closed on him as the jaws of a vise. It was aloneness which had broken through Stricklin's last wall. Nature, hating the solitary thing—for the solitary thing has no function—had placed in man a sense of incompleteness which made him drift toward others; denied this closeness, he shrank and died. Not that she cared; for man was a vessel she created by the millions, and it didn't matter how many of these claypots were cracked along the way so long as a few survived to transmit the liquid she had poured into them; it was the liquid that mattered to her, not the pot. Man's dream of dignity was his own creation, not hers, and his suffering came of trying to make the dream real against the indifference of earth and sky to his individual fate.

It is certainly not required that a writer limit philosophical musings to those which he or she actually endorses. At the same time, it may be that they are inclined to do so, by comfort if nothing else; and, in Erny's case, the indifferent universe was that one he had been introduced to as a boy and, in later times, found impressed in the history of the frontier. He accepted it, and the careful, analogous reformation of the West in his writing reflected it; but that simply explained the shell of the nut, the outer coating. There remained within the meat or the seed, which had its own purpose and which he believed was capable of mighty achievement. You could be part of the forest but you could aspire to be the biggest damned tree standing, and trying to grow tall was an effort that you did have something to say about, and it was the thing that you were supposed to do. This view explained Rice Burnett and several hundred other indomitable characters that the writer created over a career just short of three decades. More than that, it explained him.

In late 1949 Erny had accepted appointment to a speakers' committee associated with a national brotherhood week, proclaimed by President Truman. He thereby committed himself to address "prominent members" of some community on that subject in 1950. His heavy commitment to the book and his illness evidently precluded the effort, for there is no record of such a presentation in any of the obvious places. But he did make a start at it, probably on some afternoon when *The Earthbreakers* had become intolerably demanding and almost any diversion welcome.

The speech draft that survives is incomplete, more a series of thoughts on the subject of tolerance in order of their occurrence to him than a well-knit message. Among these, somewhat off point, was a thought that had appeared briefly in an otherwise unimportant 1948 talk and had stuck with him, and was elaborated now as testimony, the explanation of his own search "for the light never seen on land or sea."

> We have certain obvious functions on this earth. We must earn our bread; we must create, raise and support our families; we must be useful enough to leave some kind of improvement behind us as rent for the ground we occupied while here.
>
> But beyond that we have a thoroughly personal obligation to ourselves. This brief tenure of ours on the third planet of the solar system was meant to be an adventure. It was not meant to be a mean and miserable adventure in which year by year superstitions and fears and petty qualities fasten themselves to us until near the end of life we stand shriveled and futile and wait for escape. Plan or no plan, we were meant to break these chains, to round and enrich ourselves, to acquire spiritual freedom and dignity and the capacity for enjoyment, and thus at last to be able to look back and say of ourselves: "This was my life and I made as much of it as I could." Otherwise, what are we doing here?

Afterthoughts and Acknowledgments

THE EXPLOSION OF PAPERBACK PUBLISHING AND THE POPULARITY of western motion pictures for many years beyond World War II, the advent of the television drama and the later growth of large-print and library-edition books and, lastly, of recorded literature, created a sustaining market for my father's work. Between the 1950s and 1990s, some of the novels reappeared a half-dozen times, and to this day, an occasional new volume or recording is obtainable, although Haycox is still easier to find on the western shelf of some used-book merchant. Anthologies of notable western literature continue to incorporate his work and, of course, *Stagecoach* rolls on and on.

His last novel, *The Earthbreakers*, released in January 1952, drew mostly enthusiastic reviews. Bernard De Voto would later say he didn't care for it, suggesting that Haycox was still defending the western myth and incidentally making light of A. B. Guthrie's celebrated 1949 wagon-train epic, *The Way West*. (Fearing stylistic influences, of course, Erny wouldn't have touched Guthrie's fine work while his own opus was evolving.) Most reviewers found *The Earthbreakers* a powerful story. "The best western novel of the year," said Harrison Smith in the *Saturday Review of Literature*. There was, of course, the one problem that Smith explained: "It has the quality of vigor and of freshness that may bewilder his faithful readers, who will find themselves wandering in an unknown country and involved in problems that the simple cowboy and rancher never knew."

Erny's continued popularity was due in no small degree to the determination of his wife. It was in Jill's financial interest to keep the presses and the cameras rolling, but there was more to it—involving pride and some degree of sorrow that she had not done particularly well by him as a wife. That kind of remorse often fades but hers never did, and she vigorously managed his literary estate and promoted his memory well into her eighties. If money had been the only measure, she would have sold his remarkable library, but she would gift it, and later his manuscripts, to the University of Oregon.

Jill's recollections and the resources that she both preserved and enlarged make her in many respects a co-author of this volume. And what I would say to her now is that, though I attempted to tell the story without bias, it has somewhat troubled me to limit her to a largely contrary role in the proceedings. She and Erny tried to keep their problems away from their children. In truth, it may not have been entirely the one-sided conflict between a good man and an angry woman that I from time to time observed.

I would next acknowledge my sister, Mary Ann Wallace, three years my senior and much wiser. She offered many insights and recollections in this project's early stages, and I regret she wasn't able to stay the course with me. And then my family—a wife of more than four decades who cheerfully tolerated this expedition, occasionally challenging its conclusions, and the four daughters who encouraged the effort. These are Erny's granddaughters—Elizabeth, Maria, Katherine Gay, and Brooke, the last (a third-generation Oregon J-school graduate) being a most helpful critic. I also want to recognize Jay Fultz for his invaluable editorial assistance on this project. His comments and suggestions and organizing skills led to countless useful elaborations and clarifications.

I am indebted to Richard Etulain (professor emeritus of history, University of New Mexico), who produced a doctoral thesis on Ernest Haycox while at the University of Oregon in 1966 and generously supplied me with his research. Etulain has published several commentaries on my father including a 1988 study that is part of the Boise State University Western Writers Series. Stephen Tanner (professor of English, Brigham Young University) had helpful suggestions and deserves mention for his book, *Ernest Haycox*, published in 1996 as a component of Twayne's United States Authors Series, and for other studious appraisals of the man. A number of others have examined and commented on my father's work over the years, often with favor. However, my story ends in 1950 and most of this material is of later date and, with a few footnoted exceptions, inapplicable to this account.

The Special Collections Department at the University of Oregon Library maintains my father's library and his manuscripts and has material from some other sources, the best of which was contributed by Prof. W. F. G. Thatcher (particularly those letters on writing and its problems that Erny addressed to Thatcher over about twenty years). Arthur (Ole) Larson, my father's close friend at college and ever after, saved correspondence from the Haycox interlude (1924–26) in New York; and two other good friends, writers Robert Ormond Case and Stewart Holbrook, offered glimpses of the man, Case in a very long letter to Etulain and Holbrook in two books and several newspaper columns. In the Crowell-Collier correspondence collection at the New York Public Library, many of those insouciant Haycox messages to fiction editor Ken Littauer surfaced. Of the many general reference sources utilized, *The New Encyclopedia of the American West*, edited by Howard Lamar (Yale University Press, 1998), deserves particular mention.

As books do, this one changed course occasionally and a good deal of family history didn't make the final cut. Nonetheless, countless helpful relatives—most of whom I'd not known before—deserve thanks, including half a dozen members of the Burghardt clan, particularly Willa Hipwell, who produced an abundance of letters and photographs and her uncle Charlie Burghardt's marvelous boyhood recollection. Also, Bill Burghardt, Roy and Dianne Burghardt, Veryl Stone, and Sedonia Wire. Several Haycox or near-Haycox descendants (distant cousins or in-laws or those related to WJ's second wife) dug deep, including Zilpha Haycox, Wally Holden, Betty Pritchard, Albert Kuschke, Bertha Branson, and Ruby Jean Harding. From Jill's side of the family—the Sullivan clan of her mother—records and recollections came from Stewart Sullivan, Macy Ragle and Sidnie Wilson.

Others who were helpful with grants of permission or recollections, or both, included two of Bob Case's children, Robert O. Case, Jr., and Mrs. Patricia Owen, and Sybil Holbrook, Stewart's daughter. As to permissions generally, every effort was made to obtain authorizations to reprint material directly quoted from other sources. The passage of time made this task difficult in some cases and evidently impossible in others. However, I will happily amend any future issues of this book to incorporate deserving credits that, for whatever reasons, are missing from this edition.

Finally, it is appropriate to thank many people designated as reference or research librarians at state and county historical societies in Oregon, California, Wisconsin, and New York. In Oregon, this list includes organizations in Clackamas and Columbia counties and the Oregon Military Museum at Camp Withycombe, where Private Haycox had his first target practice and bayonet drill many years back. Robb Wilson of the Columbia County Museum at Vernonia arranged an expedition with the help of Lee Enneberg along dim forest roads to the long-abandoned Haycox homestead in the hills above the Nehalem River. This was perhaps the most interesting day of the long march, but not one was dull.

Notes

MOST OF THE LETTERS AND OTHER DOCUMENTS CITED HERE ARE IN the author's possession. External sources include the Crowell-Collier correspondence collection at the New York Public Library, attributed to NYPL in these notes; Little, Brown & Co. (letters), designated LB; Professor Richard Etulain (research material), designated RE; and the Haycox Memorial Library maintained by the Special Collections Department of the University of Oregon Library (various documents), designated UOSC.

CHAPTER 1 ◆ ON A LATE FRONTIER

5 *There was a near miss:* it is uncertain whether Grandfather Burghardt, who was born Ernst and in later times favored Earnest, knew precisely when or where this trampling occurred, but such detail probably can be inferred. On July 13, 1864, while the Fourteenth was marching on the flank of a wagon column near Tupelo, Mississippi, it was surprised and overrun by a mass of Confederate horsemen.

6 *The family settled in Cleveland:* the Haycoxes appear to have been fairly prosperous emigrants, in part due to assets that Maria was said to have inherited from her mother. Family story has it that the mother, while serving in the household of the Duke of Gloucester, was impregnated by this noble gentleman and was settled upon. There is some circumstantial evidence, but not much, to support the claim.

8 *"all Eddy ever learned to do":* the record of the Burghardt family up to about 1890 comes from a long memoir prepared by son Charlie many years later. It is very much a boy's story, carefully describing meals, the

contents of wagons and his beloved ox team, while failing to mention the arrival of new brothers or sisters or his mother's activities much beyond the kitchen. Ernest was his bright star; brother Eddy appears occasionally, almost always in trouble.

9 *"The aroused fishermen":* this is from an incomplete manuscript in EH's files that WJ evidently intended to be both a recollection and a history of the Columbia River steamboat era.

10 *William S. U'Ren and Christian Scheubel:* U'Ren remains one of the best-remembered Oregonians for his advocacy of direct democracy and political reform. He was the guiding spirit behind liberal legislation that gave Oregon's citizens (and those of many other states that copied Oregon statutes) the right to initiate legislation and to recall public officials, and he is credited as well with the direct primary for senators and a corrupt practices act. Scheubel was a champion of workers' as well as voters' rights and his roots, like U'Ren's, were in the briefly popular Populist Party of the late 1890s.

CHAPTER 2 ◆ STROPPED ON HARD STONES

16 *. . . full of memories:* EH to W. F. G. Thatcher; undated copy, probably 1945.

17 *"in charge of logging operations":* from an interview (*Oregon Journal*, August 17, 1947) written by Fred Lockley, in which WJ tended to overstate the importance of various positions held and shaded other circumstances, in one example observing that he had remarried "after the death of my first wife." Lockley made a career of old-timer interviews, which, though lacking a critical eye, preserve a marvelous human record of old times.

17 *"When the bitter wind howled":* from "On Reflection," EH's column in *Spokes*, the Portland Rotary Club weekly bulletin, March 6, 1934.

19 *He would describe to his friend:* the source is Stewart Holbrook's *Lost Men of American History* (1946), 316.

19 *"I saw nothing in the system":* EH speech, untitled, Oregon Republican Club, January 31, 1945.

19 *When I was in funds:* Ibid.

20 *"never staying in one place":* EH to Thatcher, undated copy, probably 1945.

20 *"There were two hundred and fifty":* EH speech, untitled, to county school superintendents, Salem, Oregon, June 4, 1943.

21 *To this day grammar:* Ibid.

23 *Say that the customer would:* Stewart Holbrook. *The Story of American Railroads* (1947), 404. Holbrook, who never asked to be taken too seriously, grandly suggested that Erny's venture into railroad merchandising ranked with that of another great American peanut butcher, Thomas A. Edison. I remember hearing the railroad yarn from its source on several occasions but, in the father-to-son version, the instructions on short-changing were omitted.

23 "*the vow of an insolent youth*": this is from EH's 1917 *War Diary*, of which more will be heard shortly.

24 *Earlier, in 1927:* "Ambushed," *Western Story*, February 1927.

25 *Their talk went on:* from "Their Own Lights," *Collier's*, October 1933. This story also has appeared under the author's original title, "Episode—1880," in anthologies.

26 *A boy—an undersized boy:* from *Long Storm* (1946), chapter 1.

CHAPTER 3 ◆ BORDER PATROL AND THE WOBBLY WAR

27 *"At that stage of adolescence":* EH speech, untitled, to county school superintendents, Salem, Oregon, June 4, 1943.

28 *During my last year at High:* this and many following quotations in this chapter are from his *War Diary*. It is a tablet of approximately fifty lined pages, all of which he utilized between July 19 and July 25, 1917.

29 *"We expect to march":* EH to Mary Haycox (later Johnson), written in segments aboard the troop train between June 29 and July 2, 1916. He said the train was sealed at one California town because occupants of a previous train had debarked there and gotten drunk. His sympathies were at this point decidedly prohibitionist. "It was a good thing when Oregon went dry," he told his cousin, "and it will be a better thing when the U.S. goes dry, for when anything breaks down a man's will power and makes a helpless slave out of him, makes him a victim of his own depraved desire, then that thing should be kicked out of the country and kicked out fast."

29 "*having a girl to think of*": Ibid.

29 *At first they merely went:* Ibid.

30 Clackamas was an earlier name for Camp Withycombe. The facility remains in service today, though the range has been closed. It is near Oregon City on state highway 224, which, farther east, passes over Deep Creek and through Barton.

30 *"At times, farming seems too tame":* EH to Mary Haycox.

31 *"who girded his armor":* EH. "A Man's Life", *Cardinal*, probably December 1916.

31 *"Seriously, I think your stuff":* Ira Berkey to EH, August 26, 1917.

32 *The Industrial Workers of the World:* on one level, the union's demands for better wages and working conditions were not considered entirely unreasonable. Unfortunately for the rank and file, however, its leadership and literature proclaimed the destruction of capitalism to be the real goal, and industrial sabotage was encouraged. Outside of work stoppages, there probably wasn't a great deal of actual damage done in Oregon and Washington but, with western industry and agriculture called to a maximum wartime effort, talk alone was enough to justify the use of troops.

32 *Corporal Haycox's platoon:* information on the platoon's activities comes from various stories published in the *Wenatchee Daily World* in July 1917. Newspapers would shortly curtail reports of troop movements and domestic military operations under a national policy of voluntary censorship.

33 *"The people are very hospitable": War Diary.*

33 *"who stayed with their jobs": Wenatchee Daily World*; "Strikers, Chiefly I. W. W.'s, Rounded Up in Leavenworth," July 18, 1917.

33 *Wednesday night, July 17: War Diary*. Erny confiscated several pieces of IWW correspondence during the raid, including one report detailing a successful strike action at Aberdeen, Washington. There were thirty-five women working in one mill and another was out of business. "Closed down; couple of cars loading," said the IWW correspondent. "Boss driving horse." The prize of the collection was a series of gummed labels that IWW sympathizers attached to machinery and windows and other convenient vertical surfaces. Some were grim, threatening sabotage and other forms of retribution; a few were passably lyrical: "SLOW DOWN The hours are long, the pay is small, So take your time, And buck them all."

34 *"Up here they have discussed":* Ibid.

35 *"The situation seems to be":* Ibid.

35 *"about the ventilation of their bedchambers": Wenatchee Daily World*; "I.W.W Prisoners Removed to Newly Made Stockade," July 25, 1917.

36 *"I can't conceive": War Diary.*

37 *"Well, I get to go up town":* L. O. McLaughlin to EH, July 16, 1917.

37 *"Well, I think I will do":* McLaughlin to EH, August 12, 1917.

37 *"she told me something": War Diary.*

37 *"Do you think the party":* Ira Berkey to EH, July 26, 1917.

37 *"You never cursed":* This is a letter to EH dated August 4, 1917, and signed RAB. The young lady lived at Parkplace and evidently liked Erny a lot despite his bad habits. "Why didn't you slip away from Camp some time during Chautauqua and come over to the grounds?" she asked. "I looked and waited for you almost every day but I never did see you there. I suppose you had lots of duties to attend to 'tho—having charge of a small band of men as you do." Perhaps this was the lamented Ruth.

38 *"My bluest moments arise":* from a notation found with letters EH received in 1917 and 1918 and titled "Passing the Time Away."

38 *. . . I enlisted with visions of:* EH., "Soldiering, First Impressions and Later Corrections," *Cardinal*, June 1917.

CHAPTER 4 ◆ ST. AGONY

40 *"If I can get an occasional pass": War Diary.*

41 *When we arrived:* EH radio talk, "Leave of Absence," KGW, Portland, April 23, 1931.

41 *"The weather was severe": The 162nd Infantry (Old Third Oregon) in France—An Inspiration*, p. 10. This pamphlet at the Oregon Military Museum at Camp Withycombe is neither attributed nor dated.

41 *All the other companies:* "Leave of Absence."

42 *There was the usual delay:* EH, "Embarked!" This unpublished story of the crossing was written no later than 1926.

42 *"We came charging down":* Ibid.

42 *"We would crawl":* Ibid.

43 *Someone cried the alarm:* Ibid.

43 *In from the right side:* Ibid.

44 *Private Elmer Johnson:* Johnson's memoir of wartime service at the Oregon Military Museum reveals that he was quickly shipped to the front, where he would win three battle clasps. The 162nd was battle-ready, he said, for his new regular army unit found he needed no additional training.

45 *With red brassards:* EH radio talk, untitled, KGW, Portland, April 2, 1931.

46 *"We were neatly dropped":* EH, "Who Won the War? The S.O.S!," unpublished short story, 1926 or earlier.

46 *"surpassed man's wildest conception":* EH, "St. Agony," unpublished short story, 1926 or earlier.

47 *"its existence buried":* Ibid.

47 *I think no body of men:* "Who Won the War? The S. O. S!"

49 *Well boy, for speed:* L. O. McLaughlin to EH, October 16, 1918.

50 *Well, have you managed:* McLaughlin to EH, November 2, 1918.

50 *I have before me:* McLaughlin to EH, January 6, 1918.

50 *"Sonnie," she complained:* Bertha to EH, August 10, 1917.

51 *"I start today as":* WJ to Erny, October 1, 1918.

51 *"I wish you could see":* Bertha to EH, November 11, 1918.

51 *"It has created":* a note found with his letter packet.

51 *"Nov. 28. Rumors!":* Ibid.

51 *Soings, France:* Ibid.

CHAPTER 5 ◆ "HE WOULD LET NOTHING INTERFERE . . ."

53 *"that will enable me":* EH to the registrar, University of Oregon, April 15, 1919. UOSC.

57 *the early spring hanging gardens:* EH, "Vegetable Bonnets," *Oregon Daily Emerald*, April 15, 1921.

57 *a senior can be told:* EH, "Dissertation on Cords," *Emerald*, March 16, 1921.

57 *I am truly cosmopolitan:* EH, "Oh! Slush!", *Emerald*, March 1, 1921.

58 *"Our little standing army":* EH, "R. O. T. C. Rapped as Useless," *Emerald*, January 12, 1922.

60 *"No self-respecting wielder":* EH's introduction to a collection of his rejection slips, assembled in a notebook and evidently presented to Professor Thatcher about the time of the writer's graduation in 1923. UOSC.

60 *"We were hard put to":* this and the two following quotations in this paragraph are excerpted from the above-cited notebook. The first two are from letters to the writer dated July 6, 1921, and April 12, 1922. UOSC.

61 *"tone it down some":* Herbert Bashford to EH, May 8, 1921. UOSC.

61 *Quite the best thing about Eddie:* EH, "A Persistent Writer's Success," *The Writer*, September 1922.

62 *And if this were not sufficient:* One of these stories, "Crimson Wheat," was attributed by *Emerald* literary weekly's modest editor to two others, OW and RN. This was sufficiently transparent for the purpose, being the abbreviated identification of The Oregon-Washington Railroad and Navigation Co.

62 *"slightly built but wiry":* James Case to Richard Etulain, April 26, 1963. Jim was the younger brother of writer Robert Ormond Case, who graduated from Oregon before Erny arrived. RE.

64 *Erny probably was recalling:* from "Sir Walter Excepting . . ." which appeared in the February 1942 edition of *Writer's Digest.* Max Wilkinson was a *Collier's* fiction editor.

65 *The beginning writer:* Ibid.

CHAPTER 6 ◆ THE GIFT OF PROSPECT PARK

68 *"one piece of awfully workable":* Jessie Scott to W. F. G. Thatcher, October 13, 1950. UOSC.

68 *"What does it matter":* "Kalamans Divide Speeders' Fines," *Oregonian,* December 11, 1923. This is an unlikely utterance from someone facing a traffic court judge and one suspects it is an example of Erny's what-he-meant-to say rule of quotation. The Haycox method worked best, of course, when—as in this case—the speaker wasn't identified and, therefore, couldn't complain.

69 *"the swing and the vigor":* EH book review, *The Writings of Theodore Roosevelt,* by Herman Hagedorn, *Oregonian,* October 14, 1923.

69 *"with the zeal of":* EH book review, *My Journey Round the World,* by Lord Northcliffe, *Oregonian,* October 14, 1923.

69 *"There is, however":* EH book review, *Strenuous Americans,* by Roy F. Dibble, *Oregonian,* December 30, 1923.

70 *sat in the office of:* "Bride Arrested in Poison Case," *Oregonian,* March 2, 1924. This and preceding quotations in this paragraph from other *Oregonian* accounts are offered as examples of police-beat reporting's engaging style at the time. Reporter Haycox is probably represented here, but that can't be confirmed.

70 *"The man who ran the place":* EH speech, untitled, Oregon Republican Club, Portland, January 31, 1945.

71 *"to check up on daily work":* initially, this ledger enclosed a record of Erny's revenues, expenses, investments, and the like. However, most of the pages involving miscellaneous financial data were ripped out and, starting in 1928, it became a log of stories written and sold that he would maintain for the rest of his life. Albert Wetjen, mentioned in the November 29 entry, was a writer and one-time Oregonian whom Erny would later describe as both unusually talented and off-the-wall.

73 *"temples dedicated to mangling":* EH radio talk, "Further Confessions of a Bohemian," KGW, Portland, May 14, 1931.

74 *"was batiked in nine odd colors":* Ibid.

74 *"Once [a writer] began":* Ibid.

75 *"There is a tension":* EH, "A trip to Washington, D. C. June 27, 1926." This two-page note, perhaps intended for a diary, included a grim assessment of Philadelphia, "a city sprawled all over God's creation, with beautiful suburbs that will soon be slums if something is not done to arrest the mass building of one- and two-family dwellings, built into each other for endless blocks . . ."

75 *the Chords and the Sullivans:* these two families, like the Burghardts and Haycoxes, were late-frontier arrivals in Oregon, settling in and around Baker City between about 1870 and 1900. Unlike Erny's progenitors, they were acquainted, but they were not uniformly friendly. Some of Jill's uncles, who were second generation but still Irish as could be, greatly disliked Jill's father, James Chord, a reserved descendant of Scotch immigrants, an accountant, and an accomplished musician. After his death in 1911, their sister Mary's boarding house further offended Sullivan sensibilities, and her later achievement in the business world was likewise begrudged.

CHAPTER 7 ◆ "HAVE YOU READ THOSE STORIES?"

80 *He had company:* EH to Ole Larson, 1925, undated.

81 . . . *feeling better than:* EH to Ole Larson, late 1925, undated. Larson preserved the correspondence and made copies for Jill in 1974. There are about fifteen letters, mostly written in New York in 1926.

81 *My desire is to hit:* EH to Larson, February 8, 1926.

81 *I give you two years:* EH to Larson, mid-1926, undated.

82 *I don't like realism:* EH to Larson, February 8, 1926.

82 *I think most people:* EH to Larson, March 8, 1926.

82 . . . *did you follow:* Ibid.

82 *Speaking of coming home:* EH to Larson, February 8, 1926.

83 *I do not deny:* EH to Larson, January 5, 1926.

87 *Case knew something about:* Bob Case's view of Jill comes from a long letter he wrote to Richard Etulain, then a graduate student and thesis writer at the University of Oregon, on February 1, 1964. It is principally a

warm appreciation of Erny but contains a number of bleak references to Jill (which Case said, if published, would have to be moderated). "The most charitable appraisal of Jill, I suppose," he concluded, "is to say that she wasn't Ernest's intellectual equal." RE.

89 *Zane Grey and Frederick Faust:* details in this paragraph concerning these two titans of western adventure in its heyday are found in Frank Gruber's authorized biography of the master (*Zane Grey*, 1970) and Gruber's autobiography (*The Pulp Jungle*, 1967), in which Faust appears at some length. Himself a novelist and later a screenwriter, Gruber thought Erny "probably the best western *writer* of all. His prose was sparse and beautiful. His pages rang with authenticity. As a craftsman, he was greatly admired and imitated by his fellow writers" (*Zane Grey*, p. 108). As a fledgling author in the 1930s, Gruber said he wrote to Erny, confessing that his own attempts at western fiction seemed artificial. "He wrote back and suggested a number of factual western books that might be of help . . . [and] gave me the name of a rare book dealer from whom I might obtain these books. I spent $200 at this dealer's on my first visit" (*The Pulp Jungle*, p. 152).

Gruber also thought well of Frederick Glidden (Luke Short) as a western writer, as do many others. A list of other notable western storytellers whose careers intersected with Erny's and whose work appeared in slick magazines and in book form would include James Warner Bellah, Harry Sinclair Drago, Alan LeMay, William McLeod Raine, and Eugene Manlove Rhodes.

90 *This shortness of limb:* EH, *Return of a Fighter,* Chap. 2.

90 *"a typical example":* New York Herald-Tribune, February 17, 1929. Hometown assessments were somewhat more generous. Haycox was "an able and interesting writer . . . [and] a student of history," said *Oregonian* reviewer Ep Hoyt, who could have said no less of his close friend's first book. (*Oregonian*, March 3, 1929). Portland's *Oregon Journal* thought it "a thrilling, wholesome book for the whole family" (February 17, 1929).

90 *There's two ways:* EH to Larson, November 7, 1926. Both sender and recipient were in Portland at this moment and one assumes this written communication was intended for emphasis. Ole wanted to write but hadn't done much, and his friend was losing patience. "You may have been able to pull me all over the tennis court, but by Godfrey I'll pull you all over the literary roads before I'm through with you," Erny bellowed. "Now don't let me have any more of that old brand of oatmeal. Next time I see you I want to see something on paper that I can sink my teeth into."

91 *"Have you read":* this is from several pages of undated notes Larson prepared late in his life. UOSC.

93 *September 5. 1930. I begin:* EH's personal diary, which runs about forty typewritten pages, was a sporadic thing, gaps between entries sometimes spanning several years. "The Manhunter" (September 19 entry) was retitled "McQuestion Rides" in *Collier's* but wasn't Erny's first appearance in that magazine. "Dolorosa, Here I Come," which *Collier's* next bought in October, was first to run, in its issue of February 28, 1931. In good company, it might be added—preceded by the first installment of a Sax Rohmer thriller and shortly followed by the concluding episode of Erich Maria Remarque's *The Road Back.*

96 *"Two thousand words!":* Edison Marshall to EH, January 11, 1930. "I didn't [write] it because you did a favor for me. People are always doing favors for me, and I do favors for no one. I did it only because I'm weak-willed and find it hard to say no—particularly to an old friend."

96 *"as we have only two days":* James Norman Hall to EH, March 24, 1931.

96 *"I may fill a notebook":* Ibid. Also from that letter are all of the other brief quotations in this and the following paragraph. Hall's comment that he wasn't fond of "breathless action" is hard to take at face value. He was writing *Mutiny on the Bounty* (1932, with Charles Nordhoff) about this time, and it certainly didn't lack for heart-thumping and spine-tingling passages. Joseph Joubert (1754–1824) was a meditative Frenchman, an observer of life and literature in their abstract forms.

CHAPTER 8 ◆ OLD VOICES

111 *The other day:* EH radio talk, untitled, KOIN, January 28, 1930.

111 *Possibly you will wonder:* Ibid.

112 *"a long-haired, poetical-looking creature":* EH speech, untitled, Baker Kiwanis Club, July 26, 1927.

112 *what I'd like to get over:* Ibid.

113 *Let us lay all the fancy words:* EH, "On Reflection," *Spokes*, September 25, 1934.

114 *"I suppose I am some sort of":* EH to A. L. Strand, October 6, 1949.

114 *"And now Franklin Roosevelt":* "On Reflection," *Spokes*, January 14, 1936.

118 *"You seem to forget":* Jack Chord to Jill and Erny, April 9 [1938].

119 *"The Charm you created":* Ken Littauer to EH, January 7, 1935. NYPL.

120 *"When any writer gets":* EH to Littauer, January 12, 1935. NYPL.

120 *We're pretty close:* EH to Littauer, June 22, 1934. NYPL.

122 *"That famous ride":* Maurice Fitzgerald to EH, October 5, 1938.

123 *"I would not know":* Lew L. Callaway to EH, September 14, 1940.

123 *Charles H. Sharman:* Sharman's narrative letter to the author appeared in edited form as "A Very Special Party" in the Spring 2001 edition of *Montana*, a quarterly publication of the Montana Historical Society.

123 *"I was highly honored":* Lee Howard to EH, undated. Mr. Howard's many contributions to EH's research file included the following, hair-raising description of frontier medicine: "When we had a toothache we took a bit of cotton dipped in camphor, arnica or even crude carbolic acid and inserted it in the cavity, then danced and cussed until it burnt out the nerve." For boils, exceedingly common in this saddlebound society, poultices of bread and milk or slippery elm bark or cow manure were first applied to bring the beast to a head. "This was the crucial stage when you kept the fellows awake at night with your groans as long as they could stand it. Then they poked your head into a salt barrel, stripped your lower garments . . . and operated [using a knife sterilized with tobacco spit] while you in muffled curses told of the tortures you would inflict on them when you got loose."

124 *"Perhaps it is kindest":* EH book review, *The Old Wild West. Adventures of Arizona Bill,* by Raymond Hatfield Gardner (Arizona Bill) in collaboration with B. H. Monroe, *New York Times,* June 9, 1944.

124 *"He'd been through a mass:* the writer's library included three dozen books and government reports on the Little Bighorn massacre, including transcripts of the courts-martial of two officers, Reno and Benteen. There were also about one hundred separate volumes and documents dealing with post–Civil War army campaigns, personalities, and facilities.

124 *almost all the experts:* EH to Raymond Everitt, July 14, 1943. Little, Brown editor Everitt did in fact ask Fred Dustin to read *Bugles in the Afternoon* and Dustin generally approved, saying the author was obviously well informed and "may himself have experienced some of the vicissitudes of wind and weather he describes." However, he added, the manuscript was reminiscent of Teddy Roosevelt's strenuous prose in its "use of bad language and exaltation of that phase of American life that has a little of the heroic in it, but a vast deal of the raw, the crude, the vile . . . " (Dustin to Everitt, February 1, 1944). Erny found Dustin's comments generous and his objection to profanity typical. "I have met so many men of the old

school who dislike verbatim portrayal. Had he gone through the army, he would have perhaps not objected" (EH to Everitt, February 9, 1944).

CHAPTER 9 ◆ THE GARDEN OF ALLAH

130 *"schedule for season, 1938–1939":* An undated typewritten page.

131 *"Yourself and Jill done":* WJ to EH, December 20, 1935.

132 *"Outside of a few more buildings":* EH to Jill, February 28, 1937.

133 *"Now there's a fellow":* EH to Jill, March 1, 1937.

133 *Marshall had said something:* EH to Jill, March 4, 1937.

134 *"Of course she wanted to know":* EH to Jill, March 1, 1937.

134 *"We have had a lot of luck":* EH to Jill, March 4, 1937.

135 *The first motion picture sale:* The two 1939 releases are probably the best remembered of Erny's motion pictures: *Stagecoach* rescued John Wayne from B movies, earned Thomas Mitchell a best-supporting-actor Oscar for his portrayal of a drunken doctor, and was for many years ranked among Hollywood's best pictures. *Union Pacific* (Joel McCrea and Barbara Stanwyck) was well-received too, although not critically acclaimed. Erny's opinion of the former was expressed in a letter (March 23, 1939) to Ken Littauer: "It's as good a western as anybody will see. John Ford did a marvelous job of directing. Dudley Nichols did a marvelous job of adapting and, by this manner of modest indirection and spurious praise, may I convey to you the thought that I was marvelous too." NYPL.

136 *Sheilah Graham and Scott Fitzgerald:* several items in this and the following paragraph were taken from, or resuscitated from ancient memory by Ms. Graham's charming book, *The Garden of Allah* (1970).

137 *I lay down two premises:* EH to Ken Littauer, May 3, 1939. NYPL.

140 *a thing to be called Seventh Cavalry:* Ibid. NYPL. It's not clear whether it became a motion picture. A film by that name appeared in 1956, starring Randolph Scott, but the thumbnail plot description doesn't remotely match the Haycox version.

140 *a film treatment of "Stage Station":* it was twice produced, first as *Apache Trail* (with Lloyd Nolan and Donna Reed) in 1942 and then as *Apache War Smoke* (Gilbert Roland and Glenda Farrell) in 1952.

141 *Now this is 1939:* EH to Littauer, January 11, 1939. NYPL. The Hemingway work referred to probably was *The Fifth Column and Four Stories of the Spanish Civil War*, published in 1938.

142 *"Could we, for a little while":* Littauer to EH, Jan 31, 1939. NYPL.

142 *"I can see you tilting":* Littauer to EH, August 2, 1939. NYPL.

142 *"I tried to write":* EH to Littauer, August 16, 1939. NYPL.

142 *"Everything he put his hand to":* R. O. Case to Richard Etulain, February 1, 1964. RE.

143 *The engine pushed a load of rails: Trouble Shooter*, Chap. 4.

144 *Some might have found:* Director Ford's recollections of the film are found in *John Ford's Stagecoach* (Universe Books: New York, 1975).

144 *The stage stopped:* "Stage to Lordsburg."

145 *Suddenly [Hazel] heaved himself erect: The Border Trumpet*, Chap. 14.

CHAPTER 10 ◆ SCENES FROM A DOUBLE LIFE

150 *that Jim Marshall said:* Marshall had a good deal of fun with friend Haycox in a tongue-in-cheek tribute, "Books and Saddles," which ran in *Collier's* on November 29, 1941, coincident with the first installment of *Alder Gulch.* "Haycox likes big things," Marshall wrote. "He smokes the biggest cigars he can find, wears a tentlike overcoat in winter, drives a huge car. His dog, a 200-pound St. Bernard, is built along the lines of a lioness. This dog is rather a trial, because every guest asks Erny where the brandy cask is, and the whole thing is a bit repetitious. His friends used to say that the Haycox bedroom contained a badminton court and a sleeping nook, but this is exaggerated. The net has never been put up."

151 *he made do with long rows:* his 1947 garden, detailed in a letter to Mary Ann, included several rows of berries, peas, carrots, onions, lettuce, beets, cabbage, celery, peppers, corn, and tomatoes. By this time, he may have given up on rhubarb, which he planted profusely for several years and then—the supply far exceeding his family's ability or desire to consume—forced on neighbors, his secretary, his stockbroker, and anyone else who wandered into his office.

154 *"the direct, inevitable result":* from a partial draft in a collection of his miscellaneous writings—possibly an early version of his letter of June 28, 1940, to the *Oregonian.*

155 *Undoubtedly, Mrs. Roosevelt:* from an undated, and apparently unprinted, editorial letter.

156 *If we wish to exist:* "Ernest Haycox: The Road Ahead," letter to the editor, *Oregonian*, June 28, 1940.

156 *the Forty-first needed a postmaster general:* it was probably just as well he didn't go. The Forty-first took heavy casualties in New Guinea, where neither side bothered with prisoners, and many of its survivors contracted malaria. Among notable literary casualties of the war was Max Brand. Frederick Faust went to Italy in 1944 as a war correspondent and was killed by a German shellburst.

157 *Board 1 administered:* "Selective Service Anniversary," editorial, *Oregonian*, October 16, 1945.

157 *"those who were able to state":* EH speech, untitled, at a Portland dinner honoring Oregon's wartime draft board members, March 5, 1946.

158 *If you, as a nondefense business:* EH speech, "Manpower on Main Street," Eugene (Oregon) Rotary, September 15, 1942.

158 *compensating the "captain":* about 1945, Earl gave Jim an unarmed hand grenade that had been tossed into the board's office by a high-spirited returnee. It was an unnerving moment, Sarge said, watching the infernal thing roll across the floor toward him and remembering the anger of some who, having been denied deferment, spoke bluntly of retribution.

159 *The only point of doubt:* EH diary, December 19, 1942.

160 *It is slightly possible:* Erny's introductory remarks at a Republican gathering in Portland April 13, 1944, which featured Ohio Governor John Bricker, then seeking the party's presidential nomination. The "Hopkins method" was, of course, associated with FDR's friend and confidant Harry L. Hopkins, a highly visible New Deal administrator, presidential emissary, and briefly (1938–40) secretary of commerce.

161 *The story of our state capitol:* Dwight Griswold (EH, actually), "The Nebraska Story," *Saturday Evening Post*, September 4, 1943.

162 *Maybe I have lost some faith:* EH diary, September 1945.

163 *The snow whipped against him:* "Deep Winter," *Collier's*, January 1943.

164 *At the same time:* "Dark Land Waiting," *Collier's*, July 1940.

CHAPTER 11 ◆ AS GOOD AS IT GETS

165 *"as much of a characterization":* EH to Raymond Everitt, January 23, 1941.

166 *"once we were convinced":* Everitt to EH, January 30, 1941. LB.

166 *"If I embarked on it":* EH to Everitt, February 5, 1941. LB.

167 *"exceedingly fine treatment":* EH to William Chenery, March 10, 1943. NYPL.

168 *"The tradition of the powerful hero":* EH radio interview, "Ask Your State Library," KOAC, Corvallis, Oregon, November 4, 1942.

169 *With you, there can be no:* EH to W. F. G. Thatcher, in 1932 or 1933. The writer's letters to Professor Thatcher, twenty-five or so in all, were reproduced en mass by Thatcher about 1951, preparatory to a book he planned to write about his former student. Unfortunately, in this reincarnation, dates were excluded. The book didn't proceed, but a few letter excerpts did appear in *Dear W. F. G.*, a promotional pamphlet issued by Little, Brown & Co. in connection with the publication of *The Earthbreakers* in 1952.

169 *"the meaty, detailed inclusive":* EH to Thatcher, circa 1934.

169 *With me, and I suppose:* EH to Thatcher, circa 1937.

170 *"added the Hamlet strain":* Bernard De Voto, "The Easy Chair," *Harper's* Magazine, December 1954. This is perhaps the best-known encapsulation of the Haycox legacy from a man who considered western fiction preposterous and said that Erny, "the old pro of the horse opera," was unable to overcome its mythology and sentimentality. "He turned to other parts of Western history, the emigrant train, the mining camps, the Columbia River steamboats, the Indian wars. He did much better with them and two or three times he came close to breaking through the mythology and writing fiction. *Bugles in the Afternoon*, which incidental to its purpose is a sound history of the Little, Bighorn campaign, is almost a good novel, and a number of his short stories are the real thing."

171 *"This, I think, is the precise note":* EH to Ray Everitt, May 24, 1940, Tom Lea made his mark both as a western painter and writer, the latter work including *The Brave Bulls* (1949) and *The Wonderful Country* (1952).

171 *The other day I began:* EH's diary, October 24, 1944.

172 *Maybe two or three: Long Storm*, Chap. 6.

173 *"a romantic juvenile":* EH To Thatcher, circa 1940.

173 *There is a man:* EH to Thatcher, written while *Long Storm* was in the typewriter, probably September 1944.

174 *He was a smaller man:* James Algar, written under the pen name James Fargo, "*The Western and Ernest Haycox,*" *Prairie Schooner*, Summer 1952.

175 *"a bitter and impoverished":* R. O. Case to Richard Etulain, February 1, 1964. RE.

176 *"Is ham all right":* Ibid.

176 *"I will yield on the matter":* EH to Ray Everitt, July 18, 1940.

177 *but "much more iconoclastic":* EH to H. G. Merriam, July 9, 1932. Professor Merriam established a highly regarded writing program at the University of Montana. On this occasion, Erny declined to join a panel discussion, suggesting Wetjen or Stewart Holbrook in his stead.

177 *"Boy, if you want to rest":* EH commencement address, Lincoln High School, Portland, January 18, 1945.

178 *When we moved them away:* EH speech, untitled, Woodburn (Ore.) Rotary Club, March 23, 1944.

178 *The one shining contrary example:* EH speech, untitled, Oregon Republican Club, Portland, January 31, 1945.

179 *Now it is our time:* EH speech, "Peace Has a Price," Medford (Ore.) Rotary Club, June 25, 1945.

182 *We are, we feel, a region:* EH speech, "Is There a Northwest?" Writers' Conference on the Northwest, Portland, November 1, 1946.

CHAPTER 12 ◆ THE ACCIDENTAL PROFESSION

198 *The Hawaiian vacation put Jill:* Jill to Mary Ann, January 9, 1947.

198 *Governor Oswald West:* West's action preserved Oregon's beaches for public use and he was colorfully tough on crime, on one occasion sending his secretary to reestablish order in a small eastern Oregon town where gamblers and other ne'er-do-wells were temporarily ascendant.

198 *"As with any other writer":* EH to Ray Palmer Tracy, December 29, 1947. Tracy was a minor writer, but Erny admired him for other accomplishments, which included bronco-busting, ranching, and storekeeping in early rural Oregon. EH knew a few other western writers but none of his well-known contemporaries. His literary acquaintances in Oregon, in addition to Bob Case, Richard Wetjen, Jessie Scott, and Ep Hoyt, included John and Ward Hawkins and Ellis Lucia. He was reasonably close to Frank Richardson Pierce in Seattle and fond of several of his *Collier's* counterparts—Jim Marshall, of course, and also Max Wilkinson and Frank J. Taylor. As a Hollywood writer, John Hawkins would script "A Day in Town," which, as *The Windmill* (General Electric Theater, 1954), is said to have featured Ronald Reagan's last television acting role.

199 *It comes close to 400 pages:* EH to Sydney Sanders, March 19, 1947.

200 *It's down from 395 pages:* EH to Sanders, June 17, 1947.

200 *We return to the thing:* EH to Sanders, June 26, 1947.

200 *You comment on the two brothers:* EH to Sanders, July 3, 1947.

201 *Two or three things:* EH to Sanders, February 21, 1947. The "Hollywood project" involved Erny's offer to do a motion picture treatment of *Santa Fe,* a book written by Jim Marshall. He put a high price on it, and there were no takers.

201 *On the Wanger deal:* EH to Sanders, May 7, 1947.

202 *I've never gotten:* EH to Mary Baker, May 27, 1947.

202 *The first story (1864):* EH to Sanders, July 14, 1947.

204 *Can you close your eyes:* EH to Phil Metschan, July 31, 1947.

204 *Harney has turned into nothing:* EH to Metschan, October 27, 1947.

204 *It is not dramatic to say:* EH to Raymond Armstrong, January 2, 1947.

205 *You are trying:* EH to Lawrence Neault, July 11, 1947.

205 *I guess the answer now is:* EH to Clarence Wyman, May 19, 1947.

205 *The proponents of the AAA:* EH to George Holcomb, February 6, 1947.

206 *It is a strange thing that writing:* EH to Professor Philip Souers, March 27, 1947.

206 *Everybody wants to read:* EH to Dr. J. A. Van Brackle, July 30, 1947.

207 *I had no intention:* EH to Sanders, May 7, 1947.

207 *I write so painfully:* EH to Sanders, August 19, 1947

207 *It's been a long hard year:* EH to Jim Marshall, June 12, 1947.

208 *I have been over in the islands:* EH to Senator Harry P. Cain, February 6, 1947.

208 *Almost every businessman:* EH to Senator Guy Cordon, February 7, 1947.

209 *I can think of a good many ways:* EH to Roy Vernstrom, April 23, 1947.

209 *I do strongly wish to see:* EH to Representative Helen Gahagan Douglas, August 18, 1947.

210 *When we pulled out:* EH to Mary Ann Haycox, October 7, 1947.

210 *I've been watching folks:* EH to Mary Ann, November 11, 1947.

211 *I did some commercial fishing:* EH to Jay Allen, February 6, 1947.

211 *I noticed in Spokes:* EH to Andy Patterson, March 10, 1947.

211 *With cubbing we now start:* EH to Alfred Parker, May 14, 1947.

212 *We have little breathing spaces:* EH to Phil Parrish, September 25, 1947.

212 *Were I a minister:* EH to Marshall Dana, October 21, 1947.

212 *I do appreciate your feeling:* EH to Ellis Lucia, May 5, 1947.

213 *"The trip will have some prestige":* EH to Sanders, October 1, 1947.

CHAPTER 13 ◆ "THEY ARE ALSO TERRIFICALLY DEMOCRATIC."

214 *The test of our policy:* EH to Fred Baker, July 15, 1947.

215 *He was a widower now:* Jack Chord to Mary Ann Haycox, November 30, 1946.

215 *There's no radio:* EH to the family, November 13, 1947.

216 *"an excellent Governor":* EH, "The Greeks Have Many Words for It," a manuscript. In a much-shortened form, this article appeared in the March 1948 issue of the *Atlantic Monthly*. The published version excluded both of the quotations that appear in this paragraph.

216 *You must be having a fine time:* Jill to EH, November 16, 1947.

216 *There's one smell:* EH to the family, November 22, 1947.

217 *He's one of those fellows:* EH to the family, November 26, 1947.

218 *Just three years ago:* EH to the family, November 29, 1947.

218 *"A striking guy":* EH to the family, December 2, 1947.

219 *"If the guerillas captured Dwight":* EH to the family, November 17, 1947.

219 *a pretty wild looking cooky:* Ibid.

220 *But the interpreter warned him:* Ibid.

220 *As we left:* EH to the family, November 17-18, 1947.

220 *"One by one men":* EH to the family, November 26, 1947.

221 *"My policy in this thing":* EH to the family, November 22, 1947.

221 *This morning, we went ashore:* Ibid.

222 *The greatest roadblock:* EH to Senator Morse, December 26, 1947. In a December 31 telegram, the senator would thank him for "one of the most helpful reports on Greek situation I have received from any source." It helped, of course, that Erny's letter "coincides so completely with observations I made when in Greece a year ago . . . ."

CHAPTER 14 ◆ "I SAID I'D NOT WRITE ONE OF THOSE AGAIN..."

224 Predating Erny's trip to Greece, the *Reader's Digest* article, "Fear Is Out of Date," appeared originally as a guest editorial, "Monsters over the Hill," in the December 1946 issue of the *Rotarian*. The writer's thesis was that

ancient fears residual in modern man impeded civilization's progress, and might even do it in.

224 *Atlantic Monthly:* the article, simply titled "Greece," was the first item in the magazine's column, "The Atlantic Report on the World Today," in its April 1948 issue.

224 *I voted for the guy:* EH to Fred Baker, July 15, 1947. Erny and the senator met by chance at the Portland train depot in the late '40s and chatted briefly. After Morse departed, the writer said to his son in a stage whisper that surely carried the lobby: "I do not trust that man."

225 *"I don't think we could use":* Elliott Schryver (*Cosmopolitan's* fiction editor) to Jo Stewart, Sanders Agency, November 11, 1948. NYPL.

226 *Having professed ourselves adherents:* EH to Ben Hibbs, March 9, 1948.

227 *Truman, frankly:* EH to Dwight Griswold, March 29, 1948. Griswold contested unsuccessfully for a U.S. Senate seat in 1946 but won a special election (caused by the death of an incumbent senator) in 1952. He died in office in 1954.

227 *Confidentially, do you know:* EH to Walter Wanger, April 1, 1948.

227 *To be fair with Syd and Mary:* EH to William Herndon, April 20, 1948.

228 *I've had a letter from Sanders:* EH to Herndon, May 1, 1948.

228 *Syd, I find, first tried:* EH to Herndon, May 29, 1948.

228 *I think the root of the trouble:* EH to Mary Baker, May 29, 1948.

229 *Your criticism is a better job:* EH to Howard Cady, December 16, 1948.

230 *You'll recall that:* EH to Ken Littauer, April 24, 1948.

230 *Never was a spring:* EH to Littauer, April 30, 1948.

231 *I'm finishing a serial:* EH to Littauer, December 7, 1948.

231 *In Oregon, in the early days:* EH to Ted Shane, October 23, 1948.

232 *In the matter of taboos:* EH to John Ford, February 12, 1948.

233 *I understand very well:* EH to Rex Stout, December 1, 1948.

233 *It's conceded that Stassen:* EH to Walter Davenport, May 27, 1948. The Dewey-Stassen contest had been a close one before Oregon, but Dewey won the Republican nomination and, as is well known, narrowly lost to HST.

234 *At this point the evidence:* EH to Ralph Cake, March 29, 1948. In February 1948, Portland's City Club reported widespread gambling, prostitution,

and bootlegging in the city. Mayor Riley, it said, was at best indifferent to the situation, but the strong implication was that he was sharing protection money with a corrupt police force.

234 *The senator with us tonight:* this excerpt is from EH's remarks at the event, which was a Portland Junior Chamber of Commerce dinner in Portland on January 8, 1948.

235 *We both know:* EH to H. K. Newburn, January 16, 1948.

236 *The thing is loaded:* EH to Newburn, April 1, 1948.

236 *Haven't seen dad:* EH to Bertha, October 11, 1948.

236 *There has been:* EH to Leo Pasewalk, November 9, 1948.

237 *No, I don't believe:* EH to Marshall Dana, January 5, 1948. The Townsend Plan was an old-age pension scheme designed to end the Depression by giving those over sixty a monthly government stipend (financed by a special income tax). Had it become law (it didn't), the recipient would have been required to quit working and to spend each month's payment within thirty days.

237 *I have your letter suggesting:* EH to a Mr. Bromfield. Menachem Begin, later a prime minister of Israel, was at that moment largely associated with Irgun, a Jewish terrorist organization, though he had recently entered politics as a leader of the Herut party.

237 *After much messing around:* EH to Donegan Wiggins, November 23, 1948.

237 *Last night I found:* EH to Marde Sanders, December 22, 1948.

238 *She fell silent:* "Beach Fire" was the last item placed in the writer's reject file. It contains about three dozen manuscripts, mostly work from the 1920s and '30s.

CHAPTER 15 ◆ HARD RULES IN THE GOLDEN LAND

240 *"we both look back":* EH to Bertha, November 29, 1949.

241 *"Writing is not a simple businesss":* EH to Graham Dean, November 28, 1949.

242 *There were two ways to go:* EH to Howard Cady, February 10, 1949.

242 *[R. C.] Hutchinson's latest book:* this was *Elephant and Castle*, published by Rinehart & Co. in 1949 and reviewed by William Soskin in the *Saturday Review of Literature* issue of January 29, 1949, p. 19. Hutchinson was a well-regarded English novelist.

243 *"I wish to tell the story":* EH to Cady, February 10, 1949.

243 *And on the tail end:* Ibid.

243 *The first will be the story:* EH to Max Wilkinson, April 5, 1949. Emerson Hough, both novelist and conservationist, was one of the early producers of romantic western fiction.

244 *Two shorts sold in January:* these were "The Land That Women Hate" (*Saturday Evening Post*, July 1949) and "The Misfit" (*American* Magazine, October 1949), both written in 1948.

244 *"I would like to do some more moderns":* EH to Marde Sanders, January 29, 1949.

244 *As you say it is sad:* EH to Sanders, March 21, 1949.

245 *As you know my last:* EH to Angus Cameron, February 21, 1949.

245 *"For many years I gave":* EH to Sanders, February 28, 1949.

246 *It was to avoid the suspicion:* EH to Ken McCormick, March 4, 1949.

247 *I shall say again:* EH to Cady, May 4, 1949.

247 *It must be the novelist's:* EH to Cameron, April 9, 1949.

247 *They brought the seeds:* EH to Cameron, May 5, 1949.

248 *In writing a short story:* EH to Cameron, July 14, 1949.

248 *"I begin now to see":* EH to Cameron, November 28, 1949.

248 *I am returning:* Ibid. Little, Brown published seven anthologies in all (hardcovers, shortly followed by Pocket Books paperback editions), giving new exposure to many of the *Collier's* and *Saturday Evening Post* shorts. These were *Rough Justice* (1950), *By Rope and Lead* (1951), *Pioneer Loves* (1952), *Murder on the Frontier* (1953), *Outlaw* (1953), *Prairie Guns* (1954), and *The Last Rodeo* (1956). Some of these were later repackaged as *The Best Western Stories of Ernest Haycox.*

249 *she decided shortly after becoming engaged:* In 1949, Mary Ann married James N. Wallace, later a foreign correspondent for the *Wall Street Journal* and a senior staffer at *U.S. News and World Report.* They were divorced after a dozen years.

249 *Yes, Mary quit:* EH to W. F. G. Thatcher, exact date uncertain.

250 *The original Mercys:* EH to Harry Paxton, March 9, 1949.

250 *The readers of your page:* EH to Ralph Knight, March 21, 1949.

251 *I presume from the tone:* EH to A. J. M. Norman, April 4, 1949. The story was "*Violent Interlude*" (*Saturday Evening Post*, February 1949) in which the Mercys are informed by a peevish trapper that the entire countryside, their claim included, belongs to him.

252 *I took the Sat. Eve. Post:* Oswald West to EH, July 23, 1949. The Palouse is fertile, high-desert wheat country in southeastern Washington and western Idaho.

252 *"then I suppose I have":* EH to West, July 29, 1949.

253 *a father has come to me:* EH to H. K. Newburn, January 5, 1949.

253 *[Drinking] is as much:* EH to Mrs. W. S. Love, February 14, 1949.

254 *I'm afraid the idea:* EH to state Senator Richard L. Neuberger, January 26, 1949.

254 *[Dorothy McCullough] Lee:* EH To Don Eddy, December 16, 1949. As should be obvious, the Texas Charley paid off. The writer's favorite punchboard was, of course, at the cigar store.

CHAPTER 16 ◆ BEYOND THE OBVIOUS FUNCTIONS

257 *Quite by chance:* the quoted article, "Ernest Hemingway," appeared in the October 8, 1950 book review section of the *New York Herald Tribune.* Several years later, the Francophile writer and editor Joseph Barry would tell Jill that one of Hemingway's more notable Parisian acquaintances, Gertrude Stein, had a few Haycox books on her shelf. Barry said he had introduced Ms. Stein to the writer and claimed the volumes from her apartment after her death in 1946.

259 *Katherine got pushed away:* EH to Angus Cameron, January 3, 1950. *In Sicily* was a highly regarded effort by Italian writer Elio Vittorini (New York: New Directions, 1949). The volume included introductory comments by Ernest Hemingway.

259 *The kids:* EH to Bertha, January 3, 1950.

260 *Jim H. is working:* EH to Bertha, February 21, 1950.

260 *Therefore, between editor:* EH to Howard Cady, April 4, 1950.

261 *A writer. . . has to discount:* EH to Cady, April 6, 1950.

262 *I got about 100 pages:* EH to Cameron, April 29, 1950.

262 *The clue to this conflict:* EH to Cameron, June 5, 1950.

262 *I am in a cabin:* Jill to EH, August 2, 1950.

263 *We have worked out:* Jim to EH, August 16, 1950.

263 *I have returned:* EH to Bertha, undated but late July.

264 *Bob Case moved into:* EH to Jill, August 20, 1950.

264 *Perhaps I had better:* EH to Jill, August 27, 1950.

265 *Night moved in: The Earthbreakers*, Chap. 2.

266 *We have certain:* undated and untitled speech draft—at a guess, composed in December 1949.

AFTERTHOUGHTS AND ACKNOWLEDGMENTS

267 *"The best western novel":* Harrison, Smith. "Pioneer Settlers—The Earthbreakers," *Saturday Review of Literature*, (March 1, 1952): 17

The Published Works of Ernest Haycox

OF THE TWENTY-FOUR HAYCOX NOVELS, THE FIRST TWENTY-ONE appeared initially as magazine serials, with the hardcover version issued one or several months following the final serial installment. With one exception (*Rough Air*), all of the novels were reprinted in various hardcover and paperback editions over several decades. Of the writer's approximately 270 published magazine shorts and novelettes, about 175 reappeared in anthologies (and a few singly). Most of these also have seen multiple paperback printings, occasionally with a title change. The dates used here are in all cases that of first U.S. issue in book form.

BOOKS ◆ *Free Grass* (1929), *Chaffee of Roaring Horse* (1930), *Whispering Range* (1931), *Starlight Rider* (1933), *Riders West* (1934), *Rough Air* (1934), *The Silver Desert* (1935), *Trail Smoke* (1936), *Trouble Shooter* (1937), *Deep West* (1937), *Sundown Jim* (1938), *Man in the Saddle* (1938), *The Border Trumpet* (1939), *Saddle and Ride* (1940), *Rim of the Desert* (1941), *Trail Town* (1941), *Alder Gulch* (1942), *Action by Night* (1943), *The Wild Bunch* (1943), *Bugles in the Afternoon* (1944), *Canyon Passage* (1945), *Long Storm* (1946), *The Earthbreakers* (1952), *The Adventurers* (1954).

ANTHOLOGIES AND SINGLE NOVELETTES ◆ *Rough Justice* (1950), *By Rope and Lead* (1951; later, *Stagecoach*), *Return of a Fighter* (1951), *Head of the Mountain* (1952), *Pioneer Loves* (1952), *Rawhide Range* (1952), *The Grim Canyon* (1953), *Murder on the Frontier* (1953), *Outlaw* (1953), *Guns Up* (1954), *Prairie Guns* (1954), *Secret River* (1955; the 1990 version has a different second story), *Vengeance Trail* (1955), *Gun Talk* (1956), *The Last*

Rodeo (1956), *A Rider of the High Mesa* (1956), *Dead Man Range* (1957; later *Clint*), *On the Prod* (1957; originally *Fighting Man*), *Brand Fires on the Ridge* (1959; later, *Wipe Out the Brierlys*), *Guns of the Tom Dee* (1959), *Lone Rider* (1959), *Best Western Stories of Ernest Haycox* (the 1960 issue incorporates the thirty-six stories in *Rough Justice, By Rope and Lead, Pioneer Loves*, and *Murder on the Frontier*; the 1975 version, the first two anthologies only), *The Feudists* (1960), *The Man from Montana* (1964), *Outlaw Guns* (1964), *Winds of Rebellion* (1964), *Sixgun Duo* (1965), *Trigger Trio* (1966), *Powder Smoke and Other Stories* (1966), *Guns of Fury* (1967), *Starlight and Gunflame* (1973), *Frontier Blood* (1974), *Burnt Creek* (1996), *New Hope* (1998).

Bibliography

BOOKS ◆

Abbott, Carl. *Portland—Planning, Politics, and Growth in a Twentieth-Century City*. Lincoln: University of Nebraska Press, 1983.

Brier, Howard M. *Sawdust Empire—The Pacific Northwest*. New York: Alfred A. Knopf, 1958.

Case, Robert Ormond. *The Empire Builders*. Portland: Binfords & Mort, 1949.

Chittick, V. L. O., ed. *Northwest Harvest, A Regional Stock-Taking*. New York: Macmillan Co., 1948.

Dinan, John A. *The Pulp Western: A Popular History of the Western Fiction Magazine in America*. San Bernardino, Calif.: Borgo Press, 1983.

Graham, Sheilah. *The Garden of Allah*. New York: Crown Publishers, 1970.

Gruber, Frank. *The Pulp Jungle*. Los Angeles: Sherbourne Press, 1967.

———. *Zane Grey, A Biography*. New York: World Publishing Co., 1970.

Hall, James Norman. *Mid-Pacific*. Boston and New York: Houghton Mifflin Co., 1928.

Holbrook, Stewart H. *Lost Men of American History*. New York: Macmillan Co., 1946.

———. *The Story of American Railroads*. New York: Crown Publishers, 1947.

John Ford's Stagecoach, Starring John Wayne. Edited and with an Introduction by Richard J. Anobile. New York: Universe Books, 1975.

Lynch, Vera Martin. *Free Land for Free Men, A Story of Clackamas County*. Portland: Artline Printing, 1973.

Maddux, Percy. *City on the Willamette—The Story of Portland, Oregon*. Portland: Binfords & Mort, 1952.

McClelland, John, Jr. *Wobbly War—The Centralia Story*. Tacoma: Washington Historical Society, 1987.

Mills, Randall V. *Sternwheelers Up Columbia—A Century of Steamboating in the Oregon Country*. Palo Alto, Calif.: Pacific Books, 1947

Oliver, Egbert S. *Homes in the Oregon Forest—Settling Columbia County*, 1870–1920. Brownsville, Ore.: Calapooia Publications, 1983.

Pollard, Lancaster. *Oregon and the Pacific Northwest*. Portland: Binfords & Mort, 1946.

Powers, Alfred. *History of Oregon Literature*. Portland: Metropolitan Press, 1935.

Pratt, Laurence. *I Remember Portland*, 1899–1915. Portland: Binfords & Mort, 1965.

Tanner, Stephen L. *Ernest Haycox*. Twayne's United States Authors Series No. 666. New York: Twayne Publishers, 1996.

Tyler, Robert L. *Rebels of the Woods: the I. W. W. in the Pacific Northwest*. Eugene: University of Oregon, 1967.

Wildmen, Wobblies and Whistle Punks, Stewart Holbrook's Lowbrow Northwest. Edited and with an Introduction by Brian Booth. Corvallis: Oregon State University Press, 1992.

PAMPHLETS, ARTICLES AND OTHER SOURCES ◆

De Voto, Bernard. "Phaethon on Gunsmoke Trail." In "The Easy Chair" column. *Harper's* Magazine (December 1954).

Etulain, Richard W. *Ernest Haycox*, Western Writer Series No. 86. Boise, Idaho: Boise State University, 1988.

Fargo, James [James Algar]. "The Western and Ernest Haycox." *Prairie Schooner* vol. 26, no. 2. (1952).

Fowler, Kenneth D., ed. *The Roundup*. A Special Ernest Haycox Anniversary Issue, vol. 21, no. 10 (October 1973).

Haycox, Ernest, Jr. Introduction to *Bugles in the Afternoon*. Boston: Gregg Press/ G. K. Hall, 1978.

———. Introduction to *New Hope*. Unity, Maine: Five Star, 1998.

Haycox, Jill, and John Chord. "Ernest Haycox Fiction—A Checklist," *The Call Number* Fall 1963/Spring 1964. 25, nos. 1 and 2, Eugene: University of Oregon Library. Includes appraisals of the author by Luke Short, Saul David, and Frederick Nolan, and a brief commentary on the Haycox Memorial Library Collection by Thomas Easterwood.

Haycox, Jill Marie. *The Light of Other Days*, The Roundup, 21, no. 10, Western Writers of America (October 1973.)

———. Introduction to *The Border Trumpet*. Boston: Gregg Press/G. K. Hall, 1978.

———. Introduction to *Canyon Passage*. Boston: Gregg Press/G. K. Hall, 1979.

"Hi-yu kloshe muck-a-muck, hi-yu wa-wa hi-yu hee-hee!" [Plenty of good food, much talk, much laughter]. Portland, Ore.: Portland Chamber of Commerce promotional brochure, undated, circa 1941.

The 162nd Infantry (Old Third Oregon) in France—An Inspiration. (This booklet of about seventy pages does not disclose its author, publisher, or date—but probably Portland in 1919 or 1920.)

Index

NOTE: Where a book or short story title follows a name, the individual is a character in that story.

www.ingramcontent.com/pod-product-compliance
Lightning Source LLC
LaVergne TN
LVHW091020080826
845145LV00002B/304

* 9 7 8 0 8 0 6 1 9 4 8 5 1 *